BALKAN BLUES

NEW ANTHROPOLOGIES OF EUROPE

Michael Herzfeld, Melissa L. Caldwell, and
Deborah Reed-Danahay, *editors*

BALKAN BLUES

Consumer Politics after State Socialism

YUSON JUNG

INDIANA UNIVERSITY PRESS

This book is a publication of

Indiana University Press
Office of Scholarly Publishing
Herman B Wells Library 350
1320 East 10th Street
Bloomington, Indiana 47405 USA

iupress.indiana.edu

© 2019 by Yuson Jung
All rights reserved

No part of this book may be reproduced or utilized in any form or by any means, electronic or mechanical, including photocopying and recording, or by any information storage and retrieval system, without permission in writing from the publisher.

The paper used in this publication meets the minimum requirements of the American National Standard for Information Sciences—Permanence of Paper for Printed Library Materials, ANSI Z39.48–1992.

Manufactured in the United States

Cataloging information is available from the Library of Congress.

ISBN 978-0-253-03671-1 (hardback)
ISBN 978-0-253-02914-0 (paperback)
ISBN 978-0-253-03674-2 (ebook)

1 2 3 4 5   24 23 22 21 20 19

*To my parents
with gratitude and love*

CONTENTS

Acknowledgments ix

Note on Transliteration and Translation xiii

Introduction 1

1 *Mente*: Consumer Grievances 25

2 Needs, Rights, and Protection 46

3 Consumer Activism? 81

4 Consumption as Civic Engagement 109

5 Consumer Politics after State Socialism 131

Epilogue: "Enough Is Enough"—The Moral Commitment of the State 150

Appendix. An East Asian Ethnographer in Eastern Europe: Notes on Fieldwork and Positionality 157

References 179

Index 191

ACKNOWLEDGMENTS

It seems almost clichéd to say that this book has been long in making. But in this case, it has indeed been a seemingly endless process, and I owe much gratitude to many people across three different continents. In Bulgaria, I have learned so much about how one deals with life and dignity especially in the midst of dramatic social and cultural changes. A heartfelt thank-you to all my Bulgarian friends, colleagues, and interlocutors: you have always found time to share your stories with a probing anthropologist. This book would never have come to fruition without your insights. My foremost gratitude goes to the executive director of the Bulgarian National Association of Active Consumers (*Aktivni Potrebiteli*), Bogomil Nikolov, who has tirelessly shared his experiences and facilitated access to numerous consumer issues and events. He and his staff, especially Veni Peycheva, went out of their way to make me feel welcomed and made sure that I had access to everything I needed. I am deeply grateful for their unflagging friendship over these many years. My Bulgarian anthropology colleagues in Sofia have also assisted me in numerous ways. Ilia Iliev, in particular, deserves special mention for always lending an ear to my stories, answering my questions, and offering a sharp eye to my manuscript—he has generously read through the drafts and offered critical comments. Tanya Boneva, Evgenia Blagoeva-Krasteva, and Orlin Todorov have always been there with their boundless encouragement and insights. I am also very fortunate to have met Iskra Velinova in Budapest during a workshop organized by the Central European University many years ago. I cannot express how much I value her friendship and sound counsel whenever I need it as well as the many meals and drinks we have shared together and with her wonderful friends, *kakite* (older sisters). My long-term engagement with this project and Bulgaria would not have been the same without Ana Bankova's generosity in letting me stay with her anytime I went to Bulgaria.

My host families during my first extended fieldwork did not hesitate in sharing their living quarters with a stranger when it was uncommon to do so. There are not enough words to express how much I appreciated living with them—I felt privileged to have been included in their lives. There are many friends and numerous interlocutors, including my two Bulgarian language teachers, whom I cannot thank by name following the professional and ethical standards of my profession: I hope you know how much it meant to me that you welcomed me into your lives and shared your experiences with me. I would like to acknowledge Kalina, my Bulgarian sister and confidante, who always lends her uncanny wisdom and offers a sense of comfort to me. Without "Joto" and "Jonka," who never hesitate to share a glass of wine, and Vase's great sense of humor and big heart, my return trips to Bulgaria would not have been the same. I also thank Ivan Bakalov for giving permission to reprint images from his magazine. It was Maria Todorova who got me hooked on Bulgaria. Her Balkan history class, which she offered as a visiting scholar at Harvard University, inspired me to learn Bulgarian and delve into Bulgarian culture.

At Harvard, I had the incredible fortune to be nurtured by the most brilliant minds and kind souls: Manduhai Buyandelger, Melissa Caldwell, Nicolas Sternsdorff Cisterna, Paulette Curtis, Saroja Dorairajoo, Vanessa Fong, Tracey Heatherington, Irving Johnson, Eriberto (Fuji) Lozada, Vaso Neofotistos, Nicole Newendorp, Ilay Ors, Tianshu Pan, Bernie Perley, Andrew Preston, Maple Razsa, Levent Soysal, Wen-Ching Sung, Sarah Wagner, and Min Zhang. My doctoral advisor Michael Herzfeld's inspiration, patience, and steadfast mentorship and friendship have no match. Without his unflagging support and encouragement over these years, I would not have adapted to and understood the true meanings of different cultures and overcome personal difficulties. Few people are fortunate enough to have a mentor and friend on whom they can call anytime for any problem. I am also thankful to Nea Herzfeld's warm presence that always made Cambridge a more comfortable place. James (Woody) Watson and Rubie Watson have taught me so many things beyond anthropology. My love for teaching was cultivated in Woody's classes as a graduate teaching fellow. I have learned so much from Engseng Ho, the late Mary Steedly, Jennifer Cole, Nur Yalman, the late Stanley Tambiah, and the late David Maybury-Lewis. The staff in the anthropology department, especially Monica Munson, Elizabeth (Penny) Rew, and Cris Paul, were always there, and I deeply appreciate their lasting friendship.

Because this project spans many years, funding has come from a variety of sources: the US Department of State (Title VIII), the Mellon Foundation, and at Harvard, the Davis Center for Russian and Eurasian States, Minda de Gunzburg Center for European Studies, the Department of Anthropology, and the Graduate School of Arts and Sciences. Wayne State University provided additional financial and administrative support, and I also appreciate the support from the Center for East European, Eurasian, and Russian Studies at the University of Chicago and especially from Victor Friedman.

I thank my fellow Bulgarianists, especially Gerald Creed, Deema Kaneff, Kristen Ghodsee, and Elana Resnick, for their support and wise counsel. Thanks to Elizabeth Dunn, Gaby Vargas-Cetina, Neringa Klumbytė, and Jakob Klein, who have also contributed to this project, perhaps more than they know. Nan Kim-Paik and Peter Paik have made life in the Midwest so much more enjoyable. The unfaltering support from Korea has always anchored me: many thanks and love to Ahran Park, Soyoung Yoon, and Suhyeon Jeon. I am tremendously grateful to Jungwon Kim and Kiwhan Kim—they may not realize how much they helped with making this book happen. Our shared memories in Cambridge are deeply cherished.

Detroit and Wayne State University have been greatly inspiring places to be. I am fortunate to have such supportive and collegial colleagues: Allen Batteau, Tammy Bray, Steve Chrisomalis, Tom Killion, Julie Lesnik, Mark Luborsky, Barry Lyons, Guerin Montilus, Andy Newman, Andrea Sankar, Jonathan Stillo, and Sue Villerot. Sherri Briller, Jess Robbins, and Krysta Ryzewski in particular have read the manuscript and offered many valuable insights which was very much appreciated. My life and workplace would not have been the same without their presence as not only colleagues but also great friends. I am incredibly grateful to the anonymous reviewers who have provided insightful and meticulous comments. Needless to say, any remaining shortcomings are mine.

Indiana University Press has been immensely supportive—I thank the unfailing support of the book series editors and especially my editor, Jennika Baines, and her assistant, Kate Schramm. I understand that it is not a given to have such ease and efficiency with communication. Their professionalism and accessibility is deeply appreciated. A sincere thank-you to my copy editor, Kathleen Deselle, too, for such a fine and meticulous job in making the book more readable.

Melissa (Lissa) Caldwell and her compassionate family, Andy Baker and Kaeley Baker, have truly been examples of kindness and thoughtfulness. Words fail in expressing my gratitude to Lissa, who as a friend, colleague, mentor, and sister has always been there to listen and put me back on track when necessary. It still puzzles me how she finds time to do everything, especially for what she has done for me and this project. Lastly, none of this would have been possible without my loving and remarkable family. To my parents, my parents-in-law, and other members of the family—thank you. This book could not have been completed without your trust and support. Life would never be the same, or would even matter, without my husband and best friend, James Jiho Kim, and my incredibly wonderful and caring daughter, Clarice—your wit, good humor, and love sustain me every day and inspire me to be a better person.

NOTE ON TRANSLITERATION AND TRANSLATION

Transliterating the Bulgarian Cyrillic alphabet into Latin letters can be challenging because there are multiple accepted traditions including the US Library of Congress transliteration system. Throughout the book, I have followed the official Bulgarian government version published in 2013. Hence, I have transliterated Cyrillic letters as follows:

в	→	v
з	→	z
ж	→	zh
ч	→	ch
ш	→	sh
щ	→	sht
ц	→	ts
х	→	h
й	→	y
ю	→	yu
я	→	ya
у	→	u
ъ	→	a

The only exception to this rule is for "Bulgaria" and names that have been conventionally spelled with "ia" instead of "ya." All translation from Bulgarian to English throughout the book is mine.

BALKAN BLUES

INTRODUCTION

Shopping at convenience stores on the busy streets of Sofia, Bulgaria, sometimes means kneeling down. Similar to the walk-up kiosks that dot the streets in Rome or Athens, Sofia's "*klek shop*" (kneel shops) are located in the half-basements of residential buildings (see figure I.1). Glass display cases protrude at pedestrians' knee level, showcasing examples of merchandise for sale. These cases flank a small window where transactions take place. Customers must kneel or squat at the window to request cigarettes, beverages, snacks, or other items from the seller. Sofia's kneel shops afford quick access to convenience items for consumers from all socioeconomic backgrounds; they are a ubiquitous part of the city's consumer experience and streetscape.

In the summer of 1999, when I was new to Bulgaria, I was fascinated by the ways in which kneel shops offered a unique shopping experience, adding a distinctive charm to the urban landscape and forcing consumers to conduct transactions at ground level. One afternoon, as I strolled along a busy street with my Bulgarian language teacher, an empty Fanta bottle in a kneel shop's display caught my eye. I squatted down to examine it. The bottle looked different than the ones I was familiar with in the United States and South Korea, my native country: it had an unusual logo, font, and style. As I lingered over the display case, my teacher whispered "*mente!*" in my ear.[1] Loosely translated as "fake" (a counterfeit or knockoff of inferior quality in this context), *mente* is frequently evoked when Bulgarians are shopping or talking about their purchases afterward.

Mente has deep roots in the region's recent history. Following the collapse of state socialism in 1989, many ordinary Bulgarians perceived their stores and markets as plagued by questionable goods that were of inferior quality and possibly unsafe. After two decades of "market economy," as Bulgarians commonly refer to it, *mente* continues to resonate in Bulgarians' everyday practices. *Mente* was often a shorthand for everything that was not right in the aftermath of socialism, from shoddy consumer goods to corrupt politicians, greedy businessmen, and broken systems. It was not only questionable goods that distressed postsocialist consumers. Public utilities

I.1 *Klek* (kneel) shops
These convenience shops that operate from the basements of residential buildings were one of the first small-scale private enterprises created immediately after the fall of state socialism in 1989. *Photograph by author, 2012.*

and infrastructure—most notably, heating (*parno*), electricity, education, and health care as well as new commercial services in the postsocialist era such as cell phones, banking and consumer credits, and housing issues—all contributed to consumer anxiety and discontent. Discerning and avoiding *mente* was a common concern for Bulgarian consumers as they made their way in the new market economy, and these experiences invariably invoked a sense of civic engagement by consumers demanding accountability and a degree of protection from the abuses of the market. In other words, they expressed acute social commentaries on the nature and role of the state under neoliberal capitalist conditions that privilege the free individual and unconstrained market competition. Everyday consumption practices, even local convenience stores or kneel shops, became sites where the discursive construction of the state appeared, where the state was experienced and reproduced.

This book is about consumer politics—namely, how citizens participate and experience the making of consumer society after state socialism.[2] It is about how consumers, by engaging in daily consumption practices such as shopping and using utilities, understand their rights and demand responsibilities of providers, including the state, in the globalized consumer society. The book departs from other consumption studies in anthropology, sociology, and history that take consumption as sites of social distinction, or ways to construct identities and modernities. These studies often highlight the expression of agency through individual choices in the marketplace.[3] Instead, I examine aspects of consumption that illuminate state-citizen relations and civic engagement, thereby expanding on other consumption studies that focus on individual desire, identity construction, and social agency. I argue that consumption practices can also be examined as mundane sites that pose risks and vulnerability to consumers because of unequal access and unreliable choices. In this regard, consumption is not solely considered in opposition to production. Nor is it viewed only as a relatively autonomous domain of individualistic practices satisfying needs, wants, or aspirations. Rather, consumption involves issues of rights, responsibilities, and accountability and, more broadly, raises questions about civic engagement in a consumerist world of goods. In the postsocialist setting, material abundance has not been equally distributed and shared. Furthermore, even consumers with relatively more purchasing power are concerned that what they buy may be unsafe and/or of inferior quality. These circumstances prompt grievances regarding access and choice in everyday consumption practices. This study calls attention to disparities in consumer practices in postsocialist contexts and discusses their implications in light of the increasing social stratification and inequality.

Prevailing neoliberal assumptions consider economic activities to be primarily in the realm of the market, thereby giving little acknowledgment to the role of the state. Consumption practices, however, do not only engage the market, even under neoliberal conditions that consider the state to be largely withdrawn. They are also entangled with multiple regimes of power such as the state and the supranational entity of the European Union (EU). These contemporary conditions produce new social relations between consumers, the market, and the state (and supranational entity), and consumer problems cannot be fully understood if we view consumption solely as a domain tied to the free market and individual choices. Consumers are not only people purchasing and using resources; they are also citizens exercising rights and demanding responsibilities in the contemporary world (Canclini 2001; Cohen 2003; Garon and Machlachlan 2006; Trentmann 2007).

Hence, the idea of a citizen-consumer refers to the linkage between consumption and citizenship, suggesting that private consumption and public benefit are intimately related (Cohen 2006: 47). Néstor Canclini notes how consumption has altered the possibilities and forms of citizenship: "Many of the questions proper to citizenship—where do I belong, what rights accrue to me, how can I get information, who represents my interests?—are being answered in the private realm of commodity consumption and the mass media more than in the abstract rules of democracy or collective participation in public space" (2001: 15).

This important observation raises questions about the nature and role of the state in modern consumption practices that are under the influence of globalization. The flourishing of consumption studies in the past couple of decades is intimately related to discussions about globalization, a process involving the exponentially increasing circulation of consumer goods that, in turn, contributes to the global production of desire for a "good life" (Miller 2012; Trouillot 2001). When citizen-consumers seek rights and demand a degree of protection from the abuses of the market under neoliberal conditions in which the state is seemingly withdrawn or absent, what kind of state are they imagining in these renderings?

This book addresses the key concerns of consumer rights, responsibilities, and accountability through an ethnographic study about everyday consumption practices in Sofia, Bulgaria, at a time when Bulgaria was preparing for EU integration and adjusting to the new post-accession environment (1999–2016; Bulgaria joined the EU in 2007). In this period, Bulgaria was transforming from a centrally planned economy into a consumer society with a market economy.

Bulgaria is a geopolitically marginal postsocialist country and the poorest member state of the EU (Bulgaria's per capita gross domestic product [GDP] was $6,993 in 2015; by comparison, the per capita GDP in the Eurozone was $32,004, and in the United States it was $56,115) (World Bank 2016). Bulgaria's recent economic and social histories are optimally suited for considering questions about how the state, the EU, and citizen relations are understood and expressed through everyday consumption practices. Postsocialist conditions offer especially productive sites for understanding state-citizen relations in this context because they raise the question of access to basic needs and choice over goods and services in the "world of goods" (Douglas and Isherwood 1979). That is, to what extent is consumption a civic right, a civic responsibility, or even a civic failure?

Postsocialist states in Eastern Europe have had a particularly interesting experience in the history of modern consumer politics. During state socialism, like their counterparts on the other side of the iron curtain, these socialist states had pursued the goal of providing a "good life" to everybody by raising living standards (Fitzpatrick 1999; Patterson 2009; Smith 2009). Just like capitalist Western societies, Eastern European states ultimately shared the vision of basic provisioning and affording better lives to their citizens. In a way, the socialist state achieved this goal, as living standards had improved for ordinary people in Eastern Europe during the Cold War era (1947–1991) (Bren and Neuburger 2012; Guentcheva 2012). As the stories of my Bulgarian interlocutors attest, few worried about basic survival during state socialism thanks to generous state subsidies for basic provisioning (e.g., food, water, housing, and utilities). In other words, access to basic goods and services was guaranteed under state socialism. Under these circumstances Bulgarians maintained basic rights to daily provisioning, and many citizens took them for granted. At the same time, socialist citizens often struggled due to the irregularity of distribution, which caused them to line up in stores, or due to the absence of choice under the deficit economy. Even during the heyday of the Cold War era, socialist citizens continued to cultivate consumer desires that were often fueled by comparisons to Western goods available to some but not others.[4] To understand Bulgarian consumption practices in the postsocialist era, it is necessary to remember these conditions of guaranteed access and limited choice during state socialism because they highlight the importance of broadening our understanding of modern consumption practices beyond individual choice matters situated in the realm of the market.

Historically, studies of consumer politics have considered questions of access and choice since the eighteenth century in Europe. According to historian Matthew Hilton (2009), with growing affluence the question of access became gradually subsumed, and consumption was increasingly framed in terms of choice. I suggest that the hegemonic discourse and practices of neoliberal capitalism furthered this tendency in which consumption was often conflated with consumerism, presuming the individual and choice as primary loci in discussions about consumption. This discourse had implications for how the scholarship on consumption developed in the past couple of decades that privileged the choice-making individual amid relative material abundance as the center for sociocultural analyses (see especially Warde 2015).

Hence, my study examines consumption as a productive site for understanding the shifting relations between the state and citizens under the co-existing conditions of material abundance and growing inequality. This approach explicitly considers the dilemma of access and choice that many societies face worldwide, and it expands the analytical loci of consumption beyond the idea of a "sovereign consumer," a perspective that has been privileged as a consequence of the dominance of neoliberal ideologies (Warde 2015: 129). The primary advantage of this approach is that it attends to the more marginalized and financially constrained consumers who are often considered excluded or limited in the consumerist and globalized market. Their grievances allow us to examine what consumption means to them. Therefore, my goal in this book is to unsettle assumptions about the nature and role of the state in everyday consumption practices in the post–Cold War era (which accelerated the processes of neoliberal globalization) and to discuss the implications of understanding consumption as a site of civic engagement.

Consumption Practices Illuminate State-Citizen Relations

In the past twenty years, anthropologists have engaged with a notion of the state that has been largely taken for granted as an analytical category without critically examining it. They have debated whether the state is a thing that is "out there" as an object of observation and whether it can be an object of study (Trouillot 2001). Some scholars have suggested that the state could be productively studied by attending to its images (cultural representations), practices, and effects (Gupta and Ferguson 1997; Sharma and Gupta 2006; Reeves, Rasanayagan, and Beyer 2014), especially as they manifest themselves legibly and spatially (Scott 1998) as well as in bureaucratic encounters (Gupta 1995; Herzfeld 1987), and by approaching it as a "relational setting" that allows ethnographic analysis about "how the state is understood, experienced, and reproduced in everyday encounters" (Thelen, Vetters, and von Benda-Beckmann 2014: 9). While the state can serve as a common analytical category, I do not presume it to be the same thing in practice or something with intrinsic meanings. Instead, following Tatjana Thelen, Larissa Vetters, and Keebet von Benda-Beckmann (2014), I approach the state as something that is historically contingent, produced and reproduced in relational setting (such as how state-citizen relations are cast in the everyday consumption context), and show how mundane consumption practices (beyond bureaucratic encounters and the context of social welfare) can be important sites in conceptualizing it. This approach allows for an examination of those who are locally seen as representative of the state power, what is considered the proper function of the state, and how state-citizen relations manifest themselves in concrete daily social interactions that are situated in specific historical moments. For example, when my Bulgarian interlocutors suspected some products to be *mente* (fake/shoddy), they often questioned why there was little state control or involvement to eliminate such inferior (and often unsafe) products from the market and protect vulnerable consumers. In their minds, the state had to play a central role in ensuring consumer safety, and it had to be held accountable when the system did not work. Mundane encounters with consumption often vividly illustrated how my interlocutors conceptualized the state. The state, in this regard, can be understood as a conceptual and cultural category associated with control (especially over product quality and safety) and accountability (ensuring that the legal and electoral systems to guarantee this control work). According to this understanding, the state becomes one of the main targets of consumer grievance.

Thinking about state-citizen relations in the context of everyday consumption is critical to understanding consumer politics after state socialism. A consumer society was not automatically created from increased access to material abundance after living through socialism's deficit economy. Experiences of socialism produced different social relationships between the citizen, the market, and the state. In fact, consumption practices were primarily channeled through the state as it controlled the production and distribution of goods (Fehérváry 2013; Humphrey 2002; Verdery 1996). In many capitalist economies, consumption is often assumed to mean practices within the realm of the market that can fulfill the desires of individual consumers and allow consumers to express their agency. When consumers in these places buy fraudulent products, for example, they seek redress from the retailers or producers and/or blame themselves for having made poor consumer choices. While product safety issues do involve the state, the state is rarely invoked as the ultimate object of blame when consumers buy poor-quality, unsafe, or fake goods in these capitalist societies. In the United States, the state uses regulatory agencies such as the Food and Drug Administration (FDA), the Centers for Disease Control and Prevention (CDC), and the Bureau of Consumer Protection (under the Federal Trade Commission), which receive signals from consumers, check faulty products and services, and notify producers who then voluntarily recall the questionable products from the market. In other words, the market is supposed to take care of the problems through consumer pressure mediated by the state. Consumer movements such as those led by Ralph Nader in the United States in the 1950s and 1960s and through the early 1980s, when citizen-consumers demanded that the state put pressure on the market through stricter regulation, gradually became obsolete.

The market is not always trusted to take care of consumer problems in other places across the world. In many so-called developing economies or in places with more authoritarian regimes, the state has a stronger presence in managing these consumer problems because of the different relationship to its citizens. A globally circulated high-profile example was the 2009 melamine-tainted milk scandal in China. Six infants died and an estimated 300,000 victims were reportedly made sick from the adulterated baby formula and dairy products sold in markets (LaFraniere 2009). While the Chinese dairy industry responded to the situation by recalling China-made dairy products worldwide, ultimately, it was the Chinese state that intervened to address the accountability issue by executing the culprits and sentencing people according to the severity of their involvement (Yan 2012; Tracy 2010, 2013).[5]

Anthropologist Jakob Klein (2013, 2014) reports that in China many consumers grew anxious about food safety and often insisted on a strong state presence to manage these kinds of consumer problems. The apprehension about food safety was not because consumers felt powerless or considered themselves passive. They thought of the state as an accountable agent protecting its citizens from the abuses of the market. This shared normative ideal was formed historically throughout Imperial China and during Mao Zedong's revolutionary times, especially because food safety concerned basic provisioning of the citizenry. The state in this context was not viewed as an oppressive regime but was identified as the ultimate power to protect its citizen-consumers and ensure their basic rights. Similarly, in Cuba, consumers' experiences continue to be entangled with the state even as the national economy has become increasingly influenced by neoliberal capitalism. Marisa Wilson (2013, 2014), for example, argues how Cubans' revolutionary ideals of equality are upheld despite the individualization introduced through neoliberal market practices that compel citizens to pursue maximizing profits for self-interest. Her Cuban interlocutors often pointed out how they preferred a universal distribution of goods (even if they were of lower quality) over market commodities because they shared a moral commitment with the state regarding the normative ideals of equality of opportunity in collective work (as opposed to an individualized market). These examples suggest how citizens relate themselves to the state and explain how they understand the nature and role of the state in their daily economic activities under changing economic circumstances.

The contexts of postsocialist (and market socialist)[6] regimes are not the only ones in which state-citizen relations are explicitly articulated through consumption. In Japan and Korea, for instance, consumers often positioned themselves as responsible citizens and embraced the cultural values of frugality and prioritized saving over spending to contribute to the national economies (Garon and Machlachlan 2006). Similarly, Lizabeth Cohen (2003, 2006) offers a compelling account of how post–World War II politics affected state-consumer relations in the United States, where consumption was promoted as a civic duty by linking acts of purchasing with creating jobs for the country. She argues that the intimate connection between the producer (manufacturer) and consumer in the United States gradually weakened as imports competed with domestic products. US policy-makers, however, continued to be preoccupied with raising consumption levels regardless of whether the goods were domestically produced or not. According to Cohen (2006), this turned the American consumer from a "citizen-consumer" into a "purchaser-consumer" who buys things for self-interest.

Even today in the United States, often considered the model of an advanced capitalist society, where neoliberal economic policies reign strong in consumer affairs to the point that the state is rarely evoked in consumer matters, the recent water crisis in Flint, Michigan, in 2016 points to how mundane sites of everyday consumption relate consumers directly to the state (Associated Press 2016). Similarly, we see an explicit state-citizen connection manifested when many American consumers discuss the quality of products: they delight in cheap prices but often lament the inferior quality of such products, explaining this situation as a consequence of outsourcing (economic globalization) and insisting that both corporations and the state share responsibilities for this situation.

The Bulgarian case thus shares a great deal with other contemporary examples of consumption in terms of state-citizens relations: how consumers across the world articulate their concern with consumption, how they relate it to the state, and how they demand that the state address their discontent. What distinguishes the Bulgarian case is that because of its historical experience and legacy of state socialism the articulation and expectation regarding proper state functions and sensibility toward state practices (or the lack thereof) in relation to everyday consumption appears to be more explicit and pronounced. And this makes Bulgaria as well as other postsocialist contexts an ideal case for thinking about consumption practices as sites where state-citizen relations manifest themselves and how consumers imagine such relations.

When it came to consumer matters such as *mente*, my Bulgarian interlocutors brought up the role of the state even as they were, at times, skeptical of the ability of their postsocialist state to rectify such consumer problems. There was always a palpable sense of civic outrage in discussions among ordinary Bulgarians regarding fraudulent and shoddy consumer products and services. Indeed, many of them viewed consumption as one of the domains in which the lack of care by the state, or the absence of the state, was experienced. And these experiences with consumer products and services highlighted the ways in which citizen-consumers conceptualized the state. Demands for normal and anxiety-free (*spokoino*) consumption was thus intimately linked to their unfulfilled expectations of the postsocialist and increasingly neoliberal state. My research with Bulgarian consumers and consumer experts suggests that the context of postsocialist consumption practices is often marked by a strong sense of distrust of the state ("politicians are corrupt") as well as a sense of regret regarding the perceived absence of the state at the same time ("unfortunately, we don't have a state"). This distrust in something that is supposedly absent is a curious conundrum, one that this book attempts to explicate. As Madeleine Reeves, Johan Rasanayagan, and Judith Beyer describe: "The state constantly has to be performed into being—it takes shape through a host of actions, mundane and spectacular, in which ordinary people are enlisted as both audience and actor" (2014: 4). In the Bulgarian context, the state is often evoked whenever citizen-consumers register a host of inactions by the state, which they interpret as the lack of will by the state to fulfill its obligation to the social contract.

The lack of care by the state in postsocialist societies is articulated frequently by ordinary citizens and noted by many scholars of postsocialism, who discuss it in terms of a discourse of abandonment and grievances often in regards to the welfare systems (Caldwell 2004, 2012; Creed 2011; Kideckel 2009; Phillips 2008) and how this discourse constantly relates citizens to the state. In Bulgaria, this state-citizen connection often appears in the everyday discourse and practice of consumption. In stating their grievances about products and services, postsocialist Bulgarians are ultimately demanding state practices that could work for them based on their historical and cultural experiences. Consumption, therefore, is one concrete domain through which ordinary people articulate their grievances and vision for state functions and practices that provide good governance. Similar to how welfare systems connect the state to citizens, consumption is a domain that materializes state-citizen relations. We need to take the Bulgarian case seriously because it calls for a different way of thinking about the configuration of market, state, and citizen relations under conditions of neoliberal capitalism and globalization.

In the neoliberal milieu that presumes rapid economic growth through a deregulated free market, the dilemma over access and choice demands a new understanding of the relationship between citizen-consumers, the state, and the market. The growing social stratification and inequality across many global consumer societies begs the question of the nature and role of the state in everyday consumption practices. The implications of consumer politics in postsocialist Bulgaria must be understood by acknowledging the state as a meaningful category in consumption practices because both access and choice continue to be important for consumer issues in contemporary Bulgaria and beyond, especially as they relate to ideas of entitlement and accountability.

Consumption as Civic Engagement

Globally, rights discourse is extended to many domains, and processes of globalization including social movements have expanded and framed the rights discourse as "new domains of political struggle by conceptualizing new relations of entitlement and obligation" (Cowan, Dembour, and Wilson 2001: 1). The case of consumer rights and consumer protection is an interesting one to examine under these circumstances because of the philosophical shifts in consumer politics. Historically, consumer issues were not merely framed as problems of the market (see especially Trentmann 2007). In pre–World War II Europe, the concern for access was primary. As modern societies became more prosperous, however, problems of access and how to protect consumers from the abuses of the market gave way to issues of choice from the abundance of goods (Hilton 2009). The antiregulatory neoliberal milieu and policies added to this historical shift, and consumer issues came to be perceived and framed as an individual matter and a matter of choice within market relations. Consumers' rights, thus, were no longer something to be advocated for but something to claim with better informed choices by individual and "sovereign" consumers. As a result, global consumer movements came to focus more on disseminating objective, reliable information to individual consumers through independent comparative testing, for example, rather than mobilizing collective actions (Hilton 2009: 18–19). Even the idea of consumer protection is premised on informed individual consumers—in other words, consumers would be protected by better access to reliable information. But if consumers are skeptical of the information provided by civil (consumer) experts or continue to feel a sense of deception in their consumption practices (as the dominant *mente* discourse points out) not only by the producers but also by the state, which failed to protect its consumers from the abuses of the market, how and to whom can they seek their rights and protection? In fact, one could further question what "rights" actually means in a context in which citizens are unsure that there is even a functioning judicial system that can enforce the law and ensure the protection of rights. Thus, consumption can be productively examined as a domain of civic engagement by citizen-consumers who seek answers to this fundamental question of rights and responsibilities.

Such questions of rights and responsibilities animate discussions on citizenship. The notion of "civic," in particular, is a productive way to think about consumption. Much discussion on civil society has taken place in the aftermath of state socialism, especially as former socialist countries in Eastern Europe and the former Soviet Union underwent intensive social transformation to Western-style democratic and pluralistic societies in which the role of the state is significantly reduced (Buchowski 1996; see also Hann and Dunn 1996; Creed 2011; Sampson 2002; Verdery 1996; Wedel 1995). Polish anthropologist Michał Buchowski, for example, views civil society in this context as a technology of governing and exerting pressure on the power of the state, whereas he refers to civic society as "social institutions embedded within civil society capable of acting as a kind of countervailing force to the state" (1996: 82). This distinction is productive in contextualizing the meanings and practices of civil society beyond the Western models. Michael Herzfeld's (2009: 79, 324) more expansive notion of civic engagement as the practices of active and general participation that are virtues of responsible citizens is also useful in thinking of consumption as civic engagement because the grievances expressed by ordinary consumers are not always grounded within the context of social institutions.

Several examples of political activism in response to the perils of the industrialized and globalized food system have been highlighted in recent scholarship on food (see especially Counihan and Siniscalchi 2014). Cristina Grasseni (2013: 3) makes a convincing case about how alternative provisioning networks in Italy (*Gruppo di Acquisto Solidale* [GAS], a solidarity purchasing group) call into question tacit assumptions about capitalism, the globalized food system, and civic participation. Buying collectively from providers nearby, consumers not only negotiate production, price, and distribution of food, but they also use these occasions for a civic reflexive self-review regarding social justice. Food provisioning is not simply a process of individualistic consumption practice but also a concrete way of civic engagement among average lower-middle-class families in Italy, raising profoundly moral questions about society and political economy.[7] Unlike Italian consumers, Bulgarian consumers have been less likely to organize collective political voices. Instead, they have consistently and frequently expressed their grievances as consumers through the mundane practices and social commentaries in public (e.g., by talking with friends and neighbors, calling in to television talk shows or posting internet comments). These articulations raise the question of what grievances might illuminate in understandings of modern consumption practices.

Civil organizations such as consumer rights advocacy groups (consumer nongovernmental organizations [NGOs]) in postsocialist Bulgaria had both successes and shortcomings. On the one hand, they did a great deal of outreach to educate consumers about the new consumer regime in light of EU integration. Frequent appearances in the national media as well as the publication of a specialized consumer magazine familiarized Bulgarian consumers with the new consumer discourse and practices in the larger Europe. These groups also represented Bulgaria in global forums regarding consumer policies both in the EU and in different international associations of consumer organizations. Despite these efforts, on the other hand, Bulgarian consumer NGOs appear to have played more of the role of filling in the institutional forms laid out by the EU than in animating citizen-consumers' direct and active participation in seeking their rights by becoming members of the organizations or by relying on the independent product and service information published in their consumer magazines. The role and function of civil NGOs in the postsocialist context is entangled with state-citizen relations (see also Phillips 2008). The limitations of consumer

NGOs in Bulgaria must be understood within this larger frame rather than attributing the constraints and limited effects to a weak or immature civil society or lack of civic engagement, arguments that are often deployed by EU integration specialists who assume a linear developmentalist logic for social change. In this book, I discuss the dominant model and ideology of the EU as it relates to consumer protection and tell the stories of Bulgarian consumers and consumer experts, all of whom have responded to the questions of rights and accountability in different ways.

Consumer Politics in Postsocialist (Supra)National Contexts

I have introduced the *mente* phenomenon in Bulgaria as a starting point for discussing questions of rights and responsibilities because consumers frequently expressed their frustrations and anxieties about *mente* problems in postsocialist Bulgaria. Through ethnographic engagements, I learned that one could easily participate in conversation about *mente* in postsocialist Bulgaria across different socioeconomic groups and circumstances. Sites of consumption in the aftermath of state socialism revealed the material conditions of the postsocialist era, very often characterized as disappointing and disillusioning by postsocialist citizens. *Mente* is a term that symbolizes these political-economic conditions and serves as a sociocultural critique against new forms of power, both domestically and internationally. This is not to suggest that Bulgarian consumers only complained about consumption practices. On the contrary, they also conveyed excitement, joy, and happiness with material acquisitions and used them both to express identities and social status and to identify with certain lifestyles that affirmed a sense of belonging to global consumerism (Jung 2012, 2016). But here I focus more on consumer grievances because they illuminate different aspects of consumption that have not received much attention.[8] The eagerness and demand to address these widespread concerns in everyday consumption practices continue to loom large among ordinary Bulgarian consumers, who often feel constrained in the choices available to them due to financial reasons or the lack of quality control (i.e., even for consumers who can afford the products and services, the question of *mente* persists). And these consumer concerns have implications beyond Bulgaria as many contemporary capitalist economies feel compelled to address issues of inequality that expose the juxtaposition of material abundance and poverty in problematic ways.

These consumer issues are essentially questions of both access and choice. For example, while there are numerous goods and services in the postsocialist era, the things that the average Bulgarian consumers can afford or trust in terms of their quality are relatively limited, which makes consumers more prone to purchase *mente* items or feel relatively powerless vis-à-vis the producers. This makes them anxious about their consumer choices. Under neoliberal capitalist conditions that favor individual agency in a free market regime, abundant consumer choices are often celebrated as empowering and expressing agency (Freeman 2000; Hansen 2000). Yet discussions on consumption often overlook how these choices are actually conditioned upon access. Consumption practices cannot be discussed only in terms of the individual consumer: they require discussions in relation to the larger political economy that shape the balance between access and choice by citizen-consumers. This suggests that consumption can be seen as a productive space of civic engagement. What Bulgarians refer to as *mente*, for instance, provides illuminating moments of civic engagement regarding the question of access and choice.

The problem with fake goods is, of course, not new or unique to Bulgaria. Many other countries, including some in the West, have experienced counterfeit goods or consumer fraud at different times and in different contexts (Hilton 2009; see also Lin 2011; Crãciun 2014). While discussions on fake materials are often related to capitalist strategies, the production and consumption of so-called knockoffs point to a wider range of issues beyond status and profit-seeking individuals. For example, Yi-Chieh Jessica Lin (2011) found that the production and consumption of knockoff goods in China is also related to *shanzhai*, a cultural value that literally means "mountain fortress"; figuratively, it refers to bandits in mountain hideaways who take things from the established power and redistribute them to ordinary folk à la Robin Hood. Thus, while the market economy certainly unleashed entrepreneurial energies, some of which are directed to profiteering from knockoffs, there was also a shared sense of cultural intimacy (Herzfeld 1997, 2005a) among those engaged in this copy culture (producers, distributors, and consumers), which meant Chinese citizens often viewed the copy culture as a way to resist and reclaim control of meanings from a changing economic system (Lin 2011: 6). This cultural notion of *shanzhai* can therefore be understood as an expression of civic engagement and not simply an individualistic behavior in pursuit of self-interest and various aspirations.

By juxtaposing the authenticity of selves with the inauthenticity of objects, Magdalena Crăciun also explains "fakes (fake brands)" in Turkey and Romania, not in terms of capitalist strategies but as materiality that brings people and objects together as an ongoing dialectical process of objectification (2014: 10). For her research subjects, too, fakes are not simply a matter of identity politics through choice but have to do with the constructed nature of authenticity. The diversity of fakes analyzed in numerous anthropological studies demonstrates the wide-ranging variability of this phenomenon.[9] In this book, I analyze the *mente* phenomenon in postsocialist Bulgaria by exploring a number of critical questions that it raises regarding rights and responsibilities. Discussions of contemporary consumption practices and consumer culture have not examined this aspect of fakes. My Bulgarian interlocutors frequently asked themselves questions such as these: Do we have a better life now because of democracy and capitalism? Yes, we have the abundance of goods, but can we all afford or trust them? Even if we can afford them, how do we know that what we consume is safe and good for us and that we won't waste our income on *mente* products? Who will be responsible for all these crooks (*moshenitsi*) whose only interest is to make quick money from us? Why is the state not doing anything to control them? How can we have a normal life and be free of anxiety (*spokoino*)?

Consumption in the era of globalization with seemingly abundant choices thanks to free market competition is usually considered a rich arena to understand how desires are expressed and how agency is exercised by different individuals and social groups despite the workings of power that privilege some and constrain others (Miller 2012; Freeman 2000; Hansen 2000; Warde 2015). Postsocialist everyday consumption practices, however, bring to the fore questions that are not simply about individuals and choices. Instead, the questions asked by many Bulgarian consumers are about choice and access in relative terms (relative to the past, relative to other countries) and about how the complicated relationship between access and choice has implications for consumers' social relations to multiple regimes of power involved in everyday practices.

Questions regarding access and choice continue to be relevant today in the lives of ordinary Bulgarians even after over two decades since the transition from a centralized planned economy to a free market economy. Purchasing power remains relatively low compared to other EU member states, and the rising inequality between the haves and the have-nots has exacerbated an ontological sense of normality among ordinary citizens, resulting in continued aspiration for a normal and anxiety-free life. While the country harmonized its political and economic structures with the EU to gain membership, Bulgarians feel that the new system continues not to work in Bulgaria—that is, it does not raise the standards of living of many ordinary citizens. Neither does the new system restore the fundamental social trust that many feel is broken because of rapid social transformation led by antiregulatory neoliberal policies and political corruption.

When state socialism collapsed and a capitalist market economy started to prevail in postsocialist Eastern Europe, everyday consumption practices became central in people's experiences with the swiftly changing society. Many studies on postsocialist societies have reported how consumption was a deeply politicized field even during the Cold War. Consumption was ultimately seen at that time (although not officially positioned, due to the productivist bias of the socialist regime) as the measurement for economic growth, indicative of the successes and failures of state socialism (Bren and Neuburger 2012; Caldwell and Patico 2002; Humphrey 1995; Mazurek and Hilton 2007). Communism was dedicated to fulfilling the needs of the population, yet relatively little attention was given to such needs, highlighting a paradox of state socialism (Haney 1997; Steiner 1998; Verdery 1996; see also Fehérváry 2013 and Rogers and Verdery 2013 for more recent discussions on needs under communism; cf. Feher, Heller, and Markus 1983). The stereotypical contrast between consumption under socialism and capitalism in Bulgaria as well as in other postsocialist societies was often depicted as shopping amid a scarcity of goods with long lines and empty shelves versus shopping amid an abundance of goods but with little money. How consumers under these circumstances resort to creativity and savvy to cope with the uncertainties and difficulties of daily life was well-documented (Caldwell 2004, 2009a; Chelcea 2002; Klumbytė 2009; Mincyte 2009, 2014; Patico 2008; Shevchenko 2002, 2010). Yet these are not the only aspects that everyday consumption practices can illuminate in the globalized contemporary consumer society, as the *mente* phenomenon in postsocialist Bulgaria suggests.

In my encounters with Bulgaria's postsocialist consumer society, I observed aspects of consumption that were not simply cast in terms of individuals' creative expression of desires, identity politics, or expressions of modernity and globalization (Freeman 2000; Hansen 2000; Liechty 2002; Mazzarella 2003; Miller 1995b, 1995d; Rausing 2002). Rather, consumers' experiences highlighted debates about the consumerist market and their relationship to the state and the EU. This tendency is important to note in light of the fundamental shift in consumer policies across the world brought about by the end of the Cold War. Since the 1990s, consumer policies have adapted to the neoliberal ideologies that privilege a free market over a regulatory state. Unlike in previous decades, the state was no longer considered the ultimate accountable subject protecting consumers from the abuses of the market. Consumer protection thus gained new meanings compared to earlier consumer regimes. Overall shifts in neoliberal policies also affected the EU and its consumer protection regime, which until the 1980s and early 1990s was largely based on social democratic goals from the 1950s and 1960s with an emphasis of access and welfare protected by the state (Hilton 2009: 54).

EU policies since the 1990s regarding consumer rights and protection, however, were no longer premised on a regulatory state. Instead, they followed the neoclassical economic philosophy that "individual satisfaction is obtained through greater choice" (Hilton 2009: 17). Additionally, consumer protection regimes were to guarantee such consumers' rights by providing reliable information that could enable greater choices. Ultimately, it was the consumers who were held responsible for their choices. The role of the state was more ambiguous in these consumer policies.

If consumption was implicitly framed in terms of raising the standard of living for everybody during socialism, in the context of EU integration, consumption was explicitly framed as a development agenda for the candidate countries wishing to join the EU. According to the *Acquis Communautaire* (the body of EU law and regulation), the consumer sector comprised a separate chapter to harmonize the systems among EU member states. This meant that candidate countries such as Bulgaria had a clearly modeled path of social transformation from state socialism and had to meet specific requirements dictated by the EU in order to gain membership. One of the popular discourses among EU policy experts in this context was that poor countries like Bulgaria did not have a "consumer culture" and therefore had to develop one to join the EU (Pritchard 1994).

Bulgaria, like many other former socialist Eastern European countries that applied to join the EU, had to adopt the *Acquis Communautaire* with little negotiation. These external circumstances generated tension within the newly forming consumer sector in postsocialist Bulgaria. Because of the EU dictates, Bulgaria was obligated to develop a consumer sector consisting of government agencies responsible for consumer affairs, new consumer laws (state socialism did not have consumer laws) conforming to EU standards, and NGOs representing consumer interests in a developing civil society. Yet this newly created sector was alien to the majority of consumers because it hardly resonated with their past experiences. Perhaps unsurprisingly, despite persistent consumer anxiety and frustration, the new consumer sector in Bulgaria neither mobilized consumers for collective actions nor facilitated EU's consumer policies that conceptualized consumer protection in terms of consumers' access to reliable, independent consumer information to protect themselves. The EU model of establishing an infrastructure so that consumers can help themselves with better informed choices through the guidance of consumer NGOs, for instance, has resonated little with ordinary Bulgarians. This, as I explain further in the following chapters (especially chapter 3), can be attributed to the insufficient understanding regarding state-citizen relations by multiple regimes of power, an understanding that fundamentally influenced many of the negative postsocialist experiences by citizen-consumers.

The dominance of neoliberal ideology since the end of the Cold War and the era of globalization led to reduced scholarly attention to the role of the state in economic activities (Warde 2015). I agree with Alan Warde (2015: 13), who asserts that the state needs to be examined in relation to everyday consumption practices to better understand the shifting dynamics between market efficiency and collective political decisions that impact all dimensions of the economy including consumption. As I have argued elsewhere about the importance of the state in understanding economic activities of ordinary citizens (producers and consumers alike) in the aftermath of state socialism (Jung 2014a, 2016; Jung, Klein, and Caldwell 2014), I hope the stories in this book will illuminate how so-called market logic alone cannot explain the commonly expressed grievances even as living conditions are improving in many postsocialist states.

Because of the experiences under state socialism in which the role of a paternalistic state fundamentally shaped citizens' relations to various spheres of social life and how people understood state-citizen relations, the sudden withdrawal of the state was often perceived as abandonment. Many postsocialist citizens still express a strong disapproval of this abandonment because they believe the state has breached the social contract to fulfill its promises. While postsocialist citizens express grievances vis-à-vis the state, they articulate less clearly what kind of state they are imagining in these renderings, which often leads outsiders to believe that these postsocialist citizens long for a return of a paternalistic (and often authoritarian) socialist state (see also Kideckel 2008). Yet my Bulgarian interlocutors made it explicit that they were not advocating for a paternalistic kind of state. As my middle-aged friend and interlocutor for over a decade, Nadiya put it: "It is more difficult to explain what kind of state Bulgarians want, but I know most of us feel the absence [of the state] and think something needs to be done [with the state]."

This is the legacy of socialism with which even the new generation born after state socialism continues to grapple: hope for the future is often expressed through envisioning an adequate (normal) state that can honor the social contract with its citizens. This shows how the state is a meaningful category in the social life of ordinary citizens and how its absence often becomes a source of discontent. The sentiment of abandonment and to what extent the notion of paternalism (in the name of care) is relevant in discussions about the state makes the postsocialist case a particularly productive one. Thus, postsocialism can serve as a useful analytical frame as well as a historical condition that points to the relevance and importance in understanding the nature and role of the state under conditions of neoliberal capitalism and globalization.

There have been multiple discussions over the past decade regarding the usefulness of "postsocialism" as an analytical category, especially since an entire age cohort[10] of people who have never experienced state socialism is coming of age and forming their own families. In particular, scholars have asked whether postsocialism is a temporal category (from 1989 to when?), a spatial one (primarily for the former socialist states in Central and Eastern Europe and the Soviet Union) (Buyandelger 2008; Creed 2011; Gilbert 2006; Rogers 2010; Borelli and Mattioli 2013), or if it is both. Ultimately, scholars raised the question of the relevance of postsocialism in the present when the Cold War technically ended over two decades ago. My response to this question is that consumption studies can particularly benefit from the analytic category of postsocialism because it makes the relevance and importance of the state explicit in understanding modern consumption practices and helps us to theorize the state beyond institutional and bureaucratic encounters (Ferguson and Gupta 2002; Herzfeld 1992; Sharma and Gupta 2006; Reeves, Rasanayagan, and Beyer 2014) or domains of welfare (Caldwell 2012; Muehlebach 2014).

Another key aspect that postsocialist consumption illuminates is the question of consumption and poverty. It could be argued that the relative poverty of postsocialist urbanites (the subjects of this book) and that of the Third World is different as the former are cash poor but often have resources (education and assets). However, when people are poor (real or perceived), this does not preclude the consumerism that surrounds their everyday life. In fact, as Janet Fitchen (1988) suggests in regards to food consumption practices among the American poor, even if the poor are constrained by their economic resources, they are aware of and strive to follow dominant social values and consumption practices and are not entirely excluded from the market. One might question how it is possible to discuss consumption or consumer culture when people are poor (or perceive themselves as relatively poor) or whether it is possible to study consumption under such conditions because poverty suggests market exclusion. My Bulgarian interlocutors did not consider themselves as being excluded from the consumerist world even as they worried about access and became frustrated about limited choices. In addition, as Melissa Caldwell and Jennifer Patico argue, "Consumerism is neither new nor unfamiliar to postsocialist citizens, but has long occupied a key role in consumers' relation to each other, the state, and the world" (2002: 287). If we take Juliet Schor's definition of consumerism as "an attitude and an ideology, a particular way of relating to consumer goods in which they take on central importance in the construction of culture, identity and social life" (cited in Holt 2005: 5; see also Schor 1998), poverty is not a hindering factor to studying consumption and consumer culture. The linear evolutionary presumption that consumer societies and cultures can only arise after a certain level of affluence is achieved needs to be further problematized (Goodwin, Ackerman, and Kiron 1997).

Postsocialist consumption, then, is a site in which negotiations of expectations take place. And, because the state as an institution is considered the ultimate moral agent for accountability, the processes of negotiations necessarily engage the state even under conditions of weakened political power and decreased resources compared to the socialist era. In at least a normative sense, citizens expect the state to be a kind of moral agent, and consumer discontent can be considered a moral failure of the state. As frustration and social distrust with everyday life grows, so do consumers' demands for accountability and redress. While in postsocialist circumstances people feel more alienated from the state (Kideckel 2008), they do not want the state to forgo its responsibilities to citizen-consumers.[11] EU membership did not ease people's expectations vis-à-vis the state either. Despite the institutional hierarchies owing to EU membership (in which the EU occupies a higher moral status than the Bulgarian state), the state continues to occupy an important position in terms of accountability in the eyes of ordinary consumers. These attitudes continue to inform consumption practices in postsocialist Bulgaria. Bulgarian consumers' expectations about products and services under the postsocialist capitalist market system reflect the value systems that are historically formed and continue to inform their future visions. Thus, the collective expressions of needs, normality, and anxiety-free life (*spokoen zhivot*), which are repeatedly referred to in ordinary consumption practices, are critical in the understanding of consumer expectations in postsocialist Bulgaria. As becomes apparent in the following chapters, these ideas form the basis for citizen-consumers in conceptualizing old and new rights.

Consumer anxieties in the postsocialist era were different from the kinds citizens experienced during the shortage economy, yet anxieties persisted nevertheless. Bulgarian consumers continue to ask questions about their changing relationship to the state and about rights and responsibilities in the aftermath of state socialism. They ask questions about the relationship between the market, the state, and citizen-consumers. The stories in this book suggest that postsocialist consumption practices provide a productive site to understand the tension of modern consumption regarding how to balance access and choice, and how the state, along with other regimes of power including the market and the EU, plays a significant role in navigating these tensions that present themselves as moral dilemmas over abundance in the contemporary world. In other words, consumption practices reflect the material conditions of state-citizen relations in the globalized era, and the Bulgarian case provides a productive vantage point to think about political economy in the contemporary world.

Based on a longitudinal ethnographic study in Sofia, Bulgaria, with consumers and consumer experts (1999–2015; see the appendix), I make the case that the state is considered a significant moral agent held accountable for the plight of vulnerable consumers in the neoliberal milieu. Consumption practices offer a site where social relations between people and the state are produced and reshaped. This is not to suggest that Bulgarians are nostalgic for socialism or long for an authoritarian state because of their experiences under a paternalistic socialist state. Rather, my argument is that the nature and the role of the state under conditions of neoliberal globalization can be productively examined by attending to postsocialist consumption practices in which the state has been a central and meaningful category for consumers figuring out new relationships with it. The experiences from state socialism provide a reference point as well as new resources for consumer politics in the postsocialist era.

Organization of the Book

Balkan Blues: Consumer Politics after State Socialism is organized to structure and advance my primary set of arguments—namely, (1) consumption is not only confined in the realm of the market and around issues of individual choice matters to express identity and agency but also engages the state because of the grievances over access and choice, (2) state-citizen relations manifest themselves in mundane sites of everyday consumption even in the post–Cold War context of neoliberal capitalism and globalization in which the state is considered withdrawn or weakened, and (3) consumption is not only about consumer desire and aspiration but is also a form of civic engagement through which citizen-consumers cast their ideals and conceptualize their expectations from the state.

Chapter 1 provides a sense of analytical object and ethnographic context by discussing the different instances of *mente* phenomena through which consumer grievance is acutely and consistently expressed in postsocialist Bulgaria. To understand how *mente* phenomena can be historically and culturally contextualized and to show how state-citizen relations are historically constituted, chapter 2 discusses the context of consumer politics during socialism and through postsocialism and EU integration in Bulgaria. In chapters 3 and 4, I ground my arguments further by documenting the changes in the consumer sector following state socialism and how consumer organizations were shaped in this process. Through ethnographic examinations of mundane consumption practices such as heating, housing, and seaside vacations, I also show how ideas of rights and responsibilities have been shaped in postsocialist Bulgaria, especially during the EU integration period, and how these ideas inform the expectations of the state by citizen-consumers. Chapter 5 addresses the larger questions posed in this book, particularly what consumer politics after state socialism entails in understanding modern consumption practices. Finally, in the epilogue, I provide some concluding thoughts about the nature and role of the state in postsocialist Bulgaria that has cross-cultural implications. The appendix provides more a detailed discussion of my fieldwork experiences, especially concerning my positionality as an East Asian ethnographer in Eastern Europe, in order to further contextualize the findings and arguments in this book.

Notes

1. *Mente* (men-té) is pronounced with the accent on the second syllable. It is a very broad cultural concept that is not confined to the narrow sense of counterfeit or knockoff in English. I explain this in more detail in chapter 1 and refer back to it in the epilogue.
2. State socialism in Bulgaria existed between 1944 and 1989.
3. There are many significant studies in this regard, but to list some that have contributed most to the debates on consumption up to the mid-2000s or so, when the influence of the cultural turn was in its peak (Warde 2015: 118), see, for example, Bourdieu 1984; Douglas and Isherwood 1979; Miller 1986, 1995a, 1995c, 1997, 2010, 2012; Featherstone 1991; Freeman 2000; Hansen 2000; Liechty 2002; Mazzarella 2003; Patico 2008; and Wilk 1995, 2001). More recently, there have also been notable critiques regarding the current state of and prospect of consumption studies because of the concept's unclear definition and broad scope (Graeber 2011; Colloredo-Mansfeld 2013; Trentmann 2007).
4. In socialist Bulgaria, so-called foreign currency stores (CORECOM) offered limited Western goods to citizens who were entitled to shop with foreign currency, such as American dollars. See further discussion of CORECOM in chapter 2. For more studies on consumer desires during state socialism, see especially Gronow 2003, Patico 2002, Patterson 2009, and Smith 2009.
5. For a comparative contamination case regarding Coca-Cola and Pepsi in India, see Vedwan 2007.
6. Scholars of China, Vietnam, and Cuba have questioned whether "postsocialism" adequately describes these societies because they are still socialist. Klein (2014: 118) prefers to use "market" or "reform" socialism following Hann and Hart 2011 to describe China, and Nir Avieli (2014: 146–147) refers to contemporary Vietnam as "late socialist" following Harms 2011 and Endres 2007 to distinguish the present period from the previous more "orthodox" socialist stage. Wilson (2014: 182–183) uses "(post)socialism" to describe contemporary Cuba.
7. See also Wilk 2001: 277, which explains how the motives and outcomes of consumption by individuals inevitably raise moral debate.
8. Different forms of grievances by ordinary citizens during socialism have been explored by Sheila Fitzpatrick (1996, 1999) and Vieda Skultans (2001).
9. Crăciun (2014: 36–4) provides an excellent overview of scholarly examinations of fakes across the world including India (Nakassis 2012), Côte d'Ivoire (Newell 2013), Russia (Patico 2002), Guatemala (Thomas 2009), and Vietnam (Vann 2006).
10. I prefer to use the term "age cohort" rather than "generation" because it is a more flexible concept.
11. See Ganev 2007 regarding the role of the state in Bulgarian politics and Kaneff 2002 on the relationship between the Bulgarian state and the individual as reflected in funerary practices during socialism and postsocialism.

1

MENTE

Consumer Grievances

Deception and Risk

Many of my friends in Sofia were getting ready for their annual seaside vacation at the Black Sea in the summer of 2002. Irena, an energetic journalist in her mid-20s, suggested I accompany her to some shoe shops to buy sandals. She wanted a particular Western brand, Salomon, known to be sturdy and of reliable quality. We started our quest in the former Central Department Store building, *Tsum*, which had been turned into a Western-style shopping mall. As we entered the modern-looking mall with empty spaces, Irena led me to the third floor where Salomon had a direct sales store. The store sold outdoor gear and sports equipment, including shoes. Irena examined several pairs of sandals carefully but did not try on any of them. As we left the store, she said that they were nice but too pricey. She also wondered whether some of them could be *mente* because they looked flimsy. I protested, indicating that since it was a corporate store housed in a nice, newly renovated shopping mall, the products ought not to be *mente*. Irena grinned and reminded me that we were in Bulgaria and everything could be *mente*. Next, we went to a few small neighborhood stores on busy downtown streets, where she examined sandals carefully (some from the brand that she was interested in) and checked price tags. Finally, we arrived at an outdoor and sports specialty store a few blocks down from *Popa*, the central downtown landmark with a statue of an Orthodox church priest, which was not too far from where she lived. The establishment maintained a neighborhood-store feel in terms of its intimate space, but it also displayed specialty gear for hiking and swimming. Irena selected a particular pair of sandals and asked the owner to bring her the right size so that she could try them on. Although she looked at them carefully, she did not seem to examine the displayed pair with the same scrutiny as in the other stores. When the storeowner brought her the sandals, Irena tried them on and looked at me contentedly. She wondered what I thought of them, although it was quite obvious that her mind was set on this particular pair. Because payday was several days away, she told the owner that she would be back soon. The owner assured her that he would put them on hold for a few days. She had obviously shopped in this store before, and the owner was not a complete stranger. When I inquired how she could be sure that this smaller neighborhood store did not carry *mente* (especially given my experience with another friend who had also purchased from a small neighborhood store and felt cheated, though in her case she was not acquainted with the store or the owner), Irena told me that this store was a "serious" one and that the owner had been doing business for some time here. If he carried *mente*, customers from the neighborhood like herself would have already stopped shopping there. The importance of store reliability was reminiscent of stories my other interlocuters told me, and Irena took the fact that the store had been around for a long time very seriously. Compared to the prices in the larger, corporate stores in the mall, these sandals were also a little cheaper, which made her even happier. I was surprised that she would spend more than two-thirds of her entire biweekly paycheck (230 leva for the sandals out of wages of 300 leva)[1] on this particular purchase. Although single, she contributed financially to her family's household in significant ways. This was why, Irena emphasized, careful shopping was so important in postsocialist Bulgaria—the stakes were high for an ordinary consumer with limited purchasing power in a market flooded with *mente* products. Eventually, she made good use of the sandals, and the pair lasted her two summers with lots of mountain biking and hiking along the rocky seaside, confirming her assessment that the sandals were authentic and of "high quality." Consumer savvy rather than the brand name itself turned out to be vital in avoiding a *mente* product. I asked Irena why she went to the other stores when she had already made up her mind to buy the sandals from her neighborhood store. She responded that even though she trusted her local store, she just needed to reconfirm that she was not wasting her paycheck on *mente* since there was no working system in place that protected her as a consumer. "They" (referring to the state), she smilingly said, "don't do their work of controlling bad stuffs in the market, don't you know? I need to be certain [as a consumer]." Other Bulgarian interlocutors pointed out that once the authenticity of the Western brand was proven, its authority could replace that of the state in controlling quality in the postsocialist environment. Proving authenticity, however, involved an astuteness often based on one's own experiences of consumer competence in the (perceived) absence of a state that could protect consumers from the abuses of the market (see also Jung 2009).

This incident illustrates how the sense of being cheated in mundane consumption practices plays a central role in conceptualizing citizens' relations to and expectations about the state in the postsocialist era. The initial enthusiasm for flashy-looking[2] foreign goods that flooded Bulgarian markets with the end of socialism soon waned as people became dismayed by what they referred to as "garbage products" (*bokluk*) being offered to poor, ordinary Bulgarian consumers. As in the case of the "Ossies" (East Germans) who, a few years into German reunification, as Daphne Berdahl (1999: 177) notes, started to wake up from early illusions of the "Golden West," Bulgarian consumers also began differentiating imported products around the mid-1990s. Unlike East Germans, however, Bulgarians did not become quite as disenchanted with the West because they learned that the *bokluk* products that they could afford were not actually Western. They started to notice that the cheap (and sometimes fraudulent) products were made in China, Turkey, or even Greece[3] and that the quality products were made in Germany or France (see also Patico 2002, 2008 for similar observations in Russia). What they increasingly became disillusioned with, however, was their own state ("they") and its inability to address the rampant market spaces fraught with deception and risks. This Bulgarian reaction differs from what Melissa Caldwell (2002) observed in Russia, where the sense of deception was primarily expressed as market fraud without explicit reference to the lack of the state's control. Although Bulgarian consumers quickly became aware that "market economy" did not mean all goods and services were "good," the majority of Bulgarian consumers could not help but buy second-rate things because of financial limitations. Cheap items often meant poor quality, which Bulgarians translated into the notion of fake. Although *mente*[4] was used for a range of things that were not original and therefore fell into the realm of fraudulent, counterfeit, or inauthentic, essentially the term referred to things that were not of good quality (*nekachestveni*), including spoiled products, or not real (*neistinsko*) and thus unreliable and risky. Everyday consumer experiences have been intimately intertwined with encounters of *mente* (real and perceived) in postsocialist Bulgaria and highlight two main anxieties of citizen-consumers: first, the limitations of reliable choices despite the relative abundance of goods compared to the socialist times and, second, uncertainty in how to conceptualize the new postsocialist state in relation to new regimes of power such as the market, NGOs, and the EU.

What is important to note in this context is the notion of choice, so prevalent in the popular discussions of contemporary consumer society with its implication of free and greater choice amid material abundance. Choice in this latter case assumes a level of affluence that enables free choice. In this context, choice actually indicates "preference" (Hilton 2009: 250). In comparison, many postsocialist Bulgarian consumers face a different kind of choice, one that is not about preference but about avoiding deception (buying something that is not authentic exposes one to potential danger). Understanding how this language of choice is used by different consumers and consumer experts in the postsocialist context is important in order to grasp the consumer politics after state socialism. To what extent are citizen-consumers fully able to act as social agents, or to what extent are they weak victims in need of protection? What kind of state is imagined in these renderings?

If Irena's concern about potentially buying *mente* was more reflective of the general sense of vulnerability for consumers with financial constraints, the following cases of *mente* demonstrate a palpable sense of frustration, anxiety, and even anger, and how some of my Bulgarian interlocutors dealt with the constant feeling of deception in their everyday consumer choices by attempting to identify targets of blame and responsibility.

Yulia, an aspiring journalist with a cable television station, had been wanting a new pair of winter boots and was waiting patiently for her next payday. She worked as a reporter on an ad hoc basis and was paid per reportage if it was accepted by the editorial staff. As such, she did not have a consistent salary, but this time she expected just enough money (about 60 leva, approximately US$30 in 2001) with which she could afford some boots to get through the upcoming winter. After visiting a number of different shoe stores around Pirotska Street (the old market street) and Stamboliiski Boulevard, she finally bought a pair of black high-heeled boots that looked sturdy and stylish. Because I accompanied her on numerous shopping trips, I witnessed how carefully she examined the boots before spending almost her entire paycheck for them. Unfortunately, the second day she wore the boots one of the heels broke in such a way that gluing it back would not have fixed it. With teary eyes, Yulia complained about the lack of quality control that she attributed first to the producer, then to the merchants, and ultimately to the state that did not take consumer safety or consumer protection seriously. After all, she said, the state allowed a poor-quality product to be sold at such an expensive price (at 50 leva in the winter of 2001, her boots belonged to the upper median price range). When I asked whether the state still held the ultimate responsibility in what my Bulgarian interlocuters frequently referred to as the new "market economy," she admitted, "I don't know. Maybe it is me, the buyer, or maybe it is the businessman, but do you understand how upsetting it is to spend money and feel cheated [*izmamena*]? I still have some clothes from the socialist time, and they look better than those I can buy now. So sometimes I don't know whether now is better than then, really." Yulia belongs to the younger cohort who celebrated her *abiturientski bal* (high school graduation ball), a culturally meaningful social event in Bulgarians' lives and a marker of adulthood, a few years after the democratic changes in 1989. Although Yulia first identified the state as the target of blame and the object of accountability, she was also aware that there were, in fact, multiple objects of accountability—more than one "they"—herself, the capitalist manufacturer, and the state.

At the same time, she brought up the point about purchasing necessities (*podrebnosti*) that went into the garbage soon after and emphasized the sense of betrayal she felt on such occasions. The provision of necessities or needs—most notably shelter, food, clothes, and jobs—was considered a major function of the socialist state (see also Feher, Heller, and Markus 1983; Haney 1997; Steiner 1998). Yulia's comparison of the past and present and her conflicting moral judgments were informed by this historical understanding of needs and who should be the agents responsible for those needs. Historic socialist ideas concerning necessities (Velinova 2004) are crucial in the understanding of shifting social values in postsocialist Bulgaria (see chapter 2). Even if the role of the postsocialist state was not about guaranteeing access, it could not be excused from its obligation to its citizens. Thus, a relatively young person like Yulia, who spent her formative years already under a market economy and is deemed culturally more fluent in everyday consumption practices than the older cohort, still needed to negotiate the social values inherited from her older cohorts with new values she was learning under the changed environment. The neoclassical view on consumer sovereignty argues that supply responds passively to the dictates of consumers whose preferences rule through their purchasing power (Fine 1995: 138). Bulgarian consumer sovereignty is being informed by further negotiations of social values such as needs (access) and expectations of the multiple "they." Some of these negotiations do not occur within the realm of the market, as the expansion of capitalism and neoliberal globalization debates may anticipate. In the postsocialist context, negotiations of values and social relations outside the market, such as consumers versus the state, are important because they help us understand how new meanings of rights and responsibilities are shaped in daily consumption practices that are often fraught with a sense of deception.

Mente i Originali: The Informed Consumer?

To what extent is this *mente* problem, widely accepted by Bulgarian consumers as an everyday consumer grievance, a matter of individual choice as opposed to a matter of access? Furthermore, how can consumers who feel cheated defend themselves? The following example is particularly interesting because it suggests an early civic response to these problems of *mente*, raising questions of consumer redress, consumer protection, and the role of the state from the perspectives of postsocialist citizens, which differed from the EU's stance on consumer policies. Whereas the EU's viewpoint is informed by neoliberal policies that highlight the responsibility of individual consumers to protect themselves, Bulgarian consumers responded with a different mindset.

In the summer of 1999, I went with my friend Elena, a teacher in her early 40s and the main breadwinner in her family, to a liquor store to buy a bottle of brandy (*rakiya*) to take back to her place as an accompaniment for *meze* (appetizers such as salads, cold cuts, and cheese that Bulgarians pair with alcohol). The large liquor store was located in a residential area a little south of downtown Sofia and looked respectable in the sense that it was neatly organized, quite spacious, and well stocked. I grabbed a bottle of *Sungurlarska Rakiya*, which was a well-known Bulgarian brand. When I was ready to check out, Elena asked me whether she could take a look at it. She started to examine the bottle carefully and at my look of curiosity whispered, "just to make sure that it is not *mente*." She actually took the bottle back to the shelf and gave me another one. The second bottle also said *Sungurlarska Rakiya*, and other than the style of the label, it did not look much different from the first bottle I had selected. After we left the store, she immediately pulled me to a nearby newspaper stand. I recalled a simi-

1.1 *Mente i Originali* magazine covers
Left (1999, no. 7): headlines include "What Is There in Coca-Cola" and "Rakiya Twins."
Right (1998, no. 4): headlines include "Hunt for Counterfeit Alcohol" and "From Grapes [wine/brandy] to Whiskey: What Is in the Plastic Bottle?" *Reproduced with permission of Ivan Bakalov.*

lar encounter with *mente* water at the Black Sea resort earlier that summer when I heard the term *mente* for the first time. In an effort to explain what *mente* entailed, Elena directed me to *Mente i Originali* (Fake and originals) a magazine published by the Mente Society (the society's name is written in Latin letters, not in Cyrillic) (figure 1.1). This specialty magazine was apparently issued to respond to the numerous *mente* phenomena in Bulgaria.[5]

Interestingly, in the issue Elena pointed to, we found an article that discussed the same *Sungurlarska Rakiya* bottle that I had almost bought, and it was identified as *mente* (figure 1.2). *Mente*, in this particular context, referred to counterfeit (knockoff) products and not simply something that was of shoddy quality, although it could also indicate that the product was unsafe.

Mente i Originali guided consumers through different kinds of fraudulent products comparing them with the originals ("the authentic" or "the real") and advised consumers how to shop sensibly. In some cases, it also

1.2 *Mente* and authentic *Sungurlarska Rakiya*
The photos on this magazine spread show the difference between the authentic and *mente* bottles and bottle caps. (*Mente i Originali* 1999, no. 7, pp. 26–27). *Reproduced with permission of Ivan Bakalov.*

clarified how global brand products such as Coke could, in fact, still be authentic but taste differently if bought in Bulgaria because the Coca-Cola company used "different recipes" for different markets. For instance, in the article "What Is There in Coca-Cola," the author compared a Coke bought in Greece with a Coke bought in Bulgaria and noted that the Greek version had higher sugar content and the Bulgarian version tasted less concentrated in terms of flavor. Essentially, they tasted different, according to the author. While the Bulgarian Coke was still the "real thing," the author indicated that Bulgarian consumers might perceive it to be *mente* because it was not the same as the Greek product. In this particular case, *mente* referred to something that was simply not the same as in "other" (usually implying Western) markets.

In any case, by offering objective, reliable information, this magazine was a form of consumer advocacy before most of the consumer organizations in Bulgaria even existed. (As I discuss in the Introduction and chapter

3, most of the consumer organizations started their activities in late 1999 and early 2000 when Bulgaria's new law for consumer protection was adopted.)

Mente i Originali seemed to be partly sponsored by various companies that had an interest in informing consumers about *mente* products that claimed to be theirs. According to the featured articles, the range of *mente* products was wide, and virtually everything was subject to *mente*: alcohol, foodstuffs, soft drinks (most often Coke and Fanta), soap, toothpaste, tires and various car-related accessories, electronics, computers, money (banknotes such as US dollars, German marks, and Bulgarian levs), and so on.[6] In an editorial note, editor-in-chief Ivan Bakalov wrote: "Publications like the magazine '*Mente i Originali*' exist in many countries. They differ from each other, however, because in the civilized states [*tsivilizovanite*],[7] the sale of counterfeit goods is a felony and we cannot see '*mente*' products in the markets [there] in such a massive scale like in our country" (1998: 5).

Comparing Bulgarian markets, which were flooded with *mente* products, with those in the "civilized states" (which in the Bulgarian context means the West), the editor emphasized the lack of control by state authorities (in the West, counterfeiting goods is a felony) over the products sold in Bulgaria. Indeed, many Bulgarians were afraid of buying *mente*, and if they found out that they had, they became very upset and frustrated. At the same time, their limited financial means made them very susceptible to *mente*, which perpetuated a deep sense of deception and vulnerability, echoing the public sentiments of demanding control by the entity in power. As has been documented in many post-Soviet consumption practices, experiences of deception (Humphrey 1995; Shevchenko 2002) have been a central image associated with consumption after the political changes. In fact, people living under socialist regimes commonly experienced deception as well (Verdery 1996), which influenced state-citizen relations. Socialist citizens had ignored the state's insistence that living standards were constantly rising since the 1970s and especially in the 1980s when they were allowed a glimpse at the West, whose technological development exceeded theirs and whose stores displayed an abundance while theirs increasingly exhibited a constant shortage. In the postsocialist period, feelings of vulnerability and betrayal persisted not only because of scarcity or inferior quality of goods but also because of the perceived lack of control of market abuses. As some of my interlocuters argued, they were not so naïve as to think that there were no "bad products" in other countries (with more "developed" capitalism). They nevertheless insisted that there could not possibly be a state like postsocialist Bulgaria that did not care enough to control quality.

In the post-Soviet case, deception was primarily associated with imports (Humphrey 1995); postsocialist Bulgarians' reactions to deception, however, did not merely derive from foreign sources. While true that many of the fraudulent products were made in China or Turkey, a good number of domestic products—most notably counterfeit wine, brandy, and banknotes—were offered to Bulgarian consumers. Recently, in 2013, the so-called imitated dairy products scandal produced endless *mente* stories in the media and among my friends. This imitation cheese was essentially a processed cheese containing nondairy vegetable fat (think Kraft American cheese) that was not illegal but nevertheless considered *mente* because it was not made by "real" and "authentic" cheese-making methods. In this case, *mente* did not indicate a counterfeit but something that was chemically processed and thus of lesser quality. Even though the state did act in this particular incident to force producers and stores to differentiate real (*istinsko*) cheese from fake cheese by requiring strict labeling for "imitation cheese" and dictating its display in a separate section from real cheese (figure 1.3), the fact that the state tolerated this *mente* and made it legal to be circulated only reconfirmed consumers' discontent with the postsocialist state.

Interestingly, Chinese, Turkish, or Bulgarian *mente* producers were not the ultimate objects of blame in these instances. Consumers repeatedly vented their frustrations against the Bulgarian state, which was incapable of controlling these *mente* and which let them appear in the market and thus exposed consumers to risks. The editor of *Mente i Originali* made this point clear by emphasizing that in Bulgaria, people (merchants and producers alike) could get away with *mente* products without going to prison because of the inaction of the state.

Bulgarian consumers had an ambivalent relationship with their socialist state that carried over in their relations to the postsocialist state as well. As much as they saw the socialist state as a deceiving subject,[8] they also pointed out that they appreciated its ability to control *mente* (like in the "civilized states") and protect consumers. Protection here was primarily associated with the regulation of fraud, which allowed citizens to have a sense of social trust in terms of the authenticity (if not high quality) of goods (see also Giordano and Kostova 2002 for discussion on social [mis]trust).

1.3 "Imitated products containing processed milk"
Bulgarian law requires processed ("fake") white cheeses to be labeled and displayed in a separate section in grocery stores. Bulgarian consumers describe this kind of cheese as *neistinsko* (not real) and thus *mente*. Photograph by author, 2013.

Furthermore, the state's ability to control standards is also associated with reliance on the socialist law in the production of goods (Jung 2009). My Bulgarian interlocutors such as Irena, Yulia, and Elena perceived socialist standards as superior to the present standards in the market economy (which, more accurately speaking, were believed to be absent). During socialism, they said, the products were cheap and maybe of poor quality but not fake. The quality of products during socialism was believed to correspond to their price.

Many Bulgarian consumers continue to feel deceived and vulnerable about the services and products they choose and consume. Consumer choice for many ordinary postsocialist citizens does not imply free choice based on preference. Whenever I accompanied friends like Irena or Yulia to shop for groceries, for example, I often saw how they scanned the different shelves, eliminating the top (usually more expensive) and bottom (usually cheaper) shelves and tried to find items on the middle shelves. Numerous other interlocutors, including my other Bulgarian language teacher, Gergana, commented how they orient themselves as consumers when they shop, which was essentially the same tactic that Irena and Yulia employed. Some of my interlocutors, such as my landladies, however, also picked things that were the cheapest (from the bottom shelf) and lamented that though the products could be *mente*, they had to risk it because of their financial limitations. This is the social context in which Bulgarian consumers relate to the state and express their daily frustrations and demand control by an accountable state. Such public sentiments, however, collide with what Western-influenced consumer advocacy supports in the era of neoliberal globalization. Consumer regimes in the advanced capitalist economies in Europe or North America emphasize the significance of self-surveillance armed by better information so that consumers can protect themselves and rely less on the regulatory state. Consumer experts in postsocialist Bulgaria repeatedly echoed the same idea: consumers should inform themselves and protect themselves rather than expect the state to do so. The question was, how could this be achieved?

Accountability and the State

In 2007, I found myself once again in the middle of a *mente* debate with some friends, all middle-aged working mothers, and this time it was about yogurt. Coincidentally, I had some newsletters with results from comparative tests on dairy and meat products conducted by the Bulgarian National

Consumers Association (BNCA), a consumer advocacy organization where I volunteered during my fieldwork (see notes on my fieldwork in the appendix). Galina, who worked as a public relations specialist in an NGO, opened to the yogurt page in one newsletter to read dairy product reviews that contained tables with different yogurt brand names, their weight per unit, their retail prices, water percentage, and most importantly, the number of active yeasts (bacteria) such as *Lactobacillus bulgaricus* and *Streptococcus thermophilus*. Bulgarians take exceptional pride in their yogurt because, as the name implies, *L. bulgaricus* originates from Bulgaria.⁹ The newsletter explained at length what the differences between these two active bacteria were and why one was "real" (authentic in this context) and the other not. In other words, a "real" Bulgarian yogurt would contain mostly *L. bulgaricus* and little *S. thermophilus*, but because the latter was cheaper, easier to work with, and preserved better, many industrial manufacturers reversed the ratio.

All the women looked over when Galina said triumphantly, "No surprise . . . Danone yogurt is *mente*! Look, it has only 4.5 *bulgaricus* and 250 *thermophilus*." In contrast, three smaller local brands contained 9,500 *L. bulgaricus* and 95 *S. thermophilus*. Ida, a self-employed lawyer, confirmed that she had tried one of those three brands and agreed that it definitely tasted "authentic" like in the old days. The other popular local brand that was widely available in grocery stores proved to be compromised as well (with a smaller amount of active *L. bulgaricus*), albeit not as much as the Danone brand, news which brought a sigh of relief from Diana, a retired economist and former NGO employee, who only purchased that particular brand. She commented: "This information is very useful—but, geez . . . how do we access this? If you did not bring [the newsletter] to us, we would never be able to know, except, well, the extreme case like Danone where the texture, taste, and never-spoiling quality speaks itself to its fakeness. . . . Shouldn't they [the consumer organization] distribute this kind of information more widely?"

Encouraged by their positive response to product testing results, I also informed them that the consumer organization was going to start a consumer magazine primarily focusing on comparative testing results, but it would be for sale and not distributed for free. I added that such practice was common in many Western countries. Unsurprisingly, my comment generated skeptical reactions, and Yana, a schoolteacher, questioned how the comparative product testing was actually done and who paid for the testing. Winking in a half-joking manner, she wondered whether the testing results themselves were *mente* and those producers with better results had actually paid for the testing. I tried to explain that these tests were financed independently by the consumer organization without any corporate funding or advertisement, and the organization only used independent labs to test the products. Yet the fact that one needed to pay in order to access the testing results (which were supposed to be for the public's benefit) did not sit well with my friends. Interestingly, these women had no qualms about buying newspapers or lifestyle magazines to access information. Galina summed up the common sentiments: "You know, it is bad enough that our state cannot protect us from *mente*. If they cannot regulate those immoral producers, they at least should be able to provide the public with this kind of information so that consumers can exercise some control and protect themselves, don't you think?"

These sentiments were expressed again in 2009 when I was invited to observe a focus group interview, co-organized by BNCA and a market research company. In this interview, two groups of ten people each were having discussions after reviewing the information in BNCA's consumer magazine *Potrebitel* (Consumer) that had just launched earlier that year (although a shorter version in newsletter format under the same name had been published since 2007 [see chapter 3]). Generally, the participants, most of whom had not seen the magazine before, felt that it provided useful, credible information that was not "bought" by companies. Many of them voiced, however, that they were not willing to buy the magazines for the same reasons my friends had given: Shouldn't the state disseminate this kind of information for free for the public's benefit? A couple of people mentioned that they would rather rely on their own competence in gathering information from the internet to protect themselves as consumers. When asked how they knew whether the internet offered trustworthy information, they responded: "Well, there is no guarantee, but how can you guarantee that paid information is better and more objective? As consumers, we have rights to access credible information without paying [for it]." The right to be informed as a consumer in the postsocialist context meant that reliable information should be available to consumers for free, and the state ought to oblige its citizens in this matter of accountability.

Bulgarian consumers' attitudes regarding their expectation for free, credible information provided by the state has been very consistent. In the same summer of 2009, I had a fortuitous meeting with the founder of *Mente i Originali*, Ivan Bakalov, who turned out to be an established journalist. He was surprised that I knew about the magazine and told me that it was a good project then because Bulgarians craved this kind of reliable information about consumer products. He explained that he had issued the magazine from 1997 to 2002, after which time he felt that it could not sustain itself any longer due to the difficulty of financing its publication. Initially, to partly offset publishing costs, he sought financing from companies that had stakes in disseminating this kind of information—those that did not want to compete with *mente* products. When he started to issue the magazine in the late 1990s, consumers did not pay too much attention to the independence of the testing results and did not think it was a big deal that the magazine had paid advertisements from manufacturing companies. Ultimately, however, sales were low, and Bakalov could not make ends meet even with paid advertising. Although he never tracked down the exact sales figures, he knew that he did not make any profit from the magazine. He said he even had some old issues that he could not sell. His final remark was telling: "Do you remember how much *Mente i Originali* cost? Less than 2 leva, or $1, and Bulgarians still did not want to buy it!"[10] Yet he was aware that many Bulgarians circulated the magazine among friends and family sharing the knowledge of how to distinguish *mente*. Despite low sales, he still considered the magazine a successful experience that responded to the needs of that time. When I told him that BNCA had the same problem with low sales of its independent and professionally tested product reviews, he shrugged and said, "Bulgarians will never be ready to buy that kind of information. They feel entitled to have access to it for free."

Two sides of the consumer protection issue are expressed in Bakalov's last comment: Should information, especially that which is related to protecting consumers from the abuses of the market, be considered a commodity for sale or public property to which citizen-consumers should be entitled to access without paying?[11] This sense of entitlement vis-à-vis the state, often expressed by citizen-consumers as demands for accountability by means of better state control of the market, was commonly verbalized in all the *mente* cases examined in this chapter. But how has this idea been shaped to the point that my interlocutors took this sense of entitlement for granted? Moreover, what is "the state" that they constantly referred to in the postsocialist Bulgarian context?

"They versus Us": Who Is Accountable and Why?

While living in Sofia, I learned a lot about Bulgarian culture and society by chatting with cab drivers. Cab rides were a relatively cheap and efficient way to navigate through the sprawling urban space. The drivers I met represented a diverse cross-section of people from recent rural migrants to those with a college education, young and old, and it was interesting to hear their opinions about their country. During one cab ride in 2007, the driver, a man who looked like he was in his late 50s with greying hair and who had an intelligent way of talking, complained about difficulties providing for his family. He explained that he had a college degree and during socialism had worked diligently as an engineer, which provided a decent income with which he could raise a family relatively anxiety-free (*spokoino*). Things had changed, he grumbled: "If a person like me can't find proper work in my trained profession and has to drive a cab to buy bread, . . . to survive, . . . whose fault do you think this is? It is not mine. I worked hard my whole life, and I'm working hard now. *They* are the guilty ones. How can *they* let this happen?" (emphasis by speaker).

Although I assumed, given my extensive conversations with many Bulgarians thus far, that by "they" he must have been referring to the state, I nevertheless questioned who "they" was, conveying a foreigner's naïve curiosity. The driver looked at me through his rearview mirror and raised his eyebrows and right arm and said, "You don't know? The state [*darzhavata*], of course." He repeated his earlier point that he was not the guilty one, but clearly there must be someone or something that was accountable for so many people's misery in this country. I was somewhat reminiscent at the moment thinking that I could possibly recall several dozens of commentaries and reactions exactly like his, in almost identical wordings, from my fieldnotes in the early 2000s.

For ordinary people, such frustrations were persistent and manifested themselves in various domains of everyday life. And these mundane social commentaries often connected consumption with something more than the individual as a shopper with choice. More specifically, the frequently mentioned "they," as the cab driver indicated, referred to the state (*darzhavata*), a conceptual and cultural category that could include those in power who governed the state but was differentiated from government (*pravitelstvo*), a term that Bulgarians used to indicate the governing body. The state, for my Bulgarian interlocutors, was a broader, more abstract cultural category shaped by state socialism and reproduced through everyday consumption practices even for those consumers who did not have firsthand experiences with state socialism. As such, the state was not a bygone conceptual category from the socialist regime but continued to be perceived as a meaningful social and cultural category through which citizens articulated ideas about accountability and entitlement.

Looking through the lens of those everyday consumption practices, the state can be broadly understood as a regulatory body with the authority to control and protect its citizens from market abuses, including the will to enforce the law. Therefore, it is not only the concrete practices of the state but also the lack of such expected practices that contribute to the understanding and experience of the state. When Bulgarian consumers evoke *darzhavata*, the state is not merely conceived as images or cultural representations (Gupta 1995; Sharma and Gupta 2006) but more in terms of practices and effects (Gupta and Ferguson 1997; Mitchell 1999; Reeves, Rasanayagan, and Beyer 2014; Scott 1998). It can be productively discussed in what some scholars have called a "relational setting" (Thelen, Vetters, and von Benda-Beckmann 2014; see also Lammer 2017) because it bridges the problematic gap between analyses that focus either on state images or its practices and allows for a "stategraphy"—namely, an ethnographic analysis about how the state is understood, experienced, and reproduced in everyday encounters (Thelen, Vetters, and von Benda-Beckmann 2014: 2–9).[12] Unlike these scholars of the anthropology of the state, however, I move beyond the fields of welfare services (Caldwell 2012; Muehlebach 2014; Thelen, Vetters, and von Benda-Beckmann 2014) or bureaucratic encounters and political elections (Herzfeld 1992, 2005b; Gupta 1995; Reeves, Rasanayagan, and Beyer 2014) and call attention to sites of everyday consumption in which the state manifests itself in meaningful ways.

What Bulgarian consumers referred to as the state was not just confined to an abstract administrative entity or structure but included the subinstitutions within the state apparatus that could exercise control and achieve a resolution in the social life of citizens.[13] The notion of control informs the dichotomy of they as the controller versus us as the protected. But the idea of protection here is not so much because citizen-consumers are infantile and in need of paternalistic care. Rather, protection implies a more active demand by citizens that the state fulfill its obligation to the social contract.

The *mente* examples I have described frequently reference this "they." Similarly, when the Sofia cab driver said, "How could *they* let this happen?"

he identified "they" as the state and indicated that he did not have control over what happened to "us," the Bulgarian people (*narod*). Such an understanding of the state in terms of control actually allows multiple actors to be labeled as "they" in postsocialist circumstances, including capitalists, the EU, or even an abstract symbolic entity such as "the West." Critiques have pointed out that this dyad of "they" and "us" in the postsocialist literature is too simplistic (see, especially, Yurchak 2006: 1–35). As political scientist and scholar of Bulgaria Venelin Ganev (2014a: 529–532) argues, however, the seemingly crude interpretative framework of "they versus us" can actually serve as a sharp instrument. When it came to issues of accountability, this "they versus us" dyad was instrumental in delineating rights and responsibilities. Nonstate institutions such as NGOs become a fuzzy category under these circumstances. Frequently in Bulgaria, NGOs are identified with "they" because of their presumed connection to the state. Consumer NGOs, for instance, are often miscategorized as state institutions such as the Commission for Trade and Consumer Protection (CTCP; *komisiya po targoviya i zashtita na potrebitelite*) or the Consumer Protection Department, which operates under the Ministry of Economy. My interlocutors in Sofia often admitted that they were not always clear about the function of NGOs but believed that they were connected "somehow" to the government. Consequently, consumer NGOs were often understood in opposition to the "us" with whom Bulgarian consumers actively identified. And this perception was certainly reflected in their expectations for consumer organizations. When consumers visited the consumer NGO, they often left in frustration as they came to understand the NGO did not have the power to control *mente* or solve their problems. Many interlocuters did not consider mere assistance to solve a problem as compelling enough to turn to a consumer organization, let alone becoming a dues-paying member. Conversely, for the NGO activists, it was equally frustrating to explain that they were actually in the "us" camp and were trying to represent consumers' interests. As I discuss further in chapter 3, taking Western categories (such as NGOs, consumer rights, and human rights) for granted in postsocialist contexts posed serious limitations in putting such concepts into actions. One reason Bulgarian consumer advocacy NGOs were not easily perceived as representing "us," for example, was related to the fact that most of them did not begin as grassroots organizations but rather originated to meet the needs of top-down reform efforts sponsored by the EU and other Western donors. Moreover, many consumers remained unconvinced of such imposed needs for consumer NGOs when they realized their problems would not be resolved by them.

The notion of control in the dichotomy of "they versus us" is important in understanding the everyday consumer frustration and demands for accountability. And the legacy of state socialism looms large when it comes to the issue of accountability. During the socialist regime, it was always the state that was accountable for both the successes and failures of social policies. This is why in the postsocialist era, despite the multiple faces classified as "they," the state continues to be a meaningful social and cultural category, even though its power is certainly diminished. The state is still considered (if only at the normative level) the authority to control commodities and allow its citizens to afford everyday needs. Why does the state continue to be the major target for consumer complaints even though in the present "they" can also indicate stores (merchants), the market economy, or capitalism, all of which are considered objects of accountability and sources of consumer discontent?

David Kideckel's (2009) comparative observation of activist practices through the discourses of citizenship in postcolonial India and postsocialist Romania is insightful here. While the postsocialist state has been commonly portrayed as weak, having lost its paternalistic characteristics that were central to the socialist state (e.g., Verdery 1996; Gal and Kligman 2000; Hemment 2007), Kideckel (2009: 117–122) describes the relationship between the citizens and the state in postsocialist Romania as "alienated" because of the growing divide between state and people owing to the rejection of the past. I find this characterization useful in understanding the form of the postsocialist state as experienced by Bulgarian consumers. Moreover, Kideckel describes this type of citizenship as one based on "grievance" in which citizens issue complaints and demands to the state. Thus, he suggests, postsocialist protests can be understood as "redress of grievances." In comparison, postcolonial citizenship is based on discourses of "rights." As a result, he concludes, "Postsocialist states, rejecting their past, top-down collectivities, will become more wedded to the global system while postcolonials, reminded of their past subalternity, reject it even further" (127). Ironically, alienation from the state brings postsocialist citizens closer to the global system (such as neoliberal capitalism) while simultaneously maintaining the divide between the state and people (they versus us) in the postsocialist context, thereby continuing to label "the state" as the ultimate bearer of accountability. This aspect of redress that Kideckel points out in describing the relationship between the postsocialist state and its citizens is closely related to the idea of accountability that Bulgarian consumers assign to their state (see also Skultans 2001).

In this chapter, I examine concrete instances of the *mente* phenomenon to illustrate how consumer grievances are expressed in postsocialist contexts and how everyday consumption practices become sites fraught with consumer anxiety and where understandings and the visions of the state and state-citizen relations manifest themselves. The range of meanings of *mente*—from counterfeit, knockoff, relatively low and shoddy quality, to inauthentic and unoriginal—demonstrate how postsocialist consumers experienced deception and risk in concrete, everyday encounters and how such experiences shaped their understandings of the state and accountability. Chapter 2 looks more specifically at the historical formation of the normative ideals regarding the state to show how postsocialist Bulgarians understand and articulate the state and its relationship to citizen-consumers.

Notes

1. The lev (plural: leva) is the unit of Bulgarian currency. In 2001, Bulgarian currency was fixed to the euro. Although currency rates have fluctuated, 1 lev was approximately 0.50 euro, and 1 euro was roughly US$2 throughout the 2000s and early 2010s.

2. Local people often described the new market environment as "colorful" (*shareno*) compared with the monochromic look during socialism.

3. Many Bulgarians consider Greece to be part of the Balkans, and while it was part of "Western" Europe during the Cold War, it is considered not quite "Western" enough like those other Western European countries. See also Herzfeld 1987 for similar discussion on Greece's relationship to Europe.

4. The origin of the word *mente* is unclear. Apparently, it was not used much in the socialist period and according to my Bulgarian interlocutors appeared only after the changes in 1989 for everyday usage. The Gaberoff 2010 Bulgarian-English dictionary does not list this word, whereas the more recent (2014) edition lists only *menta* (as a noun) and defines it as (1) peppermint, and (2) lie, trick, et cetera. One of my friends related this word to the old (pre-socialist) Bulgarian slang term *menta*, which means a lie. For instance, *ti me mentish* means "you lied to me."

5. I purchased three issues of *Mente i Originali*, which was sold in most major kiosks in Sofia, during the summer of 1999. When I returned to Sofia in 2000, I could not find the magazine anywhere. My friends could not explain to me who the editor was, but they speculated that he was someone who capitalized on the *mente* phenomenon for a little while and then stopped. The magazine cost about 2 leva (a daily newspaper cost 0.60 leva), and while it was not regarded as very expensive, my skeptical friends did not think many people would buy the magazine, since most Bulgarians were financially very constrained and the magazine

would be an unnecessary expense. Years later, in 2009, I met the founder and editor-in-chief of *Mente i Originali*, which I discuss later in this chapter.

6. My friends even added apartment construction (i.e., material that looked "flashy" on the outside but would crack soon after construction) and, as Bulgarian humor goes, politicians to the list of things that could be *mente*.

7. The expression "civilized states" can be used with much irony in the everyday discourse and may not necessarily reflect an evolutionary bias of linear progress.

8. My Bulgarian friends and interlocutors frequently relayed this common joke of socialism: "They lie that they will pay us, and we lie that we work." This reflects a similar sentiment during socialist Hungary according to the movie *Sunshine* (1999) by István Szabó in which the main character declares, "The state lied to us that everything was okay and we lied to the state that we believed them." Paradoxically, this mutual deception also reflects a level of trust between the state and its citizens in that both parties could reason with each other regarding mutual expectations. In the postsocialist period, this kind of fundamental trust between the state and citizens was often thought of as being eroded.

9. Yotova 2014 provides a cultural history of Bulgarian yogurt and also discusses issues and politics of authenticity.

10. Bakalov told me during this interview that the reported average monthly income between 1999 and 2002 was US$180.

11. Property is one of the key concepts that has been critically examined in the literature of postsocialism, especially because decollectivization and privatization processes after the collapse of state socialism called for a careful understanding of property (see especially Verdery and Humphrey 2004; Verdery 2003). I discuss the question of free consumer information more fully in the following chapters.

12. Specifically, Tatjana Thelen, Larissa Vetters, and Keebet von Benda-Beckmann (2014) propose three venues of analyses for the study and theorization of the state: relational modalities, boundary work, and forms of embeddedness of actors. This approach allows for an understanding of the state that is historically contingent and grounded in social interactions.

13. Kaneff 2002 describes how state-citizen relations are manifested in funerals, for example.

2

NEEDS, RIGHTS, AND PROTECTION

CORECOM ("*Correction of Com*munism"): The Paternalistic State

One afternoon in 2002, Yulia, Tsvetelina, and I were strolling down the street from NDK, the National Palace of Culture, a socialist landmark located in the city center. Being the only smoker in the group, Yulia asked if we could stop by a neighborhood store so she could get cigarettes. As soon as we entered the store, she grabbed me by the arm and whispered, "This is the smell similar to CORECOM . . . this store smells like CORECOM."[1] I sniffed the air around me. It smelled clean and aromatic, a combination of disinfectant and air freshener, not at all unusual. I detected no hints of other smells common in older neighborhood stores, such as from ham, sausages, or stale bread. Yulia bought her cigarettes and urged us to go. Tsvetelina was curious. Yulia turned to Tsvetelina and whispered, "Tsvete, you remember the smell of CORECOM, right? That store had a very similar smell." Yulia's eyes lit up as she remembered when a visit to CORECOM was such a treat for her as a child. Tsvetelina stared at Yulia a little puzzled but then acknowledged that the store did smell "very clean and aromatic like CORECOM." Yulia was excited to finally show me what she meant by the "different smell" of that particular store, CORECOM, compared to the other Bulgarian stores during socialism. She tried to describe the special sensory experience she used to get whenever she visited CORECOM during her childhood. Nostalgically, she mentioned that the store had a completely different air and smelled like a mixture of Western chewing gums (mostly Wrigley's peppermint gums and Donald Duck gums for children), German chocolates (especially Kindersurprise chocolate eggs), Swiss chocolates (Toblerone and Milka), and the German soap Lux. Unlike other Bulgarian stores, which did not particularly smell "clean" but more like old wood (from the shelves) and looked drab with low-quality brownish-gray wrapping paper (for food), CORECOM apparently had its own smell evoking a sense of difference that shoppers could not help but notice. Other Bulgarian friends later confirmed that CORECOM indeed provided a unique sensory experience: in addition to the distinctive, colorful Western-style food wrappings, it smelled like aromatic soap (perfumery) and candies. More commonly, Bulgarians described it in more abstract terms such as "clean" and "new" and "different."

CORECOM was a commonly evoked place among my Bulgarian interlocutors when it came to memories of consumption and shopping during the socialist time. It was not merely recalled as a place but also as a sensory experience that contrasted with their consumption practices in ordinary stores and stimulated their consumer desires. CORECOM reflected how consumption under socialism was intimately tied to the state. More importantly, it could be considered a meaningful symbol that showed how the socialist state navigated its role as the sole provider to meet citizens' expectations in terms of access and choice as well as how it addressed the tensions arising from those expectations that were not met in the shortage economy. In other words, CORECOM served as an illustrative example of how the socialist state tried to normalize its state-citizens relations as the socialist state increasingly failed to respond to the expectations of its citizens concerning mundane consumption practices. From the perspectives of ordinary consumers, CORECOM was certainly perceived as a response by the socialist state to account for its failure in fulfilling its promises to its citizens—hence, the nickname, often recalled sarcastically but also endearingly by many Bulgarians: "*corr*ection of *com*munism." As Yulia and Tsvetelina expressed, compared to ordinary neighborhood stores that smelled "unclean/dirty" and "old/stale," CORECOM's scent was "clean/aromatic." These memories of CORECOM were often juxtaposed with recollections of dashing to a store to get in line as soon as someone heard from friends and neighbors that some products had been "just released" in such and such store.[2] And even though CORECOM was a state enterprise as any other store during socialism, citizens could experience a sense of consumer choice and privilege when shopping there.

In this chapter, I unpack the idea of the state further by discussing how Bulgarians conceptualize "the state" based on their historical experiences. Notions of needs, rights, and protection that my Bulgarian interlocutors relate to the state have been shaped in different historical moments through their everyday consumption practices. Examining consumption experiences situated in different historical moments allows me to show how concepts such as needs, consumer rights, and protection are socially constructed and negotiated and what they entail for a new consumer politics in the aftermath of state socialism.

Bulet, Bulgaria's hard currency store established in 1960 during socialism, acquired the name CORECOM in 1964 when it became an independent state enterprise.[3] By 1974, CORECOM had chain stores around major cities in Bulgaria ("Ministry Council Report no. 136" 1964; "Ministry Council Report no. 131" 1974). It mostly sold imported goods from the West. Foreigners as well as Bulgarians who had access to special bonds that could only be purchased with foreign currency, such as US dollars or German marks, were allowed to shop there. During socialism, a number of Bulgarians, including engineers, medical staff, and academics worked in foreign countries, primarily in Africa and the Middle East. International truck drivers also had legal entitlement to foreign currency. Toward the late 1980s, one could buy directly without first exchanging foreign currency for the special bonds.[4] When CORECOM first opened, the rules delineating who could shop there were more strictly observed. By the late 1970s and 1980s, however, one only needed the right connections[5] and money.

CORECOM reflected the contradictory aspect of state socialism that on the one hand insisted that the state would provide the needs of the people (access to basic provisioning) and on the other hand criticized Western bourgeois consumerism (based on choice by self-interested individuals). Although the socialist state took a critical stance against Western consumerism, it also had to compromise by creating these kinds of Western stores to satisfy the expectations of the population by granting possibilities for choices. In the larger context of the Cold War, this kind of compromise was perhaps inevitable to keep up with the promises of progress and prosperity.[6] CORECOM represented an example of the state's attempt to control the domain of consumption and how it constructed and responded to the ideas of needs by maintaining the tension between deprivation (caused by a planned system and irregular distribution through regular stores) and stimulation (by displaying and allowing citizens to choose hard-to-obtain Western goods through CORECOM).[7]

State socialism can be understood as an intensive social engineering project that prioritized industrialization and modernization as means for social progress. Although it experienced a short period of nascent modernization following its liberation from the Ottoman Empire, Bulgaria remained primarily a marginal agricultural country after World War II (Crampton 2007). The Bulgarian socialist project was premised on equal access to prosperity. While social identities during socialism generally revolved around one's status as a producer (i.e., contributing to the labor force), one's access to goods especially utilizing one's social network (rather than money) as consumers also played an important role in constructing one's social identity within the socialist system. The dominant values in the domain of consumption revolved around the notion of needs and the discourse of normality. Whenever these values were violated, they also became the basis of everyday complaining. Although aspirations for a normal life and expectations of needs could easily be dismissed as a desire to emulate a Western lifestyle (e.g., Fehérváry 2002), I suggest that these ideas of needs and normality have been rooted in social values shaped from the socialist experiences and were particularly premised on the promise of access.

State Provision and CORECOM

In 1971, the Tenth Congress of the Bulgarian Communist Party stated the goal of communism as "the satisfaction of the ever growing needs of the workers" (Ditchev 2004: 21).[8] The role of the socialist state in reaching this goal, therefore, was to fulfill the needs of the people. The question here was, who actually defined such "ever growing needs of the workers"? The unique characteristics of a paternalistic socialist state were that the state simultaneously dictated what was needed to its population and then had to supply those needs. In this regard, the idea of necessities (*potrebnosti*) is noteworthy. "Necessities for citizens" was a very important concept during socialism with a strong ideological undertone because the socialist state's political and economic strategies revolved around the improvement of those necessities. This term also highlighted the basic role that the state played in the protection of consumers: unsatisfied consumers could resort to the Decree for Complaints (*ukaza za zhalbite*), a law that allowed citizens to complain to state institutions in cases such as incorrect retirement pensions, unlawful activities of the militia, poor-quality bread sold in the stores, abuses of immediate bosses at workplaces, lack of spare parts for cars, and so on. Noteworthy is how poor-quality goods or unavailable products were treated in the same way as poor-quality work of state institutions: both were considered necessities for the socialist state. In other words, under the socialist logic, the state had to guarantee access to basic needs that would allow citizens to be not just alive but healthy and properly (*pravilen*) functioning members of society.⁹ Theoretically, a consumer during state socialism was to buy things that she or he needed to function properly in both the physical and social senses, but not because she or he wanted things or because there was an impulsive desire to buy things. In a way, CORECOM fit this socialist logic in that it offered one the "needs" to function properly as a productive member of society.

The common joke in Bulgaria that CORECOM stood for "correction of communism" (*korektsiya na komunizma*) wittily summarizes the conflicting situation of the state: as the state could not completely fulfill the necessities it defined, it had to correct its own agenda by creating stores like CORECOM that not only tacitly acknowledged the failure of the system on the one hand but also showed how the state took accountability in addressing that failure on the other. CORECOM offers a very telling example of how the state grappled with its own failure, and how this kind of coping shaped the way citizens experienced and conceptualized the role of the state.

CORECOM's centrality in the memory of Bulgarians' past shopping experiences often led to more shopping stories. Very few Bulgarians, however, actually knew that CORECOM was an acronym for *Comptoir de Representation et de Commerce* and regarded the word as simply Bulgarian (and thus, *korektsiya na komunizma*). According to the Bulgarian abbreviation dictionary (https://frazite.com), CORECOM means "foreign trade organization for import and sales with foreign currency for imports and Bulgarian goods" (*vanshnotargovska organizatsiya za vnos i prodazhba sreshtu baluta na vnosi i bulgarski stoki*). Some older Bulgarians recalled the state organizations that traded with foreign companies. Called foreign trade organization (*vanshnotargovska organizatsiya*), this institution primarily traded machines and industrial goods rather than consumer goods, but if any small surplus remained after the industrial deals, they imported consumer goods that were sold in CORECOM stores. They therefore sold various goods ranging from chewing gum and chocolates to soap, clothes, washing machines, furniture, and even secondhand cars left by foreigners.

CORECOM was first opened as a state economic enterprise (*darzhavno stopansko predpriyatie*) in Sofia. By 1974, it became a trade association with chain stores in major cities such as Sofia, Plovdiv, Varna, and Veliko Turnovo as well as in the major tourist places of Borovets (a ski resort near Sofia) and Burgas (a Black Sea resort). Eventually, CORECOM stores officially closed after the collapse of the regime between 1990 and 1991. These stores were intended at first to serve the diplomatic community, foreigners visiting Bulgaria, and Bulgarian nationals who worked abroad as guest workers and returned home with hard foreign currency earnings. In the beginning, the state strictly controlled the people who could legally shop there. They issued special bonds to be used in CORECOM that were only available with hard currency. If exchanged through official channels, Bulgarians were asked to provide documents proving their legal source of foreign currency income; otherwise, the bonds were obtainable through unofficial means that meant an exchange ratio of one to three or one to four. By the late 1970s and early 1980s, however, whoever had access to legally authorized people with hard currency could shop there as well. One simply accompanied an authorized person who would purchase the CORECOM items for the unauthorized individual in exchange for Bulgarian currency. As my friends jokingly mentioned, in a small country like Bulgaria, where everybody was a cousin of some sort and where people thrived on social networks, it was not difficult to find someone who could legally shop in CORECOM if they had the money and desire to buy the commodities from that store. Items sold in CORECOM were not cheap, but ordinary people could save up and shop there if they wanted to. The goods were not unattainable, and people with a consistent salary believed that they could save enough to make some purchases there. Also, the initial restriction from entering the store and just looking around was lifted in the 1980s, so anybody could at least do some window-shopping. Ivaylo Ditchev (2004) notes that during the 1970s and 1980s government control over CORECOM fluctuated every year: at the beginning of the year, the state would guard the entrance of the store with militia and crack down on shoppers who were not supposed to be there. Toward the end of the year, control loosened up as the state needed income to fulfill its economic plan, and consumers could window-shop or make purchases undisturbed.[10] Socialist citizens got accustomed to these kinds of state practices, and their relationship to the state continued to be shaped by such experiences.

CORECOM is a vivid marker in the memory of Bulgarians' consumption activities during socialism and is often juxtaposed with experiences of long lines or hoarding that were common consumer strategies in the socialist context (e.g., Berdahl 1999; Caldwell 2004; Humphrey 1995; Merkel 1998). While there have been popular claims that a consumer culture did not exist under state socialism, several scholars have identified an important aspect of consumption during socialism—its very politicized nature.[11] Although the political and ideological rhetoric heavily revolved around production and the relationship to it, the particular circumstances that were created by the socialist planning system made consumption highly political (Verdery 1996: 26–29; see also Bren and Neuburger 2012). The paternalistic nature of the regime offered a sense that the state was looking after its citizens to satisfy the needs of the people and that the standard of living was constantly improving under socialism. And when it did not, that state still showed accountability by addressing the failure, such as allowing access to stores like CORECOM, which in a strange way contributed to citizens' perception that the state cared. When postsocialist citizens question where the state *is*, they are essentially wondering, where is the state that actually cared—even imperfectly—for its citizens?

The paternalistic character of the socialist regimes supported by a centrally planned economy, therefore, turned consumption into an area that connected consumers primarily to the state rather than to the market as in capitalist societies. The market, as it were, meant something different under socialist economies than it did in advanced capitalist societies.[12] Studies on socialist consumption practices have explained this by focusing on the secondary economy (often called the black market) in which capitalist market principles more or less operated and on the distinct consumer strategies that developed under the socialist condition of shortages (e.g., Chelcea 2002; Caldwell 2004; Humphrey 1995, 2002; Merkel 1999; Ries 1997).[13] These studies acknowledge the central role of the state in socialist consumption practices because the secondary economy cannot exist without the presence of an official primary economy operated by the state. Such studies also focus on the "tactics of the weak" (de Certeau 1984: 51–55)—that is, of the consumers who need to confront the inefficiency of the state or system (cultures of shortages) by means of various consumer strategies as reflected in many of the "heroic shopping tales" (Ries 1997: 51–64) during socialism (see also Berdahl 1999; Caldwell 2004; Patico 2002, 2008).

The interesting thing about socialist-era hard currency stores like CORECOM is that they occupy a large space in the memory of people because these stores presented consumers with a sense of both access and choice in comparison to their routine consumption practices that was more aligned with accessing necessary products. People went to CORECOM to buy what they perceived to be "nicer" stuffs but also because they felt they needed them. For instance, Yulia's mother purchased gifts for Yulia's teachers such as the German soap Lux in CORECOM because they were highly sought-after gift items that were not available in regular stores. More importantly, they generally thought that the items in CORECOM were affordable (even though they were not cheap compared to regular stores) because they knew that they had job security and could save to buy the desired item. In a way, CORECOM epitomized socialist consumption practices of the black market mode: in other words, trying to acquire something that was rare and difficult to obtain through regular stores. Simultaneously, CORECOM was not a black market operating outside of governmental control—on the contrary, it was part of the socialist system that tried to address the "ever growing needs of the workers."

CORECOM, therefore, invoked the past in an ironic way—namely, it was rather positively associated with the past even though CORECOM in fact could represent a critique against the socialist system. The admiration for CORECOM goods as well as finding channels to access this store that was officially inaccessible to many was proof that the state took responsibility by addressing the flaw of the socialist system. The state responded and in a sense cared for its citizen-consumers through CORECOM. Consumers had access to commodities that could only be found in CORECOM and not at regular state-run stores. The state needed ventures like CORECOM to control the population by satisfying a certain level of need, thereby also supplementing its fiscal deficit through sales from CORECOM. Experiences and memories of CORECOM underscored how consumption was constantly understood and practiced in relation to the state, which was responsible for fulfilling its promises of prosperity and social progress to the people and was accountable if it failed to do so.

The ways in which my Bulgarian interlocuters described the socialist state were not always consistent because their relationship with the state during socialism was contradictory. On the one hand, the state exhibited its care by guaranteeing a level of access to basic provisioning, but on the other hand, citizens were always aware that it was also an oppressive and regulatory power that was not always as fair as it promised it to be. And yet, the kinds of state practices during socialism appeared to have established a level of social trust because the rules of the game, so to speak, were understood by citizen-consumers. This social trust, however, gradually eroded in the postsocialist period and was replaced by skepticism and anxiety that was often reflected in everyday consumption practices.

From Buyer to Consumer

For postsocialist citizens, constructing one's identity as "consumer" was not a simple matter. The Bulgarian word for consumption, *potreblenie*, was often associated with *potrebitelstvo*, the Bulgarian word for consumerism, which had strong negative moral and ideological connotations during the socialist era (Velinova 2004). Western consumerism was associated with low-quality mass cultural products (arts and literature, for example) by the socialist ideologues (see Keyzerov 1979 for a heavily ideological and moral discussion on the negative implication of consumption under state socialism).

According to Iskra Velinova (2004), the term *potrebitel* (consumer) was only used in official texts during state socialism as a technical term indicating users of public resources that implied regularity in consumption, hence, *potrebitel* for electricity, water, and heating, for instance. The word was never used in the context of everyday consumption of food, clothes, and other commodities. A Slavicized term from Latin, *konsumator*, was usually used to describe the act of consuming food.[14] Since the socialist consumer regime hardly allowed any regularity in the fields of consumption, *kupuvach* (buyer) was used in the daily discourse for consumers of commodities.[15] Another common word for "consumer" was "population" (*naselenie*) in the official rhetoric represented in print media.[16]

These differentiated usages have certainly changed in the postsocialist era. In official reports and in media representation as well as in daily usage, *potreblenie* and *potrebitel* are commonly used without the old moral and ideological connotations from the socialist era. Consumer advocacy organizations and the media, for instance, all reflect this change as they use *potrebitel* over other variants such as *kupuvach* or *klient* to refer to consumers. The change in the usage and meaning of the words *potrebitel* or *potreblenie* is partly related to the imported nature of these organizations, which did not exist before 1989. Their adoption of *potreblenie* over other variants contributed to the changes in popular usage as well. Although I noticed that elderly people tended to be reluctant to use the word *potrebitel* to describe themselves as the subject of consumption, for instance, the popularization of the terms *potrebitel* or *potreblenie* through the media enabled Bulgarians to build a new association with the words. As a result, the once morally inferior connotation of "consumption," especially compared to "production," started to fade out. This is an example of reorienting old concepts with new cultural meanings, a process that enables "cultural competence" (Bourdieu 1977: 186) in the global economy, as these words acquire similar meanings that are more compatible with other capitalist economies. Yet even as ordinary citizens started to rebuild an identity around "consumer" (*potrebitel*) rather than "buyer," conceptualizing how as consumers they could (and should) exercise their rights was not so straightforward. Sometimes they understood exercising their rights as consumers in terms of rejecting the management by the state entirely, such as engaging in do-it-yourself practices (see chapter 4). Other times, they demanded the state's more active involvement as they expressed themselves through their mundane grumblings and more formal complaints. The *potrebitel* in postsocialist Bulgaria was becoming a normative category as "a subject and object of public life" (Trentmann 2007: 150).

The seemingly straightforward questions of "What are consumer rights?" or "Do all consumers have rights?" therefore are neither simple nor clear-cut. Matthew Hilton (2009) observes that the history of consumerism had a turning point in the 1980s when the meaning of "consumerism" changed from access to choice, and when choice became the impoverished notion around which global consumer movements organized themselves. This suggests that the idea of the consumer is historically contingent and that the subjectivity of consumers is constantly negotiated. Undoubtedly, the change from seeing the consumer as the agent of access to the agent of choice was influenced by the antiregulatory agenda of neoliberal capitalism. When modern consumerism developed beginning in the eighteenth century, the consumer was considered as someone who needed protection from the abuses of the market first by ensuring access but eventually by providing choice as material abundance increased thanks to industrialization, mass production, and international trade. The question was, who should protect the consumer? In many advanced capitalist societies, consumer movements have mobilized individuals to protect themselves through consumer boycotts (e.g., Ralph Nader against US automobile companies in the 1960s). More recently, ethical consumerism such as fair trade or organics (as opposed to chemical-laden conventional production) has increasingly engaged citizen-consumers to address unfair labor practices and inequities within the globalized neoliberal market regime. Rather than addressing larger structural problems, however, here too the agent of protection is the individual consumer (as shopper) who exercises rights and responsibilities as a citizen and consumer to protect not only his or her own well-being but also the well-being of others (such as the less privileged and the disadvantaged). For many postsocialist citizens, however, such an approach based on the idea that consumption is only a matter of individual choice did not address the larger consumer issues they deemed problematic in the aftermath of state socialism.

The "Old Mentality" of Standards and Control

On a bright autumn day in 2002, BNCA invited an owner of a popular information website to its office to discuss whether BNCA could post a regular column with consumer-related information on his website to inform citizens about various consumer issues and help them protect their own rights. The website owner, BNCA's leader, another activist, and I sat across from each other on a black faux-leather couch and a couple of chairs in a small room of the NGO. The white-walled room smelled of bleach from cleaning materials and was furnished with generic-looking black bookshelves, reminiscent of a bygone standardized form and style that was observed in many offices and households across Sofia. The rattling of an old refrigerator was muted whenever a tram noisily passed by, which it did with some frequency. The atmosphere in the room was otherwise very calm and the conversation was quiet. BNCA's executive director, Bogomil Nikolov,[17] told the guest the following story as we discussed the differences between Bulgarian and European consumers:

> Let me give you an example. You know people are aware that the markets and stores often cheat them with the scales. For instance, at the Women's Market [*zhenski pazar*], many merchants are believed to cheat customers by 100 grams. They say it's 1 kilogram when in fact it's only 900 grams. Anyway, the problem is when you see a product sold considerably cheaper in one stand compared to other stands, you should expect that 900 grams sells for the price of 1 kilogram—which means that the product is sold at the same price everywhere. I say this because there is a minimum price for certain products to be sold in order for the seller to have a minimum profit—especially in the staple food sector. But our consumers are blinded by the lower price and buy less for the lower price. I know a merchant who buys white cheese [*sirene*] from a wholesaler for 3.20 leva and sells it to merchants in smaller stores for 3.40 leva. But one store, he found out later, sells it for 2.90 leva. So, can you explain this to me? How can the seller at the smaller store profit when he buys from the wholesale merchants for 3.20 leva and sells it in his own store for 2.90 leva? Would he sell the cheese in that way despite the loss? No. So how does it work, then? Very simple. The seller of the small shop would sell the cheese not by 1 kilogram but by 800 grams—cheating the consumers. This is so elementary, but everybody who sees a lower price dashes there and shouts, "Here we

go. Our white cheese." We have worked with some markets and the directors of the markets, but *there is no way to control every single merchant*. In addition, that is not the function of the state institutions anymore. The consumers themselves must understand what they are paying for. *This is hard for Bulgarian consumers to understand. They don't think they are the fools to be cheated— they blame the state and the evil merchants.* . . . So this is what we have not learned yet. We have not become familiar with the idea that everything really depends so much on our own personal choices. If the masses, the consumers, behave properly so that the rule of competition works, those unfriendly merchants and sales people will start smiling—it all depends on the consumers. *The unfriendly sales people are not guilty that they are unfriendly to us. We can choose not to go there. You know that is the difference now compared to the socialist time.* . . . This is the difference from European consumers who know when they go to a flea market they would not expect receipts, warranties, or returns policies. They simply know what to expect. They know that they may buy some garbage but for a really cheap price. Bulgarians still assume that now that communism is over, democracy and a capitalist market economy is in hand, all products in the market should be great. *But the truth is not everything in the market is great. Capitalism itself does not guarantee you the best quality with the cheapest price. It is your responsibility to find the best for yourself.* Bulgarians must learn this principle and practice it themselves. *You can't just blame the state in this case.* (emphasis added)

This ethnographic vignette presents a commonly articulated consumer problem in postsocialist Bulgaria—namely, how the state is consistently evoked in ordinary consumer matters. I draw attention to the question of why the state so often becomes the target for blame by consumers (often over merchants and producers), even though the same consumers recognize that the postsocialist state is no longer the sole provider for everyday consumption, and they also do not really believe that their postsocialist state can actually fix the problems. In what follows, I focus on articulations of state-citizen relations. Understanding state-citizen relations as reflected in daily consumption practices allows for a more critical engagement with concepts such as rights and protection that have on the one hand formed the basis of consumer politics after state socialism, yet on the other hand have often created tensions between ordinary consumers and state actors or NGO consumer experts (activists).

Bogomil's compassionate storytelling silenced the whole room until he and his colleague lit up cigarettes. The website owner nodded in affirmation and had no comment to add. Bogomil seemed to have upset himself by his own story as he spelled out his frustration of working with Bulgarian consumers. Essentially, the major point he was trying to make was about the agent of control as it related to the object of blame. As Bogomil emphasized, the state could not possibly control every single merchant or every single product in the market economy. The role of the liberalized (democratized) state had changed, and it could not be blamed. Bogomil's utmost emphasis was on the consumers. It was the individual consumer who was responsible for her purchase, and Bulgarian consumers should know this by now after decades of transition. His arguments resorted much to the contemporary Western consumer advocacy discourse that highlighted the protection of consumer rights by educating and informing individual consumers. It was a neoliberal discourse privileging the role of individual consumers over regulatory processes and structural problems. According to Bogomil, Bulgarian consumers would not achieve anything just by blaming the state because there is a limitation of state functions now—the state did not have much regulatory power. Consumers themselves needed to be more active and vigilant about their purchases.

Many of my Bulgarian interlocutors, however, still expected a guaranteed level of minimum quality standards and the state's control over them, as Bogomil's story noted, especially in light of the eroding trust vis-à-vis affordable goods in the market economy. Despite the vagaries of production and distribution of goods, the socialist state, they insisted, assured citizens that a certain level of standards would be upheld. In fact, as Krisztina Fehérváry (2013: 116–117) points out in the case of Hungary, socialist citizens were encouraged to protest things like manufacturing flaws, even though they were not supposed to protest the production plan itself (see also Lampland 1995). Coupled with the heavily subsidized everyday groceries such as bread, yogurt, and other dairy products in the case of Bulgaria, many socialist citizens came to consider affordable and decent quality standards of goods as rights and believed the state had an obligation to control these standards. These expectations for standards and control by the state often came into conflict with notions of consumer rights in the postsocialist era.

Bogomil also mentioned that consumers now have the right to choose, meaning they did not have to go to stores where sellers were unfriendly. While his argument made sense, many of my Bulgarian interlocutors such as those I have introduced in earlier chapters found it difficult to completely agree with him. My Bulgarian interlocuters still went to stores with blunt and indifferent sellers if they knew the stores were reliable because they did not want to risk buying *mente* products. "Choice" for individual consumers only works if the system works. And herein lies the daily dilemma that many Bulgarian consumers faced—namely, how to conceptualize and practice choice as consumers when they felt constrained by financial means and found themselves not knowledgeable enough about the abundant commodities available in the postsocialist marketplace. Unlike Bogomil's insistence that consumers have choice, my interlocutors perceived themselves as straddling between access and choice. If they purchased a bad product, it might mean that they could not replace it immediately if ever because of their economic hardship. This not only distressed them but also caused a great deal of civic anger and frustration.

The matter of balancing access and choice is a central theme of everyday consumption that most poignantly resonated with ordinary citizens in Bulgaria. And it was repeatedly presumed that the state was the ultimate entity that needed to protect consumers from the abuses of the market. In the absence of the state as the protector and agent of control, many citizen-consumers justified their choice in terms of minimizing risk rather than insisting on consumer rights or protection of rights by empowering themselves with information. The prevailing risks for financially constrained consumers are important in understanding why the state is persistently evoked in consumer grievances. These risks are not considered something that can be managed by individual consumers but something that needs to be controlled by the state. The following example illustrates the limited choice many Bulgarian consumers pointed out in the newly emerging consumer society in the aftermath of state socialism. The balancing of access and choice often justified why consumers felt compelled to shop at a place where the service might be bad and unfriendly but the products were reliable because the store had a consistent social record of not selling questionable products (like *mente*, as explored in chapter 1).

A neighborhood store (*kvartalen magazin*) at the corner of Shesti Septemvri and Slavianska Streets offered everyday sundries and basic groceries except fresh vegetables and fruits. It was a typical old-style store reminiscent of the socialist era in that one had to ask the seller for products over the counter unlike in the modern stores after democratic changes where customers took items off the shelves and brought them to the checkout counter. This over-the-counter type of store was familiar to many Bulgarians (e.g., the kneel shops still operate in this way), even though many Western-style supermarkets operated around the city. Until 2010 or so, such supermarkets, however, were still relatively few in number, inconveniently located in some parts of the urban space requiring a car to transport groceries. They were thus less popular (because they were less accessible) than the neighborhood stores. Since 2013, the city center has seen a noticeable increase in smaller supermarkets (like an express version of larger chain supermarkets commonly seen in other European cities), and many more residential neighborhoods across Sofia have acquired Western-style supermarkets, gradually driving out old-fashioned neighborhood stores. Still, my interlocutors in Sofia mentioned that they continued to buy basic staples from neighborhood stores as well because they trusted them more. This theme of trust is important because one of the repeatedly expressed grievances that postsocialist Bulgarians have pointed out is the erosion of social trust: they can't trust the quality of food and products, they can't trust that paying more guarantees higher quality, they can't trust what the labels on the products say (let alone understand the label itself), or they can't trust that the state does its job in protecting consumers from market abuses. Hence, a neighborhood store with a proven record in terms of the reliability of its products was compelling enough for consumers to forgo their right to choose another store.

The neighborhood store that I frequented during a ten-month stay in 2002 was not big. There was space for two or three customers to stand before the two large display shelves and refrigerator, which were arranged in the form of a Bulgarian *g* (г). The store was housed on the first floor of an old residential building (*kooperatsiya*) likely built before the 1950s given its architectural style and the history of the neighborhood. There was little natural light inside the store, and the entire space appeared quite dim, which added to the cramped feeling. Two tall, narrow beverage refrigerators storing mostly dairy products and soft drinks were squeezed into the corner space to the immediate right of the entrance. Behind the two main shelves that separated the buyer's space from the seller's was a larger space for the sellers (which could easily accommodate four people) and big shelves for products on two sides of the walls. A door between the two walls connected this space with another adjacent one apparently used for storage of the foodstuffs and other items that could not be displayed in the main room. The store offered a variety of daily consumer products: bread and yogurt (Bulgarians' staple foods), eggs, ham, sausages, prepackaged salads and sandwiches, sauces, cans, sweets, snacks, wine, beer, hard liquor, cigarettes, toilet paper, soap, coffee, tea, and so on. How they stored all these diverse items in such a small space was impressive—only one brand of each product was displayed with a visible price tag while the rest of the inventory was stored in another room. Much of the packaging on display had faded in color, which usually did not concern regular customers, who understood that the selected products would be taken from a stockroom.

Even though I had regularly shopped at this store, either by myself or with my elderly landlady, the main seller (and owner) hardly smiled at me during my stay in that neighborhood. In my subsequent visits in 2007, 2009, and 2012, her attitude remained the same even though I suspected that she recognized me from the way she gave me a knowing stare.[18] As a matter of fact, I had never witnessed her joking or even chatting with regulars, which I commonly observed in other neighborhood stores. Probably in her mid-50s, the matronly owner wore big square-shaped glasses and had short, straight, light brown hair and a stern poker face. Usually, she wore casual pants and a shirt over which she pulled a sweater during the colder months. Sometimes she was also dressed in a smock that a lot of housewives would wear while cleaning their homes—a simple knee-length cotton shirt, similar to the ones commonly worn by drugstore employees, with short sleeves or sleeveless, and worn with or without another shirt.

When customers entered her store, they usually initiated the greetings by saying "good day" (*dobar den*), a common Bulgarian salutation. The seller quickly replied with the same greeting, maintaining an indifferent facial expression and waiting impatiently (sometimes tapping her fingers) for the customer's order. I was always particularly intrigued by the interaction between seller and buyer in this store because of the inverted power relationship. The seller seemed so harsh and blunt, and the buyer seemed to be always so polite and patient. The Western model of service with friendly greetings that my Bulgarian interlocutors perceived as commonly practiced in market economies did not seem to have reached this store yet.[19] Even the way the buyer phrased the sentences when ordering the products appeared to me quite formal and official—something that I would perhaps only expect in bureaucratic settings. In other words, I always sensed a reverse power relationship between the seller and buyer where, ironically, the former was in a higher position in the hierarchy. To me, such an interaction was indicative of the legacy of socialist experiences when the power hierarchy placed sellers above buyers[20] and showed why ideas of consumer rights did not have a significant sociocultural meaning for many postsocialist consumers.

One afternoon, I entered the store and lined up behind a middle-aged female customer who was about to put in her order. I observed the following exchange between the customer and seller, which was initiated by the customer's polite *dobar den*:

CUSTOMER (smiling shyly): You know [*znachi*] . . . would you please give me a pack of flour and yogurt of Danone [brand]?

SELLER (first yells at her assistant to get the Danone yogurt, then very bluntly to the customer): We have two kinds of flour—do you want the smaller or bigger one?

CUSTOMER: Please, could you tell me how small the smaller pack is?

SELLER: 600 grams.

CUSTOMER: Right. . . . And how much is it?

SELLER: 1.80 leva.

CUSTOMER (still calmly, with a polite tone): May I ask how big the bigger pack is and how much?

SELLER (impatiently, without much facial expression, tapping her fingers on the counter): It's 1 kilogram and costs 2.10 leva.

CUSTOMER: Good. Please give me the 1 kilogram one.

SELLER: Anything else?

CUSTOMER: Hmm . . . let me think. (Continuously smiling shyly at the seller; the seller looking bored, even careless.) Yes, could I have a pack of Victoria light [cigarettes]?

SELLER: Okay. It will be altogether 4.60 leva.

CUSTOMER: Thank you. Here it is: one, two, . . . five leva.

SELLER (returned 40 stotinki,[21] did not say good-bye, and turned to the next customer, me, without any greeting, staring at me and speaking bluntly): *Kazhete* [speak].

In Bulgaria, people use the casual form of "you" (*ti*) in ordinary interactions with friends and neighbors and exchanging jokes is very common. Such informality was accepted even with people I had met for the first time. In contrast, whenever I went to a store or accompanied my friends on shopping trips, I was struck by the formality and polite exchanges between the buyer and seller (switching to the polite form of "you" [*vie*]). The seemingly reversed power relationship observed in the interaction between the seller and the consumer just described indicates not only a consumer attitude shaped in the socialist era but also a low consumer confidence that continued under postsocialist conditions, certainly influenced by the low purchasing power in postsocialist Bulgaria but also attributable to experiences of deception. When I asked my friends why people would still shop at stores where the seller was so unfriendly when there were many other stores in the neighborhood unlike during socialism, they laughingly explained that it was because the store was known to be reliable: at least they did not sell *mente* products. Again and again, stories about *mente* or deceptive behavior by merchants were commonly circulated among Bulgarian consumers, further instigating everyday grumbling and consumer complaints. Reliability, which was identified as a significant reason for frequenting an unfriendly store, is important to note here, as it relates to the ways in which Bulgarians evoke the notion of responsibility, especially when faced with experiences of deception (or risk of deception) in everyday consumption practices. This also holds true for Western-style supermarkets where checkout clerks can be as blunt or indifferent as the storeowner I just described. Yet if the store was considered reliable, consumers often tolerated even impolite behavior from sellers. In the absence of an accountable object, which many Bulgarians identify as the state, the way many consumers could minimize risks and make do within their economic ability was to rely on their own experiences (consumer competence) at the expense of exercising choices. Here, the common Western premise of understanding consumer rights in terms of a sovereign (and unconstrained) consumer is not relevant because consumer rights are understood more in terms of having trust in the system rather than having choice, per se.

Bogomil was aware of this reality, and he and other activists put much effort into educating consumers and providing them with more information about their rights and how to protect themselves, frequently appearing on TV and radio shows as part of that effort. One cloudy afternoon in 2002, Bogomil brought up another example of what he referred to as the "old mentality of standards and control," recalling his appearance on Bulgarian National Television earlier that week. Here again, we see the conflict between Bogomil's position and those of many ordinary consumers' concerning how each understands the meaning of consumer rights.

Bogomil had appeared on a morning TV show called *Questions and Answers*, which took questions from viewers live over the phone during the program. Leaning back in his chair, Bogomil recounted the episode:

One granny called and said, "I want to complain about the pretzel sticks [*soleti*] I bought—they are too hard and I can't eat them. I went back to the store where I bought them in order to return them. The saleslady grumbled and yelled at me. A pack of pretzel sticks were 50 stotinki. She would not return the money nor give me a new package. *How can they sell such a bad product in the store?* [emphasis by speaker] What should I do?" You know it was a live show and the show host said, "So, your comment, Mr. Nikolov?" And I, in that moment, didn't know whether I should hide under the desk or get up and leave in front of the camera.... What should I have done? I'm there to give consumers advice and orient them in the new system and with the new legislation. Throughout the show, I explained their rights and emphasized that they had to exercise their consumer rights—as in European countries. Do you understand? But in this case, what could I say? Well ... soak them in yogurt or water and eat them, huh? And I tell you, this granny was not crazy. She was absolutely serious, and we could not dismiss her as being a crazy old pensioner. After listening to me, she thought what she did was right. She did indeed what she was supposed to do by expressing her discontent with the quality.

Compared to the common attitudes by consumers under socialism, which deemed returning to confront the seller as very unusual (although one could file a written complaint according to the Decree for Complaints), the elderly woman took a different approach in voicing her dissatisfaction with her purchase. During state socialism, every store in Bulgaria had a ledger called "book for complaints" (*kniga za oplakvaniya*) in which consumers, in theory, could write down any complaints they had with either the service of the seller or the products.[22] Rarely, however, were the books written in, according to my Bulgarian interlocutors. Although sellers were rude most of the time, asking for the book for complaints did not improve their attitudes. On the contrary, it would further aggravate them, which would only jeopardize future shopping opportunities for the consumers. It was widely understood under the socialist system that the seller was always higher in the power hierarchy than the buyer. The book for complaints was intended to correct such unequal power relations and protect consumers, but in reality consumers chose to be practical by not risking future dealings with the store. After all, consumers relied on those limited numbers of state-run stores for their routine shopping and the provisioning of everyday necessities.

Bogomil's frustration with this "granny" who put him in a difficult situation on a popular live TV show only reconfirmed the general context in which he and his colleagues had to work. He welcomed attempts like the elderly woman's who confronted the seller with her dissatisfaction with a product. Yet, the focus of her complaint, which was about the lack of control and standards, frustrated Bogomil, who criticized consumers' reliance on "somebody to control." The pensioner's attitude is not uncommon in Bulgaria and cannot be merely dismissed as a retiree's lament. Bogomil was clearly frustrated with the "old mentality of standards and control." The more he got into the story, the louder his voice became and the more lively his hand gestures. He continued passionately:

> In the granny's mind, those *soleti* were not what they used to be. Maybe they were stale. She should have looked at the label [to check the expiration date], which, of course, she did not. But what should I tell you? . . . You know, we want to help consumers orient themselves. . . . They have not yet understood *the thoughts of the transition*, especially in terms of consumer attitudes. . . . They continue to believe in, as socialism once taught them, standards and control, . . . *standards and control* . . . —*the state* has to exercise strong control, and everything in the market should be according to the state's standards: safe, of decent quality [that is, not garbage or *mente*], *and* cheap. You won't find such complaints in Europe, will you? (emphasis by speaker)

People such as Bogomil who work closely with other consumer organizations in the EU have internalized concepts such as transition, consumer rights, and consumer protection. As the stories in the chapters that follow show, however, there was barely any explicit engagement or articulation by consumer experts (at both the EU and national levels) regarding the nature and role of the state in the postsocialist era in orienting a new consumer politics. Thus, while both consumers and consumer experts continue to evoke the state in debates about consumer problems, the only explicit thing both parties mentioned was that they knew that the state now (in the postsocialist era) was not the same as the socialist state. But then what kind of state is imagined here in the postsocialist era?

Although scholars have urged to critically examine "transition," a term that is politically charged and presumes a singular fixed future of "capitalism" as the ultimate endpoint (e.g., Berdahl, Bunzl, and Lampland 2000; Burawoy and Verdery 1999; Verdery 1996; Buyandelger 2008), for people like Bogomil, "transition" suggested an unambiguous evolutionary direction. And this position was justifiable because as a then EU candidate country, few Bulgarians saw possibilities in negotiating the EU directives to accommodate local experiences. Thus, it was a given that Bulgarian consumers must adopt this type of transition ("thoughts of transition" as Bogomil put it) and Western notions of consumer rights and protection and become like (Western) Europeans who would not complain like the elderly woman. "Transition" for the former socialist countries in Eastern Europe, most of which applied for membership and have become EU members, entailed a fixed direction because of the prescribed directives that these states had to adopt to harmonize their systems with those of the EU member states. The systems that had to be created following EU directives had implications in the ways the state functioned in consumer affairs and how the tension between consumers' conceptualization of new and old rights intensified.

Consumers Straddling between Old and New Rights

The tension between old and new perceptions of consumer rights was not merely caused by the transition. As the Cold War was coming to an end and the neoliberal agenda permeated in consumer protection policies as well, individual responsibility was highlighted over responsibilities of the state as mediator or regulator (Cohen 2003; Hilton 2009). Yet in the minds of my Bulgarian interlocutors, these consumer matters could not possibly be the responsibilities of individual consumers only.

Bogomil's stories identify a number of points regarding the present consumer problems in postsocialist Bulgaria. First, in his opinion a lot of the present dissatisfaction by consumers is caused by "the old mentality of standards and control." Under the socialist regime, every consumer item was subjected to a certain standard, and the state both defined and controlled its adherence to that standard (see chapter 3 for a discussion on the law of standardization). Thus, consumers became used to the basic quality of different products. By basic, Bulgarian consumers do not mean good quality, but neither does basic translate into bad/poor or garbage, let alone fake. Indeed, it is important to note that when Bulgarian consumers talk about quality, it is in relative terms. For instance, my elderly Bulgarian friend Paulina, a former low-level civil servant, explained that the quality of products was worse in Bulgaria than in the West or in neighboring Yugoslavia, which had "nice products like in the West." Another interlocutor, Rumi, a project manager and accountant for a private company, showed me her bright green hooded jacket that she was wearing in 2002. Her father had sent it to her from West Germany, where he has remained since defecting. She was very proud of the jacket and explained that such a nice jacket with good quality and design was not available during socialist Bulgaria in the 1980s. Even though it was over ten years old, the fabric was not worn out (and she emphasized that she wore it a lot) and the design still looked stylish (even though she received the jacket as a teenager, it still fit her). At the same time, my Bulgarian friends point out that the quality of products is worse now than during socialism. My first landlady, for example, enjoyed showing me her old dresses and sweaters that were mostly from the 1970s. They looked amazingly good, especially given how often she wore those clothes. Some of the dresses were tailor-made and based on designs from Western fashion magazines. She emphasized, however, that the fabric was made in Bulgaria. When I asked whether these tailored clothes were more expensive than most ordinary Bulgarians could afford, she replied that one simply needed to know how to access them, but that they were not more expensive.

When my Bulgarian interlocutors insist that the quality of products is worse now than in the old days, they mean that the products that they can afford to buy now are worse than what they could afford during socialist times. Basic quality, therefore, guaranteed Bulgarian consumers a level of safety and a sense of social trust as far as quality went. The state made sure these levels of standards were controlled. Or at least the state was able to instill such perceptions in its citizens' minds. Consequently, such historical experiences influence the way people shop in the present. During the numerous occasions on which I accompanied friends and host families on their grocery shopping trips, very rarely did I observe people looking at expiration dates or reading labels for the ingredients so that they could compare price and quality. One of the neighbors, Dessi, an elderly pensioner and, according to my landlady, a devoted communist party member in "those" days, bought expired milk because she didn't inspect its label. Dessi first complained about how the expired milk could even be set out for sale. Then she remarked sarcastically that during socialism one never had to look at expiration dates because with the limited supply there would be nothing left on the shelf. When I asked her whether she went back to the store to exchange her milk, she shrugged her shoulders and said she doubted that they would do anything.

One time, I pointed out to my landlady as she was buying a pack of yogurt that she should perhaps look at the dates. This happened in 2002 when we shopped together in one of those old-style neighborhood stores where the salesperson handed the desired item over the counter when the buyer asked for it. My landlady explained to me that she had been shopping in that store for a long time, and they never gave her anything bad. Moreover, she added that that was why she preferred to go to this store where she knew the salesperson rather than to the Western-style supermarkets or other stores where a personal relationship between the buyer and seller did not exist. Hence, in her view one did not have to bother looking at the expiration date. It is interesting to note, however, that the seller in the store that my landlady frequented did not really have a personal relationship with her. She recognized her face but rarely did they exchange any personal greetings or engage in small talk. Nevertheless, for my landlady, the same familiar face she saw regularly and the fact that she never got anything bad (*mente*, which in this context could include spoiled goods) was more assuring than the unfamiliar faces in Western-style supermarkets where checkout clerks' shifts rotated.

Surprisingly, not only my elderly landlady but even younger people (who grew up in a completely different socioeconomic environment with abundant stores) gave the same kind of explanation. I was talking with friends about why they preferred their neighborhood stores over other kinds of stores for their daily groceries. Liliana, another low-level civil servant, put it this way: "In neighborhood stores, they can't cheat you because you go there every day and they know you. . . . I have never heard from anybody that they had bad experiences with their neighborhood stores. How would they give you bad milk or bread when they joke with you and they know you are their loyal customer? Places like Bila or Metro [Western-style supermarkets and wholesale hypermarkets, respectively], you can go when you have a car. . . . Of course, supermarkets like Fantastiko [a smaller Bulgarian supermarket chain] can be cheaper, but I prefer to shop in my neighborhood store even if it charges a little more than such supermarkets. I feel safer."

I asked her whether the personal relationship with the salesperson is such a decisive factor in shopping. I wondered whether she did not enjoy the right to choose directly from the shelves among various items in the supermarkets. Neither my landlady nor Liliana seemed to regard such choice (or way of choosing) as a big deal in daily grocery shopping. More important was the fact that they could rely on the products they bought from the stores. Liliana explicitly stated that she felt less vulnerable to deception under such familiar circumstances. Again, minimizing risk was considered most important over choices. For consumer activists like Bogomil, this was a passive consumer attitude, and the biggest challenge to their advocacy work has been to change the passivity of Bulgarian consumers and make them more actively aware of their rights so that they could protect themselves rather than relying on someone to protect them. Bogomil attributed the passivity to an "old mentality" that Bulgarians must eliminate if they wanted to protect their consumer rights, as in other European states. Yet as convincing as his claim sounded, such arguments did not resonate with many ordinary Bulgarians or adequately compel them to practice these right-seeking roles as consumers. My landlady, for example, questioned, "Okay, I seek my right, but who guarantees that it will be supported?" What mattered to my Bulgarian interlocutors was the fact that the state did not perform its role to protect the consumers from bad and dangerous products that could jeopardize their health. The postsocialist state was not fulfilling its role as the ultimate accountable authority, protecting consumers' basic rights to safety. It is in these concrete instances of consumption practices that state-citizen relations manifested themselves. In the absence of an accountable state, ordinary consumers saw little motivation in seeking so-called Western rights by looking for legitimate information for consumer choices in order to protect themselves from the abuses of the market. Simply put, the stores that gave them a sense of safety were considered more important for their daily consumption practices than exercising a Western notion of consumer rights by taking expired or poor-quality food products back to the store and seeking redress.

A Consumer Rights' Conference

The friction between consumers and consumer experts stemmed from the unsuccessful translation of the meanings of consumer rights in the aftermath of state socialism. This caused serious challenges for newly established consumer rights advocacy NGOs as well as for the newly formed state agencies responsible for consumer affairs. The role of consumer rights advocacy NGOs in postsocialist Bulgaria was not always clear to ordinary consumers. On the one hand, these NGOs were supposed to represent consumer interests. On the other hand, their authority was tenuous because they did not have meaningful decision-making power to fix problems in the way consumers expected them to. In light of the main argument of this book—namely, how consumer politics after socialism can be better understood by placing the state in relation to everyday consumption and by realizing how citizen-consumers conceptualized their rights and responsibilities as consumers—the following example presents a particularly common reality in the newly formed consumer sector in postsocialist Bulgaria.

In the fall of 2002, I attended a conference for the protection of consumer rights.[23] The seminar was held in a dark room that smelled stale from old fabric-covered chairs, carpets, and draperies. To Bulgarians, the setting and décor was reminiscent of local party conventions during socialism: a big sturdy metal table on the stage with a chair for the presenter and the host, an old screen for the overhead projector, and chairs for the audience neatly organized facing the stage. The room had no other decorations or colors. The windows were covered with worn-out khaki-colored drapes that could be drawn to prevent the unairconditioned room from getting overheated. What my Bulgarian interlocutors called "typical communist style" described this space—grayish, dull, monotonously monochromatic, with little decoration. Both the interior and exterior of buildings had this generic look. Communist party buildings and other official structures in Bulgarian municipalities were generally made of concrete and projected a sense of austerity.[24]

For the seminar, the room was sparsely filled with a small audience of some seventeen or eighteen people who seemed fairly elderly with wrinkles and graying hair and eyebrows, presumably in their late 50s or 60s: only about five people appeared to be in their 30s or 40s. In contrast, the presenters from CTCP's central office in Sofia looked much younger, perhaps in their late 20s to mid-30s judging by the way they were dressed. A few audience members were journalists; others seemed to be affiliated with different local civil NGOs and CTCP's Plovdiv regional branch office. Most of the people from such organizations included middle-aged women and pensioned men. A few people introduced themselves as consumers without any connection to either the NGOs or the government institutions.

This conference on the protection of consumer rights took place in Plovdiv, the second largest city in Bulgaria, located about 120 kilometers southwest of Sofia. Although my fieldwork was primarily based in Sofia, I occasionally accompanied consumer activists such as Bogomil and his colleagues Slavi or Dessislav to conferences taking place outside of Sofia. This particular conference was hosted by a Plovdiv-based consumer rights advocacy NGO during the traditional annual Plovdiv Fair (*Plovdivski Panair*),[25] and Bogomil and Slavi had been invited to attend by the organizers of the conference.

Back in the conference room, Katya, a CTCP representative from Sofia's central office, gave her presentation about the commission's work using the information technology that it had recently adopted. She spoke about the Transitional Rapid Exchange of Information (TRAPEX) system that had been shared with other Eastern European countries to protect consumers from dangerous products ranging from children's toys to domestic electronics. She used overheads to explain the system and what kinds of dangerous consumer items had been detected through this system and consequently withdrawn from the market. After her presentation, Katya started her question-and-answer (Q&A) session with the audience. A woman raised her hand and introduced herself as a Plovdiv resident and consumer. She started calmly:

> Miss, your presentation was very interesting, but I am confused. I went to a market here and bought linen sheets. I washed the linens as soon as I got back home. Then I heard on the news that some of the linen sheets in the market that were imported from China might be dangerous—the chemicals they used might cause skin allergies and troubles. I immediately ran back to the store and asked them where the linens that I had bought were from. The saleslady said they were probably from China. I told her that I wanted to return the linens because I heard in the news that they might be dangerous. Of course, I had my receipt. Of course, she refused to refund by saying that I could not return the linens when I have already used them. I cannot buy new linens again and I am afraid of using them now. . . . I was very angry. I mean how can *they* [emphasis by speaker] let such products out in the market? According to your presentation, miss, it seems that the system is there, but I don't understand how the dangerous things are still sold in the market. Why is nobody doing anything? Is there anything that the system you described can do? What can you do in my case?

Another woman raised her hand and added with an angered voice that in her case it was some children's toys that were reported in the news as being dangerous. She agreed with the first woman and repeated, "How can *they* let out such things in the market? Is this *normal*?" [emphasis by speaker] Although it was unclear to me at that moment who "they" that two women referred to was, the audience seemed to understand the reference perfectly, implicitly recognizing the "they" against which the consumers formed an "us." As discussed in chapter 1, this dichotomy was repeatedly brought up in moments of consumer grievances in postsocialist Bulgaria as it spoke to the issue of accountability. The notion of normality to which the second woman alluded also highlighted a central theme in Bulgarians' daily consumption practices.

After the comments by the two women, the audience got agitated and started exchanging their own complaints with each other. Katya tried to recapture her audience's attention and said loudly, responding to the two questions, "Please share such information with us. We cannot go around every store in the market and see whether the products there are good." Bogomil interrupted her:

May I add a few words to Miss Katya's response? I'm Bogomil Nikolov, the executive director of the Bulgarian National Association of Consumers. The question here is the system of control. I have been doing a project with a German consumer organization. What I found interesting is that the system of control is not their emphasis [*ne tehniya aktsent*]. They say they only respond to the signals from the consumers. Once they receive the signals, they contact the producers, and the producers themselves retrieve the problem products from the stores. Is this because Germans are more conscientious? No. [One woman in the audience said loudly, "Yes, because they are not Bulgarians!" This kind of self-disparaging commentary, often expressed sarcastically, is quite common among Bulgarians.] That's their system. TRAPEX is a good system for making producers aware of their image. But what you are telling me, ma'am [turning to the first woman who complained about her linens], sounds all too passive to me. I think we should not look for responsibility in somebody else. Only after being more active for rights can we ask for the work of the state.

The audience was not convinced. Almost ignoring Bogomil's comment, the attendees resumed talking among themselves criticizing the state and merchants until an elderly man in the audience took the floor. Judging from his wrinkles, white hair, and old-fashioned suit, he was probably a pensioner. He introduced himself as a member of the socialist party congregation in Plovdiv. Directly responding to Bogomil, he commented, "Okay, young man. But all goods in the market should be registered as brands. And somebody has to *control* [emphasis by speaker] them. Otherwise this system that we are talking about won't work if we don't respect the law that states such things. This country has always been operated by a stable judicial system—I mean, law, not only in the document level but with real effect."

This man was certainly calling attention to the control aspect when he commented on the significance of "real effect." Neither the audience nor Bogomil, however, responded to the older man's remark. It seemed as though his comments were dismissed as a typical retiree's lament nostalgic of the socialist past when the state exercised firm control over production and distribution of goods and had a functioning judicial system. (Whether that was actually the reality in those days or only the selective memory of this man was beside the point.) The discussion went on. Literally, everyone in the room had something to complain about: about bad services even though we are not under socialism anymore, about bad tennis shoes and consumer electronics in the market that were worse in quality than in the past,[26] about merchants cheating on the weight of vegetables and fruits, and so on. The Q&A was out of the moderator's control for some time. Then a woman from the Plovdiv branch office spoke out, saying that basically Bulgaria had to educate its consumers:

> If you go to a "one-lev" store,[27] you should know that you would rarely find a quality product. They look suspicious even from their appearance. But people buy them. They should understand that price does not guarantee quality. Somebody complained that the Bulgarian market was only for garbage. If the consumers don't buy them, the products won't be in the market anymore. We have to have well-informed and conscious consumers [consumers with awareness]. What can we do when the consumers see the products that look dangerous and still buy them and then complain that they are bad? What can you do in such a situation? We can't control everything. We ourselves demand such products out of our needs because we are poor.

The audience became quiet, and Katya took the floor again:

> My dear audience, I very much agree with my colleague's comment. Let me give you another example. It is about a receipt. My husband and I bought some batteries at the market. I told him to get the receipt. He says, "Oh, there is no need. This is *a reliable store*, so they won't sell *mente*," and so on. *Of course* [in a sarcastic tone; emphasis by speaker], when we got back home, the batteries did not work. My husband got angry and blamed the store for selling such bad products. Then he blamed the state for letting such businesses continue. Well, had he taken the receipt from them, at least he could have gone back and exchanged the batteries, or if they refused he could have argued with them and refer to the laws. Somebody earlier said the Germans were more conscientious consumers because they were not Bulgarians. I don't agree. They simply know what their rights are and how to use them. Yes, we are poor, but it's not because of someone else. We ourselves are carrying our poverty.

Katya made a strong statement about how Bulgarian consumers were accountable themselves for the numerous consumer problems. The audience, however, hardly took notice of it and their grumbling did not stop. Many of the complaints ended with deep sighs and with people recriminating the poverty of the nation and the state that put Bulgaria in such a miserable plight.

Finally, Katya gave the first woman a last chance to speak and that ended the discussion. The woman inquired about the contact numbers of the commission and asked Katya to advertise the presence of her commission to ordinary consumers so that they would know to whom they could turn. Katya gave her the telephone numbers and added, "But please remember that we cannot do all this work by ourselves. First, the consumers must 'protect themselves,' and both the governmental as well as the nongovernmental organizations have to work together to inform the consumers about their rights and how to protect themselves." The audience applauded begrudgingly as if they were still not satisfied with the responses they got from the commission staff nor convinced by their arguments. The conference was over. Bogomil came to me afterward and shook his head. "Did you see this again? Bulgarians do not have the habit of saying what the problems are, face to face. They only talk behind people's backs. And they still think there will be somebody who does something for them, somebody who controls. They don't think they have to control themselves. . . . [He sighed.] After thirty years, can we reach the level like Germany? But, frankly, I don't know whether that will happen."

When Bogomil insisted on more active rights of the consumers and less reliance on the state, he meant that consumers should think before they purchase something. After a decade of transition to a market economy, he argued, people should have learned that the price of the product did not always correspond with its quality. What made Bogomil repeatedly frustrated was the "control mode" in which most consumers (such as the elderly man in the audience) and even some consumer activists were still thinking. In other words, they still believed in somebody's authority to control and they desired that control. In fact, in his commentary, Bogomil tried to emphasize that consumers themselves had to control the market. Essentially, he was saying, "Watch out for the products you buy, and do not be blinded simply by the cheap price." This viewpoint was very much supported by the people from the CTCP. Yet consumers were struggling to define the meanings of "rights" and wanted to identify the different parties that were responsible in this case.

In addition, state officials, by explaining that they could not go into every store in the market to inspect every item, pointed out that the role of government bodies had changed. They would only inspect the products on "signals" from consumers. This role of the administration was different from the "control" role it had performed in the past when separate government institutions (e.g., Hygiene and Epidemic Institute [locally referred as HEI]) and regulations (i.e., the law of standardization) exercised control over all consumer items. No matter how often people like Bogomil advocated changing consumers' attitudes, ordinary Bulgarians still struggled to make sense of the changes that they encountered in their daily lives. Their existing values clashed with newly introduced values. They recognized that times had changed, but it was hard for them to translate the external changes into their own understandings and practices. The arguments by both state actors and NGO representatives (consumer experts) who represented the EU discourse of teaching new practices and values to citizens of EU candidate countries undergoing transition did not resonate much among ordinary Bulgarian consumers.

The consumer rights' conference was part of an effort to cultivate consumer advocacy in postsocialist Bulgaria. The concept of consumer advocacy as used in Western capitalist societies was new to many Bulgarians: its introduction came with democracy, market capitalism, and most importantly, the endeavor to join the EU. Bulgaria needed a viable consumer sector as part of EU membership requirements (Pritchard 1994). Although the concepts of consumer rights as well as the protection of those rights (consumer protection; *zashtite na potrebitelite*) were unfamiliar to a large percentage of Bulgarians, my Bulgarian interlocutors regarded them as significant. Interestingly, however, the importance was not always internalized as compatible knowledge for everyday use among Bulgarian consumers. As expressed by the participants of the consumer rights' conference, the economic hardship and frustration from an arguably long transition as well as confusion from new cultural values that came with the new situation made the issue of agency unclear to consumers. They repeatedly asked: Okay, the protection of consumer rights is important, but who will protect us vulnerable consumers? Who *controls* the quality of consumer goods to ensure safety? Who should ultimately be accountable for dangerous products in the market?

These questions constantly evoked the agent of control—namely, someone (or some authority) who could help consumers, especially with those with low purchasing power, be safe from poor-quality products and unfriendly services. They also reflected the common predicament regarding postsocialist consumer problems that occurred as central topics among families, neighbors, and friends in everyday life and appeared frequently in the local media. Consumer rights' conferences thus echoed many of the daily conversations among Bulgarian consumers that revolved around various consumption practices and their subsequent consumer complaints.

At the same time, a hierarchy of accountability is articulated in postsocialist consumption practices that further attests to the importance of examining the role and representation of the state among consumers. As was the case with the woman in the consumer rights' conference in Plovdiv who bought new linens that were later reported to be hazardous, many of the daily complaints were tied up with mundane consumption activities. Their financial limitations make many Bulgarian consumers particularly vulnerable, but according to Bogomil, it was time for them to finally have learned their lessons. These are what he refers to as "active consumers" who can protect themselves and be responsible for their own consumption activities. He acknowledged the problems that the postsocialist consumption environment produces, such as the low purchasing power of consumers, which made them especially vulnerable vis-à-vis producers and merchants. And yet he also insisted that consumers feel helpless primarily because most of them have not fully incorporated the idea that they themselves could be the controller of their own consumption thereby assigning responsibilities onto the individual. Hence, as the woman in the conference mentioned, she expected her problems to be resolved by someone else, such as the CTCP, which she perceived to be the state's representative. For those who did recognize that there is a limit to what either the commission or the state could do, they still raise common questions: How can you protect yourself when you can only afford the cheap goods that look suspicious? You know that it is most likely of lower quality, but what can you do when you don't have enough money? Am I accountable for this miserable reality?

While these questions represent the alienated relationship between the state and the citizens in the postsocialist period (Kideckel 2008, 2009), as I discuss in chapter 1, they are also instructive regarding the enduring vision of a postsocialist state that citizens share. Here, the imagined state is one that can assure citizens that there is a system that works, and if it does not, there is a mechanism for accountability. To my Bulgarian interlocutors, this assurance is the basis of social trust and can afford them with a sense of existential normality. In other words, for many postsocialist citizen-consumers, the state is essentially expected to play the role of balancing access and choice for them. More than anything, postsocialist citizen-consumers' expectation of the role of the state has also been expressed in terms of rebuilding the eroding social trust as a way to normalize social relationships between the postsocialist state and citizen-consumers. The exercise and protection of consumer rights were not about internalizing new meanings of these concepts but hinged on a normalized relationship between the state and citizen-consumers.

In this chapter, I examine how concepts such as needs, rights, and protection were shaped historically. The meaning of the consumer in the context of postsocialism differs from the socialist time where the state guaranteed access to necessities, and it is also different from Western capitalist societies in that the common assumption of the consumer as an autonomous and free agent is not taken for granted in the postsocialist context: even those Bulgarians who identify themselves as "ordinary middle-class" people find their position as consumers precarious and anxiety-ridden. Bulgarians' popular attitude toward consumption as not something emancipative but agonizing has implications in the ways in which consumers construct the meanings of rights and responsibilities and how they conceptualize the state in the postsocialist and post–Cold War context. Consequently, the postsocialist condition comes to highlight the demands for the realignment of citizen-consumers, the state, and the market, as the state is perceived as an important category in negotiating and facilitating the rights and responsibilities as consumers. The postsocialist vantage point, then, offers a meaningful engagement regarding this realignment of consumers-state-market in the era of neoliberal globalization in which the category of state is often eclipsed by the market and in which the individual is presumed to be an autonomous agent.

In chapter 3, I focus on the work of the consumer organizations and consumer experts who have been playing an important role (but perhaps not as publicly appreciated or acknowledged as they should be) in consumer politics after state socialism, especially in the context of EU integration. This will ground my discussion about state-citizen relations further by investigating the role of consumer experts who were introduced to the newly forming consumer sector in postsocialist Bulgaria as part of the EU integration process. Consumer experts, who are a group of new professionals (such as NGO activists and specialized bureaucrats) after state socialism specializing in consumer issues, often found themselves torn in addressing such consumer demands of a more active and responsible presence by the state. Caught between the model of Western civil society and recognizing the different conceptualization of the state under postsocialist conditions, these consumer experts struggled to engage ordinary consumers. Their frustrations grew particularly more pronounced as they tried to embrace the Western narratives and practices on the one hand (as I discuss in this chapter) and sympathize with and advocate for citizen-consumers with whom they shared a common historical experience on the other hand. Chapter 3 examines these tensions more concretely.

Notes

1. A chain of Bulgarian hard currency stores during socialism, CORECOM is actually a French abbreviation (*Comptoir de Representation et de Commerce*). According to Bulgarian anthropologist Ilia Iliev (personal communication, June 2, 2002), Bulgarian transliteration was French-oriented until the late 1990s when the official transliteration became English-oriented. In a similar vein, it can be speculated why older Bulgarian passports for international travels were entitled in French: *passport pour tout le monde*.

2. Suggestive here is the Bulgarian expression "released" in the context of consumer goods distribution. Bulgarians use the term "release" (*te pusnat*) rather than "sell" (*prodavat*) to describe the centralized planning and distribution system during socialism. This term implies the arbitrary and irregular nature of the distribution system—an expression that reflects citizens' subtly twisted reaction to the supposedly planned nature of the socialist economy (see also Ditchev 2004:11 n23 for a similar observation). Some of my Bulgarian friends repeatedly reminded me that the deficit economy was not so much due to the constant lack of goods than the erratic (and therefore unplannable) accessibility to the goods (caused by irregular distribution). In any case, this expression also affirmed the paternalistic nature of the state in everyday consumption practices.

3. *Intershop* was the East German variant of such special stores (see more in Merkel 1999 and Bach 2002). Similarly, the Russian equivalent was called *Torgsin* up to the 1930s and *Beriozka* since the 1950s (Lemon 1998; Ditchev 2004).

4. In addition to CORECOM, *diplomaticheski magazini* (stores for diplomats) operated with foreign hard currency. Only people with diplomat identification cards could shop there, however, and thus were much less accessible to ordinary Bulgarians.

5. "Connections" (*vrazki*) is an important concept in the everyday practice of Bulgaria both past and present. It is often expressed in terms of "acquaintances" (*poznati*), which has a more positive nuance than *vrazki*. These terms are indicative of the importance of social networks and social exchange of favors (such as *blat* in Russia and *guanxi* in China; see Ledeneva 2003, 2009; and Hsu 2005, respectively). The exchange is not always balanced, but these words do not necessarily imply bribes, which are understood more as "corruption" (*koruptsiya*).

6. In a similar vein, the so-called show-off (*pokazni*) stores in socialist Bulgaria sold "nicer" goods including exotic fruits like oranges and bananas that were normally only available during special holidays such as the New Year. The prices in *pokazni* stores were a bit higher than in regular stores (with often empty shelves), but according to my Bulgarian friends, an ordinary person with a job could afford to shop there.

7. Jenny Smith's (2009) discussion on "common luxury" (such as ice cream) in the Soviet Union is also a noteworthy example and characteristic of state socialism regarding how the state managed the tension between deprivation and stimulation.

8. This slogan was taken from the USSR in 1961 during the Twenty-Third Congress of the Communist Party (Ditchev 2004: 10). For consumption during the Cold War across Eastern Europe, see also Bren and Neuburger 2012.

9. I especially thank Ilia Iliev for clarifying and explaining this point to me.

10. Ditchev (2004: 17) further reports that CORECOM is now kept as a trademark, as is the Soviet's *Torgsin*.

11. Copious studies have addressed this. For Eastern Europe, see Bren and Neuburger 2012. For East Germany, see Berdahl 1999; Merkel 1998, 1999; and Steiner 1998. For the

Republic of Georgia, see Dunn 2008. For Hungary, see Fehérváry 2002, 2013. For Russia, see Humphrey 1995, 2002; Caldwell 2004; Caldwell and Patico 2002; and Patico 2002, 2005. For Poland, see Mazurek and Hilton 2007. For Estonia, see Rausing 2002. For Bulgaria, see Creed 2002a, 1998; and Cellarius 2004. For Romania, see Verdery 1996.

12. See also Miller 1995b, which cautions against the common assumption that "market" means the same across different sociocultural contexts. See also Humphrey and Mandel 2002, which examines this issue through case studies in various postsocialist contexts.

13. A few studies focus on consumption from the traders' viewpoint. One interesting example is Yulian Konstantinov's (1996) discussion on trader-tourism in postsocialist Bulgaria, where conditions of economic shortage provided discriminated ethnic minorities such as the Roma with an economic niche. The postsocialist shortage conditions allowed Roma traders to eliminate the class and ethnic boundaries. See also Konstantinov, Kressel, and Thuen 1998.

14. See also Graeber 2011 for discussion of the terms "consumer/consumption."

15. Velinova (2004) also observes that in the early period of transition, the word *klient* (customer) was used in place of *kupuvach* (buyer) until the term *potrebitel* (consumer) became more widely used.

16. The phrase "the needs of the population" (*nuzhdite na naselenieto*) commonly occurred in major economics newspapers such as *Ikonomicheski Zhivot* (Economic life) that were published during the socialist era and the early transition years. See also Mihaylov 1984.

17. Following the convention in anthropology to protect and respect the identity of informants, I have given pseudonyms to my interlocutors described in this book unless they are public figures. This includes Bogomil Nikolov, who gave permission to be identified by his real name. His regular and consistent media appearance in the past fifteen years or so makes him difficult to disguise. I also use the real names of the consumer advocacy organizations and state agencies because their public role and media coverage make them easily identifiable.

18. In my recent trip to Bulgaria in 2015, I noticed that the store had had a makeover with a new sign and updated interior. Some items were on shelves, and customers could serve themselves instead of asking the seller over the counter. I did not see the owner, however.

19. Anthropologist James L. Watson (2006) also notes how in China "service with friendliness" is perceived as a Western model introduced by the global fast-food chain McDonald's. Traditionally in China, if a seller is friendly it was believed that the seller was trying to cheat the customer. In Bulgaria, a seller's indifferent or rude attitude was attributed to a socialist legacy based on the experiences with the inverted power relationship in the stores during socialism.

20. For a good, detailed description of the power relationship between the buyer and seller during socialism, see Humphrey 1995: 48.

21. One lev equals 100 stotinki.

22. The actual name of this book was "book for commendations and complaints" (*kniga za pohvali i oplakvaniya*), but because stores (sellers) received more complaints than praises during socialism, most of my interlocuters simply referred to it as "the book for complaints." I thank Iskra Velinova for pointing out the official name to me. For other avenues of consumer complaints in socialist states, see Fitzpatrick 1996 (Soviet Union) and Zatlin 2007 (the German Democratic Republic [GDR]).

23. "TRAPEX and Consumer Protection in the EU," consumer conference organized by CTCP-Plovdiv and the Regional Consumer Organization of Plovdiv, October 2, 2002.

24. See Buchli 2000 for discussion on Stalinist material culture and architecture; see Reid and Crowley 2000 for the material and visual world of the socialist bloc. Fehérváry (2013) vividly describes the material culture during socialist Hungary. Her work focuses on the shifting aesthetics of quality-versus-quantity debate and how housing during state socialism contributed to this stereotype.

25. Officially called the Annual International Technical Fair (*Mezhdunaroden Tehnicheski Panair*), the international Plovdiv Fair has been taking place for over a hundred years. According to my Bulgarian friends, the fair was one of the few precommunist events that was successfully incorporated by the socialist regime and continued in the postsocialist era as well.

26. When Bulgarian consumers compare the quality of products in the socialist era to those in the present, their comments refer primarily to products that are "affordable" now and that were "available" then. My interlocutors understand that they now have access to a variety of goods, including high-quality ones, but such products are often out of reach for ordinary consumers with limited financial means. It should be understood that their comparison was not to glorify the socialist past when the products were often of inferior quality to those in the West.

27. The one-lev store is something like a dollar store in the United States. It sells everything from kitchen utensils to bathroom items such as soap, toothbrushes, and so on, for one lev. Some stores also sell stationery. The Bulgarian version primarily sells cheap consumer items imported from China. Even from the outer appearance, they look like poor-quality products of questionable safety. The stores also sell counterfeit (*mente*) items such as fake Colgate toothpaste or Lux soap for one lev. In regular stores, Colgate toothpaste and Lux soap would be at least two to three times more expensive.

3

CONSUMER ACTIVISM?

Legal Changes and Social Distrust

According to BNCA's Bogomil Nikolov, "standards and control" refers to the main principles of the socialist planned economy. The law of standardization (*zakon na standardizatsiya*), a typical and specific legal framework for the former socialist countries, determined much of the consumption experience of Bulgarian consumers and stated the principles of production under the socialist planning system. The idea of standardization was actually inspired by Frederick W. Taylor's disciplinary technique and Henry Ford's mass production and management technique, which were adopted by Vladimir Lenin, who admired such scientific management and wanted to adapt them to the Soviet's needs (Dunn 2004: 13–17). Contrary to popular belief, socialism and capitalism had much in common as modernizing projects.

The law of standardization of the Bulgarian communist state was implemented in 1964, and it meticulously defined the standards of every single product and service available to Bulgarians until an amendment was announced in 1998 and a substantial change in the form and content of the legislation occurred in 1999 (the same year the Bulgarian Parliament created and passed the Law of Consumer Protection and Trade Rules).[1] The law of standardization affected both spheres of production and consumption. I have discussed elsewhere in more detail how the standardization law worked with food products (Jung 2009: 37–40). Suffice it to say here that theoretically the state would have control over everything that went out to the market. For Bulgarian consumers, such a system assured them of basic quality and provided a level of trust in consumer products. They knew that the products were safe, not garbage, and above all, inexpensive. Buying a cheap loaf of bread did not mean that it was fake and/or dangerous. In addition, according to my Bulgarian friends, this sort of guarantee was associated with a sense of existential normality (see also Fehérváry 2013). By existential normality, my interlocutors essentially referred to a normal life without anxiety (*spokoen zhivot*), which in the context of daily consumption meant that one did not have to worry about wasting money on *mente* commodities and could have faith that a functioning system was in place to protect consumers from market abuses.

How well quality control actually worked during socialist Bulgaria is arguable. An acquaintance, Snezhanka, for instance, who in 2008 was a homemaker in her early 50s, recalled her *studenski brigardi* (student brigade) days when she was assigned work in a factory producing *burkani* (jars of pickled vegetables or fruits in syrup). Although she generally agreed that most consumer products were more trustworthy during socialism because of the state's control, she reminded me that the system was operated by people.[2] Giggling, she continued: "At first we were so disgusted to see that workers in the factory would smoke and not wash their hands in the assembly line. Once we even saw a bug going in the jar but nobody cared. They simply sealed the jar. Of course, then the students started to put some bugs in the jars, too—you know students. We thought that was fun—and since the workers didn't care about bugs or cigarette ashes going in the jars, we did not worry either. Of course, I don't know whether such jars with ashes and bugs did not pass the quality control, but after that summer experience, I never bought or ate anything from a jar that was sold in the store" (see also Jung 2009: 42).

Without doubt, the socialist system did not control everything perfectly. The problem of irregularity of distribution resulted in constant shortages and hoarding practices on the production side as well. Factory managers had to hoard materials to meet the planned goals of the state. This condition, if considered from the perspective of production, led to flexibility and creativity in given situations. Elizabeth Dunn (2004: 16–17), for instance, describes in great detail how a Polish canning factory dealt with such socialist conditions by using alternative ingredients and circumventing the prescribed standards of the state. Regardless of the realities on the production sites, however, most Bulgarian consumers I talked to believed that under the socialist system people could not get away with producing and selling fake products. In other words, *mente* could not and did not exist in the socialist economy thanks to the law of standardization and (perceived) firm state control. It is not surprising, therefore, that my Bulgarian interlocutors complain about the postsocialist state allowing companies to sell bad and fake products in the market and stores. Ironically, many of them did not regard this kind of control as a legacy of socialism that they wished to eradicate because it was indicative of a level of social trust in their provisioning activities.

In what follows, I discuss how the tension created by the inability to translate past experiences in meaningful ways affected consumer politics after state socialism. In particular, I focus on the European integration discourse and process, which were instrumental in shaping consumers' relations to consumer organizations as well as consumers' attitudes regarding consumer activism, another new concept introduced after state socialism. The EU discourse also contributed to state-citizen relations. Thus, I focus on understanding what the roles of these newly established institutions (governmental and nongovernmental) were and what they achieved.

The law of standardization has been substantially changed and minimized in postsocialist Bulgaria. To join the EU, Bulgaria had to adopt the *Acquis Communautaire* (the body of EU law) and follow a series of EU directives that required Bulgaria to establish a stable consumer protection sector with an accompanying modern legal code. Bulgaria's new consumer law, the Law of Consumer Protection and Trade Rules (*zakon za zashtita na potrebitelite i za pravilata za targoviya*), was created by translating the relevant EU law into Bulgarian in 1998. According to Stefan, who participated in this process as a lawyer, it took a team of experts from the Agency of Standardization and Metrology about four months to draft and submit this bill to the Bulgarian Parliament, which passed it on March 18, 1999. This new law replaced most of the functions of the previous law of standardization even though these two laws differed substantially in their contents. Most of the standards codified in the old standardization law were dismissed. The present law of standardization is primarily concerned with international standards in the spheres of energy, raw materials, technical terminology, and labeling (article 3 of the changed law of standardization).

The new consumer protection law introduced a number of new terms in Bulgaria. For instance, consumer rights and consumer organizations were completely new concepts for Bulgarian consumers around which the new law was framed. According to this new legislation, consumers could form organizations to protect their rights, and consumer organizations with more than three hundred members were entitled to financial assistance from the state (Pritchard 1994: 44), which was in accordance with other EU member states' practices. The problem with the new law, however, was that few Bulgarians believed that it would actually serve their interests. My interlocutors Svetla and Maria, both journalists, for instance, commented that the consumer law was just nominally there because of the EU requirements and did not work in reality. They did not trust that the law would actually help protect Bulgarian consumers from wasting money on fake and dangerous goods. The assumption was still that somebody should protect vulnerable consumers. The efforts of consumer experts who wanted to promote the new ideas of consumer rights and protection as practiced in Western Europe could not lessen the skepticism of the consumers who were not able to internalize these new concepts. A common public attitude was, Okay, we have consumer rights now, but who respects them?

There were two main reasons for the social distrust of the new law and consumer advocacy efforts in postsocialist Bulgaria leading up to EU integration. First, hardly anything in the new law resonated with the experiences of Bulgarian consumers. In other words, the direct translation of the relevant EU law without any reference to the historical and social experiences of the local people only further alienated Bulgarian consumers. Second, the politically weak Bulgarian state, which only followed what the EU told it to do, and its dysfunctional court system undermined any positive aspects of the adoption of the new law. In essence, Bulgarian consumers were not convinced that the minimal level of social trust could be reestablished without seeing the existence of any control mechanism through the state. Such common attitudes explained why the majority of my Bulgarian interlocutors did not agree with Bogomil and his colleagues, the consumer experts, who regarded standards and control as a negative legacy of socialist experiences. The following example further illustrates this common attitude.

In the winter of 2002, a middle-aged consumer visited BNCA to file a complaint about a watch that broke soon after he purchased it. In postsocialist Bulgaria, official complaints can either be filed directly with the relevant state agency (i.e., CTCP) or through a consumer advocacy organization that would help file the complaint on behalf of the consumer after consultation. While filling out the complaint form, this particular consumer uttered in familiar frustration: "How can *they* [the state; emphasis by speaker] allow such garbage to be sold in the market? Is this a normal state?" When I asked one of the staff members what that consumer meant by a "normal state," he replied, "Like in Europe—you would not pay for garbage [bad-quality] stuff in the market. European states would not allow such a thing to be sold in their markets." Later, when I retold this story to my close friends and asked, "But, don't you think if people do not buy such garbage products, the merchants would no longer sell such stuffs? Don't you think that the state does not have anything to do in this context?" all my friends sympathized with the consumer who filed the complaint. Shrugging his shoulders, Alex, an aspiring actor in his 40s, added:

> People here do not have money. We don't have a normal life like the Europeans. So what do you expect? At least, during socialism, we had a more normal life. I mean it was secure and anxiety-free for the everyday life. . . . Maybe it was a bit boring actually. We were of course not as rich as the Western Europeans, but we felt like people with normal lives. We could buy things without worrying that we would be buying garbage . . . we could afford to go to the seaside every summer, . . . we had time to go to concerts and theaters, . . . and we could afford to have guests at home. . . . That is a normal life, don't you think? Yes, the state did provide a certain level of normality then. . . . You ask about the role of the state. . . . I know that things have changed now, but I still think that the state must do something with the garbage in the market. When people do not have anything to eat, for example,³ they are susceptible to anything.

It is true that more and more people have become aware of buying poor-quality products and share knowledge about bad stores and *mente* products with friends and families as I have discussed. The popular and social media and consumer organizations also contribute in providing up-to-date information to consumers. Circulation of such knowledge is not considered as effective because of the ever-increasing number of commodities available to consumers unlike in socialist times. The financial constraints of the majority of consumers also makes it difficult for them to accept the idea that they have to protect themselves in the free market economy. They have to worry about survival (access), and they have to worry about choosing right because, for many ordinary consumers, choice is not always about preference but is related to survival.

Thus, the imposition of Western concepts has posited problems. In the Bulgarian context, where joining the EU was the primary national goal (because of the perceived lack of alternatives, see more in Jung 2010), external pressures took precedence over internal demands by the people. Although EU membership in 2007 seemed to have responded to Bulgarian consumers' concerns about the control aspect of the state or statelike entity as they would be sharing border controls for imported products with other EU members, for example, the consumer lament of *mente* and product safety control issues continue as EU's consumer protection mechanism is dictated by its neoliberal policies.[4]

Negotiating Access and Choice in the Context of European Integration

Much attention has been paid to the problematic aspects of the transition discourse in regard to the former socialist countries (Burawoy and Verdery 1999; Berdahl, Bunzl, and Lampland 2000; Hann 2002) because of the directionality and singularity inherent in the term "transition" that trumpets Western capitalism and liberal democracy as its endpoint. These studies highlight the continuing socialist practices in the postsocialist environment, which offer an explanation for failed Western aid and the possibility of different forms of non-Western capitalist developments following state socialism (see also Creed and Wedel 1997). While agreeing with the cautionary approach to a singular pattern of social transformation, I am also critical about such postsocialist literature that overlooks the EU factor and conflates the post-Soviet transformation efforts with those in Eastern Europe. Several years into what Bulgarians call *prehod* (transition), joining the EU has been firmly established as a national goal in most former socialist countries of Eastern Europe. The first wave of EU expansion accepted the former socialist states in Central Europe (Poland, Hungary, the Czech Republic, Slovakia, and Slovenia) and in the Baltics (Lithuania, Latvia, and Estonia) in May 2004. Bulgaria and Romania joined the second wave of EU expansion in January 2007. This context, then, set Eastern European countries apart in the postsocialist transition discourse because, unlike the former Soviet Union, some postsocialist African countries (e.g., Mozambique and Tanzania), and arguably China (Latham 2002), the path of social transformation from socialism was clearly modeled after EU member states. This particular context also made the Eastern European cases interesting compared to other (often postcolonial) developing countries that could adopt different hybrid models for their structural changes. In the European context, the EU dictated certain standards, rules, and its hegemonic European values according to the *Acquis Communautaire* to harmonize the systems among its member states. Candidate countries had to fulfill such prerequisites to gain membership.

This particular transition situation created both discontent and compliance, albeit reluctantly, in postsocialist Bulgaria. Bulgarian consumers complained about their deprived needs and lack of normal life in the postsocialist period. These complaints are indicative of a fundamental tension regarding access and choice because both were absolute and relative (to their own socialist past, to other countries) and were expressed through idioms of needs and normality. Unlike the experiences of many developing countries in the Third World, for example, where people bear the hardship of the present as they come to see economic progress, many postsocialist citizens found themselves questioning whether there was hope for a better future. My interlocutors explained why they were unwilling to participate in any kind of collective actions in terms of this lack of belief for a better future. The fact that many viewed EU integration as the only viable alternative for Bulgaria also contributed to the common apathy in mobilizing collective actions despite the rising levels of dissatisfaction with social changes and postsocialist governance. I call this attitude and cultural practice "complaisance," which refers to a space of agency that is different from resistance, complicity, or compliance, and argue that this is a characteristic that grew out of continuous disappointments with promised social progress (Jung 2010).[5] In other words, even though my interlocutors were ambivalent about the idea that becoming an EU member state would make life in Bulgaria better, they did not think there was a realistic alternative to EU integration. In light of the global process of marginalization, my Bulgarian interlocutors felt compelled to go along with the hegemonic powers despite their dissent to the dominant practices such powers espoused. They argued that they submitted to the hegemonic forces not because they were complicit but because of the inability not to follow them. This "inability not to follow" conveys the essence of complaisance.

In any case, for my Bulgarian interlocutors, the discourse of social progress in the postsocialist context of EU integration was understood as a guarantee of access and of having reliable choice. Yet becoming a member of the EU posed challenges in reshaping a meaningful relationship between citizen-consumers and the state and added the supranational entity of the EU into the relationship.

The Formation of a Consumer Sector in Postsocialist Bulgaria

As soon as Bulgaria set out on the path toward EU membership, it was subjected to harmonizing its structures and systems to those of other member states. In the name of the consumer sector, consumption was once again cast in a developmentalist logic in light of EU integration. Unlike during the socialist era when consumption was implicitly framed in terms of raising the standard of living for everybody, in the context of EU integration, consumption was explicitly framed as a development agenda with specific requirements that had to be met. One of the popular discourses in this context was that poor countries like Bulgaria did not have a consumer culture and therefore had to develop one to join the EU. In the foreword of *Consumer Protection in Bulgaria*, an EU integration project manager, Jean-Paul Pritchard, wrote: "One area which has undergone dramatic change is *the role citizens are now expected to play as consumers* in market economies which will soon be fully integrated into the European single market when the candidate countries realize their ambitions for full membership of the European Union (1994: 9, emphasis in original)"

In order for Bulgaria to be fully incorporated in the EU Common Market, Bulgarians needed to be consumers. Such a statement by Western European integration experts hardly took Bulgarians' historical experiences as consumers into account. As if Bulgarian citizens never played a role as consumers, EU experts emphasized the need for such a new role in the Common Market. But Bulgarians considered EU integration as the only alternative for their postsocialist state to bounce back to "normal life," thereby bringing their seemingly endless transitions—to socialism and communism and later to capitalism—to an end. Thus, despite the occasional frustration and ambivalence, many Bulgarians acquiesced to the discourse of need from the EU, which in turn legitimized a series of top-down reform policies. This discourse of need imposed from above explained the *complaisant* (namely, unable not to follow) attitude of most Bulgarians toward EU integration policy. Broadly framed as developing a consumer sector, accession aid grants were made available to cultivate consumer rights advocacy organizations in addition to establishing governmental institutions for consumer affairs and creating relevant consumer legislation. As a result, a separate consumer affairs division was established in the Ministry of Economy, and a Consumer Protection Agency was also created to regulate consumer affairs. The mushrooming of various consumer NGOs took place within this context around the time the new consumer law was adopted in Bulgaria in 1999. Both in public and private dialogues, the "European Union" (*evropeiski sayuz*) was a popular phrase in the daily lives of Bulgarians.

The *Acquis Communautaire* prescribed that all member states must have a functioning consumer sector with consumer rights advocacy NGOs. Unlike in many other industrialized countries where consumer organizations started off as grassroots movements (Hilton 2009) grown out of the civic need to protect consumer rights against corporate interests and market forces, the postsocialist EU candidate countries had to create such organizations because of the need to join the EU. The consumer sector comprised a separate chapter among the negotiation chapters that Bulgaria had to close to gain EU membership.

Consumer NGOs explained the new concepts such as consumer rights and consumer protection to the Bulgarian public and connected national organizations with global ones as part of a transnational consumer organization network. More importantly, consumer NGOs have been crucial agents in developing a consumer sector in postsocialist Bulgaria. The organizations' main missions were to help and educate consumers so that they could protect their rights through access to independent consumer information. This was a departure from how consumers viewed themselves. For instance, as previous chapters discuss, socialist consumers were not considered as right-entitled subjects even though warranties on certain products, such as appliances, existed. While Bulgarian socialist stores provided the book for complaints in which, theoretically, customers could write their complaints about the salesperson and/or the products, consumer rights as such did not even register in ordinary consumers' minds owing to the shortage economy under state socialism.

Although consumers sought for spaces to put forward their consumer complaints, the new consumer NGOs created little public interest because getting organized and standing up for consumer rights based on consumer information was an alien and unappealing idea for most of Bulgarian consumers. By 2006, Bulgaria had closed the twenty-third chapter in the *Aquis Communautaire* that dealt specifically with consumer protection. The consumer law it had passed in the National Assembly in 1999 was replaced by a new consumer law that passed in December 2006 on the eve of accession. It was not entirely clear why this change took the form of a new law instead of amendments—the differences between the 1999 and 2006 consumer laws were not very substantial. The new law included several more directives that had not been deemed relevant to Bulgaria's nascent consumer sector and market in 1999. According to Bogomil, there was very little time between when the draft of the new law was presented to the consumer organizations (one of their roles was to provide feedback to the state agencies that drafted the law) and when it had to be sent to the National Assembly. Bogomil's organization reviewed the draft and provided detailed comments to the Ministry of Economy, but little feedback from BNCA was adopted. The biggest problem that BNCA identified in the new law was its lack of details and vague legal language (eventually, a number of amendments had to be made for these reasons). While consumer organizations and state agencies were expected to work together to cultivate a consumer sector in light of EU integration, the cooperation did not always happen because their respective roles vis-à-vis citizen-consumers and how each party perceived their relationship to each other differed (discussed further in chapter 4).

As part of the EU integration process, a separate consumer protection division under the Ministry of Economy that was responsible for implementing consumer policies was established. In addition, the explicit requirements of the EU laid the foundation for newly established consumer NGOs' operations such as BNCA, the Federation of Bulgarian Consumers (The Federation), and the Regional Union of Consumers (The Union), to name a few. Instead of serving as grassroots civil organizations formed out of the particular needs in the local context, these consumer advocacy organizations were mostly established in response to the need to meet EU standards.[6] Except for The Federation, which was first established in 1990 by members of the *Otechestven Front* (Fatherland Front) from the communist period,[7] all other consumer organizations were mostly created by economists, political scientists, or lawyers, some of whom were employed by the Ministry of Economy during state socialism. After 1999 when the consumer legislation came into existence, these consumer agencies relied heavily on project funding from the EU and a nominal subsidy from the government made possible because the state recognized the need to have such NGOs in Bulgaria (for EU accession) and because EU directives stipulated that if the NGOs had over three hundred registered members, they were entitled to state subsidy. This top-down approach made implementation of reform policies more difficult. Consumer NGOs' encounters with Western partner NGOs through EU-funded projects elucidated the power dynamics within the EU integration policy and the consequent ambivalence of the candidate countries even as they continued to work with their Western partners out of complaisance (Jung 2010).

The Meaning of Consumer Culture and Consumer Organizations in Postsocialism

For many ordinary postsocialist citizens, consumer choice did not simply imply a free individual choice with which they bore an individual responsibility. As frequently reported in popular media and articulated by my interlocutors, many consumers also demanded a level of responsibility from a higher authority such as the state or the EU. This attitude was reflected in the ways in which consumers interacted with or thought of consumer advocacy organizations, which were, according to the EU directive, charged with shaping a new consumer culture in postsocialist Bulgaria as it was integrating itself to the EU.

I was invited to a friend's house for dinner in the fall of 2008, and my friend Diana had bought some Vienna sausages (similar to American hot dogs) to fix a quick, casual dinner. Smilingly, Diana admitted that she rarely bought this kind of sausage because of persistent food scandals involving this type of meat: one could not trust what it was actually made of. This, of course, was not an unfamiliar topic for me, and I was surprised that she had bought the sausages as many Sofians I knew were very careful when buying this kind of meat because it had generated so much news coverage over the past decade regarding its quality. After we had taken a bite, my friend cringed and uttered "*mente!*" She looked at me and profusely apologized while pulling the plate away. The texture of the sausage was quite rubbery, and I noticed a kind of artificial flavor. To be fair, though, I thought it was perfectly edible. Nevertheless, my friend apologetically explained that she thought it would be okay since it was a known brand and she had not heard anything negative about it. She muttered: "Until when [*do koga*] [do we have to deal with] . . . [sigh]? [This is] not normal. . . . Well, the Bulgarian way [*abe . . . bulgarska rabota*]. . . ." Again and again, these kinds of episodes served as a frequent reminder to consumers of the lack of control on everyday consumer products. And this is the social context in which Bulgarian consumers expressed their daily frustrations and demanded control by a regulatory entity. Such public sentiments, however, collide with what Western-influenced consumer advocacy supports under the conditions of neoliberal globalization. Diana, although not as explicitly as some of my other interlocutors, implied through her comments such as "until when" or "not normal" that she expected an external entity or structure to straighten out the abnormal reality. When I lightheartedly mentioned that there was nothing she could have done differently since she was not informed about this particular product, she agreed that it was beyond her ability to know what to trust and buy. The Bulgarian consumer market simply needed a "better system" and "stronger consumer culture" to weed out the poor (substandard) quality products since the individual consumer could not possibly know about every product in the marketplace.

The consumer regimes in Europe and North America in the twenty-first century emphasize the significance of self-surveillance and protection by well-informed consumers themselves and less reliance on the state or a statelike authority. Rather than expecting the state to protect the consumers, consumer experts emphasized that consumers had to protect themselves (see chapter 2). Translating past socialist experiences into meaningful practices were challenging to many postsocialist citizen-consumers and compelled them to rethink their own social values regarding what was necessary and normal. The constructions of social values, such as needs and normality, so commonly articulated by postsocialist citizen-consumers, therefore, cannot be merely seen as the result of homogenizing globalization processes and Western capitalist practices that stimulate consumer desires. Rather, ideas of needs and normality are firmly grounded on values shaped from past experiences. The economic and the symbolic must be seen as two sides of the same coin to avoid reproducing the common Western assumptions about what is necessary and what is normal. These historically constructed ideas of needs and normality were important values justifying the complaisant attitude in the EU integration process.

A frequent reaction that I received from my Bulgarian interlocutors during my fieldwork was: "Consumer culture? What consumer culture? We don't have consumer culture here. How can we have such a thing when we don't have anything to eat?" (*Potrebitelska kultura? Kakva potrebitelska kultura? Nyamame potrebitelska kultura tuka. Kak da imame takava ako nyamame kakvo da yadem?*) To explain to my interlocutors in Sofia why I was there, I generally summarized my research interest as understanding consumer culture or attitudes toward consumption after state socialism. After my brief description, they usually raised their eyebrows and broke into polite but cynical, sarcastic laughter. For them, consumer culture was something that countries with better material standards had. Or, to quote a popular phrase in Bulgaria, "what *normal* countries have." Ironically, however, some friends looked back on the socialist days (which were also perceived by them as abnormal) and cited the "consumer culture" of the times as making do in an unpredictable marketplace and expressing oneself within the constraints of the socialist economy. This suggests that the domain of consumption has always engaged people with ideas on rights and responsibilities and has especially shaped their understanding of the role of the state in mediating these ideas. The EU integration process brought in a new dimension in mediating the relationship between citizen-consumers and the state—namely, consumer NGOs.

Although there are numerous NGOs in Bulgaria, it should be noted that these groups were new concepts and entities for Bulgarians and were brought to public attention in the context of EU integration, a process that heavily emphasized the virtue and need of a strong civil society for candidate countries. Like consumer NGOs, most of the NGOs were newly established and developed by Bulgarians who saw them as new employment opportunities after the changes in 1989 (there had been massive layoffs after the collapse of state socialism), based on the discourse of "new needs" for a civil society (Cellarius 2004, 1999; Creed 2011). In other words, since the state no longer took sole responsibility of the social welfare of its citizens, postsocialist citizens were thought to need such organizations to represent their interests. The term "nongovernmental organization" never existed in Bulgarian everyday vocabulary until 1990 when the socialist regime disintegrated. Even decades since the end of state socialism, my Bulgarian interlocutors often struggled to categorize NGOs in their social classification of institutions because the NGOs' actual function vis-à-vis the citizens appeared ambiguous to them. Thus, from a Bulgarian consumer's point of view, joining an NGO (and paying membership dues) to have one's "rights" advocated for and protected still remains an alien concept. In other words, while membership (and dues) for the NGOs exist in theory, few consumers felt the need to become a dues-paying member (compare this to *Consumer Reports* in the United States, where consumers pay dues to access product information through its magazine and website).

According to Slavi, a staff member at BNCA, Bulgarian consumers do hear the term "NGO" (*nepravitelstvena organizatsiya*) frequently in the mass media, but they often confuse their functions with those of official (governmental) institutions. As a result, their expectations of NGOs are often identical to their expectations of the state or state institutions. Once consumers find out that the consumer NGOs cannot actually provide redress to their problems, for example, they get frustrated. Rather than perceiving NGOs as civil organizations actually representing the interests of the people, Slavi said that people think of NGOs as affiliated with the state and sometimes even representing it. Undoubtedly, such an ambiguous understanding is not only observed among Bulgarian consumers but also among those people who claim to be activists[8] of a nascent civil society. Some of these activists thought of themselves as experts, officially affiliated with the state apparatus rather than independent from and often against it. This ambiguity regarding their role vis-à-vis the state and vis-à-vis citizen-consumers was not helpful in cultivating a vibrant consumer sector.

Consumer protection was one of the 31 EU accession negotiation chapters (also commonly called "the adoption of *Acquis Communautaire*") that Bulgaria had to close in order to be invited to join the EU. Chapter 23 of the Aquis Communautaire specified all the rules and regulations that were needed in the area of consumer law and policy (Pritchard 1994: 33). The chapter delineated the institutional conditions that were necessary to operate consumer legislation properly (37). Furthermore, it suggested such conditions be set up along with new legislation and policies to ensure the protection of Bulgarians' consumer rights. The adequate institutional structure for consumer affairs included both governmental and nongovernmental institutions. Consumer NGOs, however, did not exist during the socialist regime.[9] Two main governmental institutions were established to oversee consumer affairs in accordance with the EU accession requirement: the Consumer Protection Department under the Ministry of Economy and the CTCP. The former primarily dealt with consumer policies, and the latter functioned as a market surveillance organ. The commission actually existed during socialism as well, but its roles and functions were largely restructured after the direction of Bulgaria's transition and reform were determined. In 2008, one year after Bulgaria joined the EU, the commission also added a separate division as part of the state institution dealing with consumer affairs—namely, the European Consumer Centre (ECC)—to assist consumers with problems stemming from a single EU market and transborder purchases. The ECC, which was part of the EU-wide network, was to assist Bulgarian consumers regarding their consumption practices while traveling in other EU member states or making cross-border online purchases (including vacation packages and hotel reservations in other EU member states). The ECC was an institution required for all EU member states.

Bulgarian consumer organizations such as BNCA were established as NGOs under the EU directives that defined their role:

> The lesson learnt within the EU is that any consumer enforcement structure requires, as one of its essential components, a strong, vibrant consumer movement. Non-governmental consumer organizations have been recognized as playing an important, indeed essential role in the consumer protection process, helping to ensure a high level of consumer protection in terms of the representation of the consumer interest to state bodies, the information they provide to consumers, the provision of advice, especially legal advice, testing, alerting state enforcement agencies as to unsafe products on the market and other threats to the consumer interest. (Pritchard 1994: 37)

The explicit requirements by the EU laid the foundation for the newly established NGOs' operations, which, in the Bulgarian context, mainly consisted of the representation of consumer interest to state bodies, raising awareness of new consumer rights and obligations, and consultancy. Legal advice was usually beyond the capacity of most consumer NGOs although BNCA always had a legal counsel as a member of its advisory board. While not grassroots, these external conditions set by the EU justified the existence and functions of consumer NGOs in Bulgaria. On the one hand, they used the developmentalist logic of "need" to justify their roles to Bulgarian consumers, and the Bulgarian state was obliged to provide a nominal subsidy to these organizations following the general European practice.[10] In this regard, NGOs and governmental institutions were not completely counterbalancing forces between civil society and the state. On the other hand, the NGOs used the same argument of "need" to receive financial and technical support from the EU and its member states, which were the primary funders for these consumer NGOs. This led to an interesting situation in regard to the relationship among the state, the NGOs, and the EU within the context of institutional hierarchy and issues of accountability. It also affected how citizen-consumers viewed and evaluated these consumer organizations.

In 2002, there were eleven registered consumer NGOs in Bulgaria, and this number increased to fourteen by March 2004.[11] Between 2011 and 2015, three more consumer organizations, primarily from provincial towns, registered anew bringing the present number to seventeen according to Bogomil. Except for the Federation of Bulgarian Consumers, which has existed since 1990, most consumer organizations were set up around the time of the adoption of the new consumer law in 1999. BNCA, for instance, was established in 1998 and has been by far the most active consumer organization in terms of operating projects supported by the EU and its member states. By 2010, it proved to be the only one recognized by the EU consumer protection circle to represent Bulgaria in Brussels for discussion on EU consumer affairs. In 2016, Bogomil was elected by his Bulgarian colleagues to represent Bulgaria in the European Economic and Social Committee (EESC), which is the EU-level body of civil representatives. Its main role is to provide opinions on the drafts of EU legislations. The development of consumer activism in Bulgaria is intimately tied to BNCA, which eventually established Bulgaria's first and only comparative product testing consumer magazine (see chapter 4).

Exercising Consumer Rights?

I have discussed how consumer anxiety and grievances were grounded in Bulgarians' frequent encounters with *mente* products. Other than complaining about this kind of consumer experience, how have consumers related to the emerging discourse of consumer rights and consumer organizations that were publicized during the EU integration process?

In 2002, as soon as Tsvetelina noticed the different colors of the two bottles of sunflower oil (a Bulgarian staple) that she had purchased, she examined the labels and the caps suspecting one or the other was *mente*. As I discuss extensively in chapter 1, Bulgarian consumers are almost obsessed with *mente*. The fixation is such that many newspapers and news reports occasionally document the fake products and show how consumers ought to protect themselves by citing expert opinions from the CTCP and consumer NGOs. For most citizen-consumers, the idea of consumer protection is often equated with protection from market abuses and how their rights as consumers can be respected. According to Tanya, a consumer expert at The Federation, this was particularly so in the beginning of the transition. During my 2002 interview with her, she took out old lab results of fraudulent products and emphasized that product testing was one of their major missions as a consumer organization. They had received project money from various "foreign sources" (she would not tell me more specifically) to help with the lab testing. She also showed me a stack of stickers of a symbol that her organization once tried to use to ensure the authenticity of consumer products. She said that the idea was to have producers acquire these stickers from The Federation and put them on their packaging, then consumers would understand that the products were not *mente*. After she described the idea to me, she sighed and explained that it did not work because the producers would not be "cooperative." Even though it was in the best interest of all parties, the producers suspected that her organization might take bribes and give the stickers to only a few of its favorite producers. This, of course, reflected a prevailing sense of social distrust. I asked whether consumer organizations would have the right to put such stickers on the products from a legal standpoint. She shrugged her shoulders and replied that they had never wondered about the legality of such actions. The problem, she quickly added, was that Bulgarians' sense of activism—in other words, a strong consumer culture—was still very immature, and consumers were often left on their own in dealing with *mente*.

In any case, Tsvetelina, on noticing the different colors of sunflower oil in two bottles, said "Oh, no. One of them must be *mente!*" She examined the two bottles very carefully. Everything including the expiration date was identical. The only difference that she noticed was in the color. The oil in one bottle was apparently darker than the other. As she had heard about the consumer organizations and what they did, despite her skepticism, she decided to call them for advice. On a Thursday morning around 11:00 a.m. on her day off, she first called the Federation of Bulgarian Consumers. Nobody picked up the phone. She tried again half an hour later—again nothing. Remembering BNCA, she called its office and a man answered. Tsvetelina stopped here and told me how it had played out: "It was very strange for me. He did not sound serious and said that he was there by himself at that moment. After he listened to my story, he said that I could try to go back to the store and return them. I said that I had already tried it but it did not work. Then, he said that there was nothing that I could do about it. He was not very friendly and made me angry, and I felt like I wasted my time." While Tsvetelina was talking on the phone with this man at BNCA, she noticed a phone number on the tag of the sunflower oil bottle. It was the producer's number. After she hung up the phone, she dialed that number—just for the heck of it, she said. To her surprise, a friendly woman got on the line and explained to her that the difference in color was not because one was fake or because one was spoiled, but because the first batch of sunflower seeds they used turned out to be darker than the second batch used for the other bottles produced at the same time. The woman from the production plant explained this to Tsvetelina and added that if Tsvetelina still did not feel comfortable with the two different colors, she was always welcome to return the bottle to them and get a new one. The only problem was that Tsvetelina would have to come to the factory located in the suburbs of Sofia. Tsvetelina was very impressed by the woman's kindness and her detailed explanation and said that she was not concerned about her sunflower oil anymore. I asked Tsvetelina how she felt about her own actions of making those phone calls. She put it this way (while shrugging her shoulders and taking a long puff from her cigarette): "I don't know, Yuson. I think I was just lucky today with that kind lady at the oil factory. It was just good luck. Look at those consumer organizations and their reactions. They can't even give advice let alone fix the problem. It was not worth my time." I then asked whether her taking action had made her feel better than merely agonizing about whether the sunflower oils were *mente*. She was not too convinced and grumbled that usually she would not have the time and energy to take action. Smilingly, she also added, "You know, life is not anxiety-free [*nespokoino*] here. But what can you really do? You only think about today and tomorrow, and that is enough for you." Tsvetelina exhibited a complaisant attitude about the whole situation, and her grumbling justified her attitude. Even though she did take some actions, rather than thinking of what she did as a form of activism to claim and practice her rights as a consumer, she considered them as something that happened by accident (she happened to have time), and the positive results of her actions as mere luck (*kasmet*). On this occasion, consumer NGOs were not able to engage her or enlighten her with their roles as representing the interests of consumers. Her attitude toward these consumer organizations, that they were neither able to give helpful advice nor fix her problems, however, was not only based on her postsocialist experiences.

On a different occasion, when I visited Tsvetelina at her apartment with some other friends, I talked to her about consumer complaints during the socialist era. Lounging around her white-walled living room furnished tidily with a new, simple-looking black faux-leather sofa, we briefed the other friends about Tsvetelina's sunflower oil incident. They were rather amused but did not seem to think that there was anything unusual about the story. Shrugging their shoulders, one of the friends reminded us of the book for complaints during socialism. There had always been a book for complaints in every store. Any consumer who was not happy about the service of the seller or products could write complaints in the book. It was meant to protect consumers from sellers who might not treat them fairly. Once in a while, a supervisor for each district would come to check these books (which usually had black covers, hence were sometimes referred to as "the black book" [*chernata kniga*]) and register the complaints.

Tsvetelina told me about her own experience with this book. When she was a child (in grade school), she was sent to buy milk from the store by her mother. She stood in the line with her friend, and when it was her turn she asked the seller for milk. During socialist times, the majority of stores were set up for over-the-counter sales. The seller barely acknowledged Tsvetelina and without looking at her quickly said that she had no more milk left. Tsvetelina was disappointed and about to leave the store when she heard the next customer buying milk. Although only in grade school, she felt the unfairness of the seller selling milk to the next customer and not to her, so she turned around and demanded the seller give her the book for complaints. The seller looked perplexed and started to murmur that she had to find the book. According to the storekeeping rules, every store had to have the book—as Tsvetelina had learned. She stubbornly kept asking for the book even though the seller tried to talk her out of it and said that she had found more milk and could sell some to her now. Tsvetelina did not give up until she received the book and wrote what had happened. Tsvetelina said, "You know, as a small kid, I thought by doing so I would really punish those sellers with their unfairness and seek justice. But you know what? Nothing happened. The seller worked in that store until the store was closed after the tenth (*deseti*).[12] You see, I learned my lesson then: not to waste my time. You can complain, but that is not going to make a big difference in reality. I would have been happier had I just shared the experience with my family and friends rather than writing in the book and waiting for something to happen." I responded whether it would be different now since there was a market economy based on competition. She replied with great skepticism and reminded me of her sunflower oil incident. Although she did get an explanation from the kind woman at the factory to whom she was lucky enough to talk, consumer organizations were neither useful nor helpful. They were not much different from those socialist bureaucrats that did nothing. This was not to suggest, however, that market forces were stronger (more competitive) in present Bulgaria and made the efforts of consumer organizations meaningless. Tsvetelina's repeated emphasis on luck spoke to her skepticism and ambivalence about both the new market relations and Western influences such as consumer organizations.

These series of interactions with Tsvetelina were interesting. It made sense why many of my Bulgarian interlocutors expressed skepticism about being able to make changes through their own actions. The constant disappointments that most Bulgarians had been going through, as Tsvetelina described, were not only about the intensive transition period. Even during socialism, people had started to accept the fact that as long as it was not your immediate friend or family who did something against you, it was not worth your time to take any action. You should just shrug your shoulders. There were lots of promises during and after socialism, but few changes, according to my Bulgarian interlocutors. It was no surprise, therefore, that people were very reluctant to file formal consumer complaints with the authorities. Their social distrust had reached a level where they expected little from the current postsocialist state or statelike entity, but they nevertheless expected a normalization of state functions that could give citizen-consumers a sense of security and normality.

Between Ambivalence and Commitment

After I heard the story from Tsvetelina, I immediately went to BNCA and talked to Bogomil about this incident. Admittedly, I was disappointed to hear Tsvetelina's experience with BNCA especially since I had explained to her several times what BNCA did and that Bulgarian consumers should utilize such organizations. Bogomil and I had discussed the passivity of Bulgarian consumers on a number of occasions before. I was sympathetic to his frustration in trying to educate and change what he called "Bulgarians' mentality." Bogomil seemed embarrassed by Tsvetelina's story and quickly tried to figure out who took her call.

The man was a member of the board of BNCA and a lawyer by profession who was known to the staff for his rather blunt attitude. He came to BNCA occasionally as a volunteer and helped Bogomil with his legal expertise. In any case, Bogomil later grumbled how difficult it was not to have enough well-trained experts or staff in his office. "Do you understand me now? Nothing works here the way it should—and I often feel lonely with my work." His plight was understandable: he was trying to translate alien Western concepts so that they would resonate with Bulgarian consumers. Although he worked in this NGO hoping to make a difference, he also often said that he had personal doubts about his activism work. Surprised at his candid ambivalence, I asked whether he was giving up, and he responded: "If I tried, but it did not work, what can I do? Change Bulgarians? Change the state? Bulgaria is still not ready for civil society. That is it. If Bulgaria was like Germany, there would be some hope, but Bulgaria is not Germany."

When I talked to Bogomil again in 2012, ten years later, I saw how he nevertheless persistently continued his work with Bulgarian consumers, doubling his efforts to disseminate reliable consumer information and protect consumers from the abuses of the market: his media appearances had become even more frequent, he actively networked with other NGOs and participated in forums regarding consumer issues, and he published the first consumer magazine featuring independent product testing, *Potrebitel*. As a consumer expert, he has had many professional achievements with his consistent and painstaking work aligning and cultivating himself in the global language of consumer activism. Since 2007, when Bulgaria joined the EU, he has also traveled to Brussels at least twice a month on different consumer affairs-related business. He reviewed EU's consumer legislations and made sure Bulgaria's interest was represented. His credibility within the EU consumer sector has also enabled him to build further global networks with Consumers International (CI) and Bureau Européen des Unions de Consommateurs (BEUC; European Consumer Organization). BNCA also become a sought-after partner for EU-funded projects with EU candidate countries such as Turkey, Serbia, Montenegro, and Macedonia.

Between occasional ambivalence and commitment as a consumer activist, in 2007, Bogomil started to publish *Potrebitel*, a monthly consumer magazine of comparative product testing results (the equivalent of *Consumer Reports* in the United States and *Which?* in the United Kingdom) to offer independent information on consumer products and services to Bulgarian consumers (see further discussion in chapter 5). This was a huge milestone in the history of Bulgaria's consumer movement because, unlike other former Eastern European countries (e.g., Poland, Czechoslovakia, and Yugoslavia), socialist Bulgaria did not have any precedence for a consumer protection regime as such. At the same time, Bulgaria, like other former socialist states in Eastern Europe that had joined the EU, had no alternative but to follow the harmonization process by reducing the consumer protection regime and policies to the lowest common denominator within the EU—namely, based on informed choice—as the main target of consumer protection (Hilton 2009: 69–72). This meant that Bulgaria and other new Eastern European members joined the rest of Europe of the 1990s where only one vision of consumer society, that of choice, was upheld. As discussed earlier, this was a break from the earlier era of protection regimes in Europe after World War II that addressed concerns of both access and choice (72). Given pressing consumer issues in postsocialist societies that found more commonalities with developing nations in Asia addressing both access and choice (Hilton 2009; Garon and Maclachlan 2006), the EU model of a consumer protection regime premised on choice inevitably created tensions in cultivating an organic consumer activism in postsocialist Bulgaria. And underlying this tension was the difficulty of translating new concepts such as consumer rights and consumer protection as the EU defined it to postsocialist citizens who were trying to balance between access and choice. This inability to make meaningful translations also influenced consumers' attitudes regarding NGOs as an ambiguous category and something not immediately useful in citizen-consumers' daily plights.

As Matthew Hilton points out, "by the 1990s, Europe had much less to say for those who could not actually afford choice" (2009: 72). This was an unfortunate and difficult circumstance for a relatively poor country like Bulgaria and explains why its consumer NGOs struggled to mobilize ordinary consumers who clearly were distressed and unhappy about the circumstances for daily consumption. Because these were civil organizations that were nevertheless formed out of need from the top, they had little agency in developing their own agenda for advocacy work. NGOs that were successful with EU-supported projects could not help but play along with the larger, EU-wide consumer ideology of choice. Ironically, the achievement of the Bulgarian NGOs was greater in the international arena than in the domestic one. BNCA, for example, continued to gain recognition in the EU and within the international consumer organization network as reliable partners, even as Bulgarian consumers such as Tsvetelina expressed skepticism about consumer organizations. This skepticism from consumers extended into a serious dilemma for Bulgarian consumer organizations: while they pushed forward with EU's consumer regime of education and dissemination of information, Bulgarian consumers expected reliable consumer information to be provided for free by the state in order to ensure the independence of the information. My Bulgarian interlocutors continued to believe that it was the role of the state, as they saw it, to be the ultimate object of accountability and agent for protecting access and choice.

Formal Consumer Complaints

Although the majority of Bulgarian consumers would certainly just complain about bad products or service rather than take further actions (e.g., the calls that Tsvetelina had made about the sunflower oil), some consumers did engage in more formal and aggressive procedures, such as filing formal consumer complaints with the state agency. For instance, according to a civil servant at the CTCP, only 60 consumer complaints (*zhalbi*) were filed in 2000 for the whole country, and this increased to 110 in 2001.[13] During a consumer conference in Plovdiv in 2002 (see also chapter 2),[14] another civil servant provided the audience with more detailed information regarding the filed complaints. Between July 2001 and July 2002, among the 512 complaints that were filed, 368 were unresolved. Also, the commission received 401 tips from consumers about "dishonest" stores that inspectors checked. Among these cases, 221 remained unresolved. These numbers have been relatively consistent to date, indicative of the normalization of official consumer complaint practices. In a conversation with one of the civil servants working at the commission in 2007, she admitted that only about 10 percent of the complaints filed reached a resolution. There are multiple reasons for this: first, the commission only has the ability to invite merchants to come to a meeting but cannot coerce them into doing so, and when the CTCP contacts the merchants once a consumer has filed a complaint, often the merchants do not respond to the commission's call. In that case, there is nothing that the commission can do without a court's action ordering the merchants to comply. Few citizens believe in the judicial system, which is still considered very corrupt. Second, even if the merchants initially agree to meet for a reconciliation conference, after a few meetings (or even just one), when they do not reach any resolution, the merchants often decide to forget about the whole thing because they do not want to waste any more of their time. Contrary to consumers' common belief, even the state agency could not fix all problems. Thus, many Bulgarian consumers indicate that they have an expectation of the state that is perhaps an imagined one yet to come true.

In most cases, consumers cannot afford to invest more time and money over a formal dispute (especially if they have to take legal action, which rarely happens in Bulgaria). Disputes over shoes, glasses/sunglasses, or small electronics, and so on, rarely get that far. This behavior was consistent with Bogomil's explanation of the level of Bulgarians' consumer consciousness or their "activeness" as consumers. Those consumers who file a complaint do so because the amount involved is relatively large—that is, more than 100 leva (US$50), which was over two-thirds of the average monthly income (132 leva [US$66]) in 2001—and the consumer has documented evidence such as a warranty card or contract signed by the sellers.[15] They also hope that the CTCP will resolve their problem (even though the commission does not have as much power as they think—as noted earlier, only about 10 percent of formal complaints reach a resolution) because they most likely cannot afford to take legal action themselves. One might think that bad publicity about a store or a product should be enough of a reason for a merchant or store owner to reconcile with the discontented consumer. Usually, however, both consumers and consumer activists attest that Bulgarian merchants are not really interested in long-term viability. It is sufficient for them to make an immediate profit. They believe that the merchants are taking advantage of Bulgarian consumers who are constrained in their choices of purchase. The low purchasing power they have in hand makes consumers choose cheaper things that are likely to be of poorer quality. The vulnerability that Bulgarian consumers feel is only natural given these circumstances, and it is no surprise that they see themselves as victims rather than as empowered people with rights.

From the commission's point of view, reconciliation meetings are one example to show that "Bulgaria is now just about to create [*praviya*] a consumer culture" according to Emilia Elchinova, head director of the market control division within the CTCP. During a formal interview at her office in June 2002,[16] she spoke animatedly about the beginning steps that Bulgaria was taking. Dressed in a simple but stylish jacket and skirt, the 40-something woman with red-dyed hair seemed charismatic and had clear pronunciation. Although very focused and attentive throughout the interview, she started to chew on sunflower and pumpkin seeds (*semki*) when she had to take an incoming phone call. In any case, from her official point of view, the fact that most consumers do not file formal complaints regarding petty matters, such as shoes, small electronic devices, and untruthful clothing labels, was one indication why Bulgarian consumers did not have any "civil position" (*grazhdenska pozitsiya*) regarding consumer problems. Moreover, another difficulty that characterized Bulgarian consumers, Elchinova pointed out, was that they did not believe much in institutions. "They think that institutions are corrupt. They want to see the results very fast, but here things are sluggish." This was an interesting comment, especially if we contrast it to the more widely held sentiment whereby Bulgarians trust institutions and organizations in a formal sense but do not trust the bureaucrats who work in them. After the interview, I mentioned this to my friend and my research assistant, both of whom were present at the interview. They both smiled and clarified that she probably meant the same thing as the popular sentiment but did not articulate it in clearer terms. Also, as my research assistant pointed out, Elchinova herself was a bureaucrat. My initial impression that the formal consumer complaints did not greatly reflect the more widely practiced daily consumer grumbling was confirmed particularly through my conversation with Elchinova. Throughout the interview, as with other officials with whom I had spoken, she repeated the official discourse of the hardship of the transition and expressed the dominant EU language based on the neoliberal ideal that focused on individual action and responsibility: people could not change overnight and it was only the people who could rescue themselves from misery and poverty. Consumers were complaining because they did not accept this truth. While she was clearly cognizant of the expectations of ordinary consumers for the state to step in and fix the problem "fast," as she put it, she too steered away from assuming any accountability and repeated the normative EU rhetoric of the individual responsibilities of consumers. Many Bulgarian consumers were acutely aware of these kinds of official responses from the bureaucrats working in state agencies, yet that did not deter citizen-consumers from imagining an accountable state in which they could exercise their entitled rights.

Standards and control were meaningful idioms for my Bulgarian interlocutors during socialism because it allowed them to gain a level of social trust regarding consumption practices. Neither the postsocialist state nor the newly formed consumer NGOs were able to translate these idioms into significant ideas that could resonate with postsocialist consumers. Consumers grew tired of the Western-oriented discourse and rhetoric of rights and responsibilities based on the principles of market economy and democracy because neither market competition nor electoral responsibility seem to be functioning properly in their postsocialist state. A persistent sense of deception and the diminished role of the postsocialist state in regulating the market underscored the growing ambivalence of postsocialist consumers in regards to the idea of right-seeking subjects. It made the advocacy work of the consumer organizations also very difficult as they found themselves caught between two sides—namely, the EU and Bulgarian citizen-consumers, whose ideas/expectations and experiences appeared less compatible. They, too, often found themselves in an ambivalent and complaisant position.

This chapter discusses the work of consumer organizations and consumer experts in the context of EU integration to further ground and examine state-citizen relations and the role of consumer NGOs under these circumstances. Consumer experts who worked for NGOs or state institutions often found themselves in ambivalent and complaisant positions vis-à-vis the dominant EU discourse and its normative ideals. On the one hand, they attempted to internalize them, but on the other hand, they also recognized how these top-down models and ideals resonated little for ordinary Bulgarian consumers. While the consumer sector that was forming based on the EU accession requirement did not seem to create a strong consumer activism as defined by the EU, Bulgarian consumers did not just remain passive. In chapter 4, I examine more mundane consumption practices to discuss how citizen-consumers in postsocialist Bulgaria continued to stay engaged and attempted to articulate what consumption meant to them in the context of EU integration and neoliberal globalization.

Notes

1. According to Stefan, a lawyer who participated in writing the new consumer law at the former Agency of Standardization and Metrology (*Agentsiya na standardizatsiya i metrologiya*), the old standardization law with compulsory standards was not effective between 1991 and 1999; it was not amended until 1999.

2. This kind of remark is a classic example of "secular theodicy" (Herzfeld 1992: 10), which refers to the principle of identity in which the flaw of individuals cannot undermine the perfection of the ideal (like the system) they share.

3. It should be noted that when Bulgarians mention people not having anything to eat, it is often meant in a figurative sense—that people don't have much means beyond survival and are engaged in basic consumption activities.

4. See Gille 2009 for a similar assessment regarding the neoliberal policies dictated by the EU in the Hungarian paprika contamination scandal. Paradoxically, the implementation of EU policies made Hungarian paprika less safe than during the socialist time. See also Dunn 2008, which reports how Georgians considered the standards during the Soviet era more reliable and safer than in postsocialism, which explained the increase of botulism in the aftermath of state socialism.

5. I have argued elsewhere (Jung 2010) that the notion of complaisance is particularly useful in understanding a space of agency that is neither resistant nor complicit, as is conventionally discussed in scholarly discourse regarding hegemony.

6. For discussions on environmental NGOs in postsocialist Bulgaria, see Cellarius 2004 and Snavely and Desai 1994.

7. This large organization included practically the entire adult population of Bulgaria as its members. The Bulgarian communist leader Georgi Dimitrov formed the group during World War II to unite all antifascists against fascism in Bulgaria. The first Bulgarian government after the war was, in fact, a broad coalition of the Fatherland Front and was not exclusively made up of communists. *Otechestven Front* was transformed after the war into a sort of a mega NGO to allow all Bulgarians to participate in the social life under communism. The main activities included cleaning around residential blocks, planting flowers around houses,

and organizing celebrations in schools, kindergartens, and neighborhood quarters. Supposedly, participation was voluntary, but it was perceived as false collectivism with pressure to participate.

8. In Bulgaria, the word "activist" is not used in the context of NGOs. Instead, Bulgarians use the term "experts" (*eksperti*) to refer to consumer activists such as Bogomil. They are entrepreneurial in the sense that by becoming experts they are also able to connect to higher officials (bureaucrats) who also identify themselves as experts in international communities. They also gain public recognition through media publicity because of their main role to educate and inform the public. The fact that the consumer protection sector was one of the areas in which the EU evaluated the progress as part of its membership criteria made their positions and functions as experts easily justifiable, but it also created confusion in the public's mind regarding what they could actually do for consumer grievances since they could not really fix consumer problems. Providing information and advice were often perceived by consumers as not enough.

9. More specifically, the EU directive explained the necessary conditions for consumer organizations as the following: setting up consultative procedures that represent the consumer interest and ensure consumer participation in the decision-making process; granting consumers efficient redress mechanisms; helping to ensure the development of nongovernmental consumer organizations (Pritchard 1994: 37).

10. In Bulgaria, consumer organizations that have more than three hundred members are given a small subsidy from the government. The subsidy can also come in the form of low rent for the consumer organizations' offices in one of the state-owned buildings. The size of the organization, determined by its membership numbers, hardly corresponds to the capacity of the organization because members are recruited through personal connections rather than voluntary grassroots interest as consumers. Membership fees exist but few pay them.

11. These numbers are relatively insignificant as some of the organizations are sister organizations of other groups and exist only on paper. Many of the registered organizations are small and only nominally operative (see also Commission of the European Communities 2004). The *2004 Regular Report on Bulgaria's Progress towards Accession* states that "two clusters of organizations can be discerned, namely one around the Federation of Consumers in Bulgaria and one around the National Union of Consumer Organisations, of which the Bulgarian National Consumer Association is the more dominant one" (114). The National Union of Consumer Organizations was not formally created until the spring of 2003, but the two groupings were evident even before the formalization. Although Pritchard (1994) reports that the Bulgarian consumer organizations are similar in their activities and characters, my observations during 2001–2002 indicate that they are quite different. A brief distinction between the two clusters can be described as the former focusing on an external "control" (often understood as the "old mentality" discussed in chapter 2) and the latter believing in consumer self-regulation and power through information and consultation with consumer organizations (see Jung 2010).

12. Colloquially, *deseti* (the tenth) refers to November 10, 1989, the official date when the Bulgarian communist regime fell. Similarly, when Bulgarians say *deveti* (the ninth), they are referring to September 9, 1944, when Bulgarian communists came to power with the help of the Red (Soviet) Army. Russians had also liberated Bulgaria from the Ottoman Turks on March 3, 1878, and thus the common saying among elderly communists: "Russians have liberated Bulgaria twice: once from the Turks and once from the fascists," which also reflect the ties between the two countries in people's historical consciousnesses. These expressions

of *deseti* or *deveti* are politically neutral temporal markers compared with more ideological labels such as "revolution" or "liberation," and so on, and are commonly used in everyday contexts.

13. Presented by S. I. [name withheld] at a BNCA-organized consumer conference, "Seminar with Judicial Experts on Consumer Protection," Borovets, June 15–16, 2002.

14. "TRAPEX and Consumer Protection in the EU," consumer conference organized by CTCP-Plovdiv and the Regional Consumer Organization of Plovdiv, October 2, 2002.

15. According to the Bulgarian National Statistical Institute (http://www.nsi.bg/en), the official average monthly income per person was 132 leva (US$66) in 2001, 430 leva (US$310) in 2007 when Bulgaria joined the EU, and 850 leva (US$480) in 2015. This monthly income does not include secondary incomes (such as the rent I paid to my host families or private tutoring fees to teachers, etc.). While living standards were improving for many Sofians, the rising inequality between those who managed to accumulate rapid wealth after 1989 and the rest of the population added to a perceived sense of poverty.

16. I took a research assistant to most of the formal interviews I arranged in case I would not be allowed to record the interview and also to have a native observer who would catch local nuances that I might miss. At this particular interview, I was accompanied by my research assistant and a lawyer friend who arranged my interview with Elchinova.

4

CONSUMPTION AS CIVIC ENGAGEMENT

The *Parno* Problem

If the EU-dictated model of cultivating a consumer sector based on neoliberal ideals of individuals making better informed choices did not resonate with ordinary Bulgarian consumers, then what did civic engagement through consumption actually look like for citizen-consumers in the postsocialist era?

Late in the fall of 2002, I had an eerie feeling as I entered Irena's apartment and saw holes in the floorboards exposing old and rustic pipes. When Irena and her brother Emil had first explained their plan of "making heating" (*pravim parno*), I could not understand what they were talking about. The only part of their plan I could comprehend was that they wanted to have heating. Having had plenty of experiences with the problem of heating in Bulgaria myself (see the appendix), I did not think that there could be any more surprises for me in that regard. I was wrong. My jaw dropped as I entered their dark apartment in downtown Sofia that day. I saw their two friends, Dimitar and Simeon, breaking a sweat trying to connect the pipes from the furnace they had just installed in the living room to the water tank in the bathroom. Some parts of the wood floor were torn up so that they could see how the old pipes were connected. The new, thin metal pipes (about 5 cm in diameter) were often seen in bathrooms around Sofia. Dimitar was a skilled professional carpenter and the boyfriend of Irena's second cousin, Tsvetelina; Simeon was an engineer and the husband of Irena's best friend, Liliana. It was already late in the afternoon, and the only light they had on was in the bathroom. While Dimitar, Simeon, and Irena's brother Emil worked on the pipes, Irena, Liliana, Tsvetelina, and Darya (Emil's wife) lounged in Irena's bedroom sipping wine, nibbling on sunflower seeds (*semki*), and smoking. Occasionally, Irena would walk out to watch the progress or to find necessary tools and plumbing items for the men. Finally, it was time to connect the pipes in Irena's room to the main furnace. Irena expressed a visceral excitement: "Finally, I will be able to sleep in my pajamas!" She implied that it had been too cold to sleep only in pajamas for several winters. The women made room for the men to work in her room and moved out to the main living room, trying to somehow sit around in the midst of exposed pipes, dust, and wood piled up by the new furnace the men had just set up. The men continued to work hard the following day until the system was completed. Irena and her brother's family did not have to go through another winter without heating.

At first I could not register the creativity of Irena and her brother. This incident could be viewed as one of the common make-do strategies by postsocialist citizens (Caldwell 2004; Shevchenko 2010). Yet there seemed to be something more in how Irena and her family and friends explained this situation. In taking these actions, they were expressing a sense of solidarity with like-minded people who opted for alternative heating. The first thing that crossed my mind, however, was whether it was actually legal to set up an alternative heating system and whether it was safe to do so. What if something were to go wrong or if it were to catch fire or even explode? Their apartment was on the second floor of a larger, densely constructed building that housed multiple apartment units. When I expressed such concerns, my friends lifted their shoulders and said, "What would you do if you were in my shoes? Isn't it nonsensical to suffer without heating? This was not a problem for our parents' generation. They have worked hard to give our generation a better life, but for what? We cannot even afford heating these days." Legalities did not seem to matter much to them at that point. They said that the state could not meddle with their personal heating methods. The government stopped providing them with adequate heating anyway. The safety issue was also beyond their concern. They considered it a matter of luck and trusted the expertise of their friends who installed the alternative heating system. To Irena and her brother, the furnace was a cheaper alternative than the central heating administered by *Toplofikatsiya*, a privatized public company in partnership with the state and municipality. They felt that heating was something that they should be entitled to as citizens, and since the state was no longer guaranteeing access, they chose this way.

After living without heating for two consecutive winters, Irena and her brother finally managed to save some money to install an old-fashioned wood-burning heating system. With help from two of their friends who were professionals, they set up a main furnace in the living room and connected it with pipes to their two bedrooms, kitchen, and bathroom. The heating method was the same as the centralized heating (i.e., it used fuel to boil water) but instead of coals and natural gas, the tanks they used burned wood. Their apartment, which they had inherited from their parents, was very old and in dire need of renovation. As with any older apartment in Sofia built in the 1940s or 1950s, the central heating system was highly inefficient. They calculated that rather than paying about 150 leva per month, which would barely keep their place warm, they could install this alternative system and spend half as much burning wood. The only problem with this method was transporting the wood purchased from a wholesaler to their place. They did not have a car themselves, but luckily, through their social network, they found an acquaintance with a car who had adopted this alternative heating method as well. In fact, they learned there were many citizens who had opted for this alternative, and this created a space of civic solidarity among them. Their acquaintance regularly drove to an outdoor market on the outskirts of Sofia where villagers sold the wood. By offering to split the cost of gas for his car, they secured a way to purchase the wood for their furnace. This method was only feasible under certain conditions: one needed to have the money and a social network to install the furnace and pipes as well as means of transportation for the wood supply. Rather than suffering in an unheated apartment and merely complaining about the state that had abandoned its basic responsibility, Irena and her brother saw their actions as a civic engagement and took comfort from the solidarity of like-minded people who chose similar alternatives. They were not alone in their heating problem.

The subject of *parno* (heating) has been a very sensitive and frustrating one for Bulgarians in the aftermath of state socialism because it was fundamentally tied to the intensive social changes from a centralized socialist economy to market economy. My Bulgarian interlocutors frequently mentioned that nobody suffered from lack of heating during socialism and that heating costs were rarely an issue. This was another mundane example of how postsocialist citizens felt that social progress was hampered: they felt denied of the necessities that even the (failed) socialist state had achieved. Somewhat nostalgically, a few of my interlocutors mentioned how they wore short sleeves during the winter because the apartments were so well heated thanks to the low cost of gas from the Soviet Union. This *parno* issue actually provided me with one of the most memorable and intimate ethnographic experiences. In my first winter in Bulgaria, I lived with a host family who had turned off the heat to their apartment because they could not afford it. At first, I was clueless as to what that actually entailed because I could not imagine the situation. It was just uncomfortable that my host family was so apologetic to me the entire time I lived with them. This incident, however, allowed me to gain new insights into something that evoked such strong emotional reactions in so many Bulgarians. The heating problem was both a private and public matter: because it was confined to the private space of home, it was not always explicitly shared or discussed in public among friends or colleagues, many of whom indicated that it was rather embarrassing to admit that they could not afford heating their home. It challenged them to live a dignified life that they felt they deserved after decades of social sacrifice in the name of progress. At the same time, it was also a deeply public matter that stimulated debates on the civic aspect of everyday consumption, as many Bulgarians knew that they shared the same plight regarding access to heating. For those who had heat, they still shared the frustration over rising heating costs. Many believed that the state colluded with the heating company in the name of EU reform policies. Above all, these discussions regarding the heating problem expressed the ideals and dreams of Bulgarians and not just their disappointments and despair.

To date, the cost of utilities such as heating, electricity, and water are considered one of the biggest burdens for household budgets in Sofia (and other urban areas), and citizen-consumers frequently brought them up in everyday complaints vis-à-vis the state. Pensioners, in particular, continue to struggle with paying for heat during the winter months as do low-income families. Even for middle-class families, heating costs take a big toll. The heating issue thus was one of the central consumption matters that had the potential of mobilizing ordinary consumers around consumer rights advocacy organizations and sparking collective actions (public benefit) as it instantly drew attention from even the most skeptical consumers who had little faith in the Western-style consumer advocacy work. The *parno* example offers meaningful insights into how Bulgarian consumers enact a sense of civic virtue despite their political apathy.

The Failure of a Consumer Movement

In the fall of 2002, the Bulgarian government started to make changes to the heating and billing system. Within the larger framework of energy reform, it installed meters on radiators in individual homes and offices that enabled consumers to control central heating so that they would not have to pay unnecessarily for overheated apartments. With the meters, they could also turn the heat off based on their ability to pay. In the past, the highly centralized and bureaucratized heating system left little room for individual maneuvering. In other words, if the heating system was turned on for the whole building, individual homes or offices could not control their indoor temperature. Similarly, if you opted to turn off the heat in your apartment for the entire winter in anticipation of not being able to pay the heating bills, you could not turn it back on in the middle of winter if your financial circumstances improved. The new device corrected these problems and would also allow consumers to watch how much energy they used. From the government's perspective, the idea behind these changes was to assure consumers that they would not be cheated by the heating company anymore. *Toplofikatsiya* was accused of charging huge sums to consumers even though some apartments were still cold. The state was also aware that many apartment dwellers in Sofia actually turned off their whole units' heating for good because of the high heating cost.

Some Sofians, however, turned off their heating for other reasons. They thought that the current natural-gas heating system cost too much and was not as energy efficient, as was the case with Irena and her brother. Bogomil Nikolov, for example, insisted that Bulgaria's heating crisis was not only the result of corruption by state officials and politicians. The sudden rise in global gas prices and the inefficiency of the Bulgarian heating system with its dilapidated infrastructure and uninsulated pipes also contributed to the *parno* problems. And this was where the state needed to step in to modernize the infrastructure. This position, though, was highly unpopular with the Bulgarian public, who viewed the heating problem largely as a matter of corruption that led to the state's failure to provide basic (affordable) access to its citizens.

In any case, those who realized the inefficiency of the old heating system coupled with their skepticism of corrupted officials opted to install alternative heating by themselves. They turned off the central heating and built a more efficient system that was less pricey in the long run using alternative fuels such as wood or a gas-electric combination. My friends Vasil and Genka, both relatively well-to-do professionals, for example, installed gas-electric heaters on the ceilings of their apartment. They looked like the heaters mounted on the vestibule ceilings of some hotels or restaurants in the United States. Unlike the radiators operating through the central heating system, these heaters warmed up quickly and could be turned on briefly whenever necessary. However, they needed electricity to ignite them and gas to fuel them, and they were not cheap to install. (Irena and her brother's wood-burning alternative was cheaper, but it required a reliable social network to install and the ability to transport the wood to use it.) As young professionals who could afford a lump sum for the installation, Vasil and Genka invested in this heating system given the long-term savings. They, too, expressed similar sentiments as Irena and her brother, who deemed that turning off the central heating and choosing an alternative consumption practice was an act of civic engagement. Irena and her brother eventually sold their apartment in 2013 and moved to two different apartments that did not require this kind of alternative system; Vasil and Genka still have their system, although since 2013, when the cost of electricity rose suddenly, they went back to centralized heating as their alternative system was aging out and no longer provided cost savings.

The heating controversy in the fall of 2002 that ensued when *Toplofikatsiya* announced that it would modernize the system could have led to a potential consumer movement. Unfortunately, it did not succeed in making effective changes after all. After the government announced its plan to install the meters, consumers who wanted to maintain central heating in their homes had no choice but to cooperate in the government's new policy. The basic premise (at least at the official level) behind the installation of the new radiator meters was to allow consumers to see how much energy they used. From the state's perspective, the ideas behind these changes were to assure consumers that they would not feel cheated anymore by *Toplofikatsiya*—the state in a superficial way acknowledged the prevailing sentiment of deception among citizen-consumers in postsocialist Bulgaria. The technicians from the heating company began installing the meters in individual homes over the fall of 2002. As more homes received meters, a rumor also circulated that it was simply a "sneakier" way of raising heating bills since with the numbers on the meter, the state could essentially justify the high heating bills more transparently. According to the rumor, each apartment had to declare how much heat it expected to use over the winter. This enabled the heating company to calculate how much heat the entire building was projected to consume. Before these devices were installed, it was impossible to know how much heat each apartment unit used exactly. The heating cost for the entire building was simply divided by the number of units in the building, and that was the heating cost each apartment had to bear. If a unit declared it wanted to "turn off" the radiators, then that unit did not have to pay for heat. With the individual meters, *Toplofikatsiya* could add up each apartment's use, and if that number did not correspond to the projected number each apartment had declared before the heating season, then the company could legitimately charge the overused portion at a higher rate, and each apartment would receive an additional bill because the two numbers did not match. This "sneaky" method encouraged neighbors to watch each other and catch the "culprit" who, after declaring their radiators were turned off (or declaring less usage than reality), used the central heating thereby burdening the neighbors with additional heating costs.

The rumors turned out to be true, and consumers, already deeply angered by rising heating bills, became even more furious when they learned that the new meter was a more cunning way to manipulate heating bills. Whatever the justification for the rising cost of heating was (e.g., Russia was no longer providing low-cost gas and oil, the heating infrastructure itself needed to be modernized, the heating company was just corrupt and evil, etc.), my Bulgarian interlocutors considered rising heating costs as a failure of the state. The absence of a state that cared was once again felt.

In the midst of this process, one consumer expert, Pavel Karlev, the executive director of the Federation of Consumers, gave a press conference to announce that every consumer who wanted to file a petition in protest against the rising heating bills should do so. His organization planned to take the petitions to the European Court of Human Rights (this is, in fact, an institution of the Council of Europe and not the EU, although Bulgarian consumers did not make the distinction). The Bulgarian state should be ashamed, so his argument went, to deprive its citizens of basic human rights to heating. He furthermore emphasized that this was what consumer organizations were for: to advocate for and represent consumers. Karlev explicitly positioned himself (and the consumer organizations) in opposition to the state. This announcement had a galvanizing effect. Many consumers, including my landlady and her friends who had been very skeptical of consumer NGOs, asked for the petition form by calling the consumer organizations (including BNCA) and brought the filled-out petitions to the offices. Even though BNCA did not agree with Karlev's understanding and handling of this heating issue (other consumer organizations also believed that the bills could be decreased by increasing the efficiency of the system itself rather than simply blaming the state for cheating on the bills and resorting to the EU), it did distribute the petition forms to consumers and accepted them to hand over to The Federation on behalf of the consumers. To the NGOs, it showed a potential for civic mobilization that could advance their consumer advocacy work. The day after Karlev's announcement, the phones in different consumer organizations rang incessantly, and within days hundreds of petitions had piled up. It was a moment of instantaneous civic engagement. The heating problem called for external intervention (as the consumer organization took the case to a European-level court), and many Bulgarians responded to it and even argued that it was perhaps their last hope.

The case was apparently sent to the European Court of Human Rights later in the year, but Bulgarian consumers did not hear anything from the court for a number of years. Once again, they found themselves opting for complaisance rather than remobilizing collectively to demand the state to fix the formidable *parno* problem that affected so many citizens. Even though the heating case generated an unprecedented instant mobilization of consumers in the postsocialist era around a common consumer issue, hence showing a potential for a consumer movement as described in the EU directives, it ultimately failed as a movement because there was a lack of understanding regarding the accountability of various stakeholders, such as the state, the NGOs, and the EU. At the same time, this incident showed an enthusiastic civic engagement in the domain of everyday consumption in that consumers publicly put forward their vision for state practices.

My former landlady, who struggled to afford the high heating costs even with the extra income she received by renting out two rooms in her apartment, explained to me in the summer of 2007 how she tried to counter the state's deviousness (even though the heating company was a private-public partnership, she did not make a distinction—for her, it was "the state"). She learned from neighbors and newspaper reports that when technicians came to read the meters at the beginning of the heating season, she could report to the technician how many radiators (each was installed with a separate meter) she intended to use in the coming winter. Apparently, if she used more than what she declared, she could be fined (that was how she understood the situation). For instance, she decided not to heat her own bedroom but instead economize by using her living room as a bedroom. Because she enjoyed falling asleep after watching TV, she figured that was not a bad idea. Her bedroom, therefore, remained closed and unheated for the entire winter. In 2006, however, her son stayed with her for a couple of weeks and she had to let him use her bedroom. Although she had already reported to the heating company staff that she would not be using that room, she turned on its radiator for a couple of hours every day during his stay. If her extra usage had been discovered during the inspection of the meters, she could have been penalized. Smiling proudly, she told me that she did not get caught, but she also expressed her concerns for the future. Compared to the control by my interlocutors who opted to remain outside of the central heating system, the tactic that my landlady adopted was subjected to the state's purview of power. It is instructive, however, to see that cheating could operate both ways: the heating company implemented a plan that would allow it to charge more, and my landlady successfully avoided a fine for her overuse.

A brief, exciting moment of civic engagement was displayed when Bulgarian consumers brought the *parno* petitions to the consumer organizations' offices. Surprised by such a sudden collective reaction, I asked my interlocutors whether they actually believed that this case would have a chance to reach a resolution at the European level. They shrugged their shoulders. They were not necessarily looking for someone to dictate to the Bulgarian state but cautiously hoped that a higher power could pressure it into addressing the heating problem. That was why, they explained, they were actively filing the petitions despite their ambivalence regarding the consumer organizations and consumer activism. Interestingly, they said that they would be willing to give the benefit of the doubt and express their civic concern because they "had had enough with the *parno!*" While few people believed that the national judicial system worked in present Bulgaria (because it was perceived to be very corrupt), they were willing to expect otherwise at the European level. Among my interlocutors, none of them questioned why this petition was going to be filed with the European Court of Human Rights and what the concrete demands of the petition were, or whether this European-level court could indeed influence the Bulgarian state in this domestic and sovereign matter. In their mind, Bulgaria's heating company was clearly violating consumers' basic rights to have access to affordable heating. It was instructive of how issues of access continued to be important for postsocialist citizen-consumers, and these issues were at the center of civic demands.

The petition was heard nearly seven years after the filing at the European Court of Human Rights. As the skeptics expected, it did not yield any results, and the case was dismissed on the basis of lack of grounds. In essence, the potential consumer movement that had resonated so widely among Bulgarian consumers failed. Some of my consumer activist friends told me that the petitions actually never constituted a "real" case—they thought it was ridiculous to label it a human rights violation in the context of the EU in the new millennium—and thus would be doomed to fail. In 2006, while my former landlady was attempting to avoid a fine, the head of the heating company was accused of embezzling public funds. As a result of the scandal, he was sacked, and this incident only reconfirmed Bulgarian consumers' suspicions of having been cheated on their heating bills over the years despite the modernizing efforts with the new meters.

In a way, neither the consumers nor the NGOs actually came up with concrete alternatives to the current system. Both groups felt that the state was complicit in the heating company's deception, but even in the petition to the European court, the consumer organization led by Karlev did not articulate any concrete demands other than that the state should make heating more affordable to its citizens. In the absence of clearly articulated alternatives, there were little grounds (or incentive) for the state or even the European court to respond to consumer discontent regarding Bulgaria's *parno* problem. In the end, the heating controversy epitomized a rather typical politics of hierarchical accountability within the framework of supranational institutions where there appeared to be a power hierarchy among the institutions when in fact this hierarchy had little impact in domestic issues and accountability. Rather than contesting such politics, however, Bulgarian consumers have been complaisant more than resistant. When they found out that no changes had been made as a result of their participation of the petition, they shrugged their shoulders and sarcastically remarked, "Of course, this is the work of Bulgarians" (*bulgarska rabota, razbira se*).

Such an attitude can be described as complaisant because citizen-consumers abide by the state or the so-called EU logic without necessarily challenging or consenting to it. They are unable *not* to follow the prescribed hegemonic rules, standards, and values (namely, the neoliberal policies and political practices of the EU and the Bulgarian state), but this does not mean they are complicit with them either. The consumer sector that was established according to the EU directives did not seem to provide any protection to consumers even though in everyday discourse the EU has always been placed higher in the institutional hierarchy. Rejecting the EU was not considered a realistic option for Bulgaria because many Bulgarians perceived EU integration as the only realistic alternative for a country whose fate had been entangled with endless transitions (to communism, to democracy and a market economy, and then to membership in the EU). While many Bulgarians did not believe that there would be a tangible improvement after they joined the EU, the ensuing disappointments with very little changes regarding their everyday consumer grievances only aggravated a sense of political apathy.

Yet these circumstances did not deter their civic engagement through the domain of consumption even as citizens' participation in the political process declined. Given the diverse and ingenuous tactics in remodeling and going around the state-operated heating systems, the *parno* problem was a central consumption practice for ordinary Bulgarian consumers expressing their civic engagement. Consumers experienced the "state" in their daily lives through heating problems that informed not only the everyday complaints against the state but also affected the perception of the state. The state, despite its weakened power, continued to be the problem as well as the key to the solution because for many ordinary postsocialist citizens consumer problems were about balancing access and choice, and the state was expected to play a vital role under these circumstances. Even though the state was perceived to be relatively absent in the postsocialist era, in the sense that it did not control the economic life of its citizens as it did before, the state was still very much part of the economic experience of ordinary people. The state was expected to fix the problem.

In the context of an institutional hierarchy, even the most skeptical consumers hoped that a supranational statelike entity of the EU would have the authority to solve the problem. The expected role of the state to provide affordable heat to its citizens did not change in the neoliberal regime. Rather, while the market system has enabled Bulgarian consumers to make do through alternative heating methods, the state has remained the target of complaint because of its neglect in addressing the problem of access. This is not to suggest that socialist/postsocialist citizens are infantile in their being used to a paternalistic state. On the contrary, this kind of craving for the state came from the tensions between balancing access and choice that was critical in the aftermath of state socialism, and this situation demanded a reconfiguration of the relationship between the state, its citizens, and the market.

The heating case, then, illustrates two important points: first, the significance and presence of the state in everyday consumption practices as reflected in the active civic engagement on the matter, and second, the imagined power of transnational governance in consumer matters. Throughout the transitional phase in the aftermath of state socialism, consumers voiced their frustrations vis-à-vis the state in terms of the lack of regulation and supervision for consumer safety and rights (Shevchenko 2002; Jung 2010). Despite disappointment with the socialist state, few people believed that the market would take care of all consumer problems according to the logic of free market competition (i.e., that consumers' purchasing power would eventually eliminate bad products in the market) in the aftermath of socialism. Many consumers still desired the state to play an active role that guaranteed access to basic utilities such as heating and ensured consumer rights in the face of cheap and lower-quality products available to the majority of postsocialist consumers. Despite the flaws of the socialist state, ideas and expectations about the role of the state and its perceived responsibilities to its citizen-consumers were nevertheless informed by consumers' socialist experiences. That hundreds of skeptical Bulgarian consumers could be mobilized so quickly by a consumer activist's argument to take the matter to the European level was indicative of the degree of civic engagement expressed in the domain of consumption.

The disappointments and frustrations with the state that consumers experienced during the socialist-postsocialist transition period had little impact on their perceptions of the state as the authority for regulation and provisioning of basic needs. Yet such an understanding of the state did not necessarily translate into identifying that regulatory power exclusively with the state. The postsocialist EU enlargement context provided Bulgarian consumers with more actors who can claim legitimacy for governance and regulation. In other words, the nation-state is not considered the only legitimate actor. In this regard, the EU, as a statelike entity, is understood to exercise regulatory power and governance over nation-states' consumer regimes. That is how Bulgarian consumers perceived the EU: they had similar expectations of the EU as they had of the state to take accountability and fix the problems. To create a viable consumer sector, consumer organizations had to embrace the expected role of the postsocialist state and position themselves accordingly vis-à-vis state practices. This was not always successfully done, but the heating controversy affirmed that consumption was an important domain where civic ideals (as opposed to individual desires and aspirations) were articulated. These ideals, too, were often expressed as needs, the theme that I explore further in the following section.

Articulating Needs in the Market Economy

Owning a residence has been culturally very meaningful for Bulgarians. My interlocutors explained to me that "building a house so you can leave it to your children" was a common Bulgarian ideal. During socialism, the three most meaningful purchases were apartment (residence), car, and villa (cottage in provincial village areas). These three items were considered signs of wealth in the socialist context, but this did not imply that acquiring them was a matter of individual choice. Although the wait was long due to the shortage economy, the socialist state guaranteed access to these items, meaning ordinary people could afford them on their salaries. The spirit of collective egalitarianism under the socialist regime put much emphasis in the fulfillment of the needs of the population. This was one of the important socialist ideals of social progress. Having social capital (*vrazki*, literally "connections," referring to networks of favors) could shorten the wait, but essentially, everybody was entitled to line up for these meaningful purchases and each would eventually be allocated regardless of social position. In this regard, it is also worth noting that home ownership in Bulgaria can be understood more as a cultural rather than an economic phenomenon. The fact that one owned a home did not preclude one from being poor. Ownership of one's residence had always been considered a cultural priority in terms of fulfilling the basic needs of life. Thus, while some foreigners might be puzzled to learn that poor Sofians would refuse to sell their residence despite their economic difficulties, many Bulgarians did not consider this kind of attitude surprising.

With industrialization and urbanization following World War II, Sofia, like elsewhere in Europe, was in need of more living space for its newly migrated population from the provinces. The state strictly controlled purchases of living quarters (which in Sofia meant apartments). Sofians with whom I interacted regularly all told their story or their parents' story of buying residences, and they were often recounted in much detail. Bulgarians had to save for a down payment, which they would deposit in the state-run investment bank so they could take out a state loan. Then, they would pay off the loan in the form of a monthly mortgage. According to my Sofian friends, about 90 percent of Sofians had a state loan: it was not difficult to get, but there was a wait time. First, one deposited the down payment (about

1,500 leva in the 1980s) and accrued interest points until one became eligible to take out the loan (initial loan amount was usually 6,000 leva; after this, one was entitled to take out additional loans).[1]

By the late 1980s, it took up to ten to fifteen years to get the loan needed to buy an apartment, at which point the shortage of residences became even more severe so that even if one had the money one could not buy a home. Unlike the former Soviet Union or East Germany, socialist Bulgaria allowed all forms of property, including private property. Because of the ideological implication, private residences were called "personal property" (*lichna sobstvenost*), which was meant to satisfy the needs of the citizens. In comparison, "private property" (*chastna sobstvenost*) referred to property that exploited labor forces beyond the family labor and carried a social stigma of bourgeoisie.

There were basically three ways to buy an apartment during socialism. First, the state built and sold apartments to people who had the money (either the entire sum or the eligibility to withdraw money in the form of a loan from the state) and who were also listed as the "most in need" because they lived in a place in which either (1) three generations had to share a two-bedroom apartment, (2) there were elderly people without families, or (3) people were disabled. To be sure, this list was subjected to corruption. The housing deficit was so acute, however, that people reacted very sensitively to housing issues and monitored the distribution process very closely. This tendency might explain why housing corruption cases did not occur in large numbers under the socialist regime. The second way to buy an apartment was by joining a group of people who would collectively borrow money from the bank (if necessary), buy a piece of land (either from the state, municipality, or private owners), submit a petition for state approval, and build a block or sometimes several blocks of buildings with many apartments. The group was usually organized by colleagues from work. These apartments were called a *kooperatsiya* (cooperative). To join the *kooperatsiya*, it was important that one had something to contribute to the construction of the building—for example, connections to construction material suppliers or a friend or acquaintance in the bureaucratic structure, and so on. In most cases, extra apartments were available because some colleagues had to drop out at the end due to individual circumstances, and other people who were not initially part of the *kooperatsiya* could join. If the *kooperatsiya* could not fill the vacant apartments from its own personal network, it announced to the municipality that there were remaining apartments, and the state would distribute them according to their most-in-need list. Finally, the third way to purchase a residence was between private parties. The state did not get involved, and only people who had the entire lump sum in cash could buy a home this way. In the urban environment such transactions were very rare because of the constant housing shortage. People simply would not sell their place once they purchased it. In fact, many Sofians named a family member as their designated recipient of inheritance for their apartments separate from their wills.[2] In rural areas, selling and buying happened more frequently between private parties as was often the case with the purchase of a villa.

Since the liberalization of prices in the housing market and the privatized mortgage system in the aftermath of state socialism, young people in Sofia, however, struggle to buy apartments. My friends adamantly insisted that it was absurd to believe that one could save enough to buy even the smallest studio apartment (*garsoniera*) in Sofia. Some of my Sofian friends were lucky that their parents or grandparents sold their apartments and bought new ones before the housing prices went up astronomically. These relatives bought a couple of smaller places in less-valued neighborhoods in the early years of transition when housing prices were much cheaper and gave these apartments to their children. Relatives with no offspring would use *pripisvane na apartmenta*, naming a niece or nephew as the recipient of inheritance for the residence. Consumers were less aware of deceptive practices in the market economy system in the 1990s. In the 2000s, however, there was a general fear of housing transactions because of so many fraud incidents with the sales of apartments; this sense had diminished in the 2010s.

In any case, Sofians who did not already own a place either rented or continued to live with parents. Most expected to inherit their parents' or grandparents' home one day, which they considered to be the only way they would ever own a residence. Few of my interlocutors in Sofia believed that it was possible to buy a residence by saving their salaries because of the constantly rising cost of living and increasing housing prices, their low and median salaries (even after they entered the EU), and the difficulty of taking out a large bank loan (affected also by job insecurity). Such circumstances, however, did not change the way people constructed their ideas of needs. A TV show *Who Wants to Become a Millionaire?* (*stani bogat*) was very popular in Bulgaria during my fieldwork in 2001–2002. The show's format was identical to the original American version; the only difference was the amount of money involved, 100,000 leva.

The show certainly sparked much discussion among my Bulgarian friends in terms of their material aspirations listed hierarchically from the most important and urgent on down. The list of meaningful purchases they hoped to make looked surprisingly similar to such lists during the socialist time: repair the apartment or buy a new apartment; repair, replace, or buy a new car; travel, both abroad and domestically. The socialist experiences clearly influenced the ways in which Bulgarians constructed and internalized needs. What was particularly striking was how they articulated their priorities as needs (access) rather than wants (choice), and they justified the distinction by referring to their past experience when housing was considered a basic necessity. They considered affordable housing "normal" and thought that basic rights were violated if an ordinary person could not work and save to buy a home (i.e., in ideological terms, "prevent one from being a functioning member of the society" as discussed in chapter 2; in other words, a functioning member of society ought to have a home). While the deficit economy affected how long it took to actually buy a home, in principle an ordinary working person could afford to own one. There was a level of social trust that fundamental material access was possible during the socialist era. The framing of needs in this context can be understood as an expression of civic ideals—what a citizen ought to be entitled to in a normative sense. Consumption, in this regard, is not so much an expression of individual identity and aspiration, neither is it about social status and distinction.

The past, therefore, was a significant point of reference for many Bulgarians, despite the flaws of the socialist system of which they were clearly aware. Stories around meaningful purchases and other consumption practices of the past provide a critique of the present and animate nostalgic memories. In Bulgaria, the experiences of socialism were very much tied with the experience of modernity, and as anthropologist Gerald Creed (2010: 30) reminds us, this association of the past and modernity helped depoliticize and normalize the experiences of the past, even as past experiences continue to be contested and negotiated. The perception and understanding of needs were especially telling in regard to the current discontent of Bulgarian consumers and influenced how they reevaluated their past experiences of which they were critical while living through them. Many of my interlocutors were aware that during state socialism the paternalistic state defined the needs of the population and tried to fulfill them. At the same time, they were also aware that the constant material shortage ranging from apartments to daily groceries instigated daily consumer complaints during the socialist era. Nevertheless, some experiences and memories of the past that were related to their perceived needs and conditions for normal life became the references for the present consumer grievances.

Bulgarians' critique of the present, often expressed in terms of a longing for the past, was not merely a nostalgia for communism as it is popularly and stereotypically explained by some local and Western experts alike (cf. Todorova and Gille 2010). It is important to understand the meaning of "nostalgia" in the context of postsocialist Bulgaria. Nostalgia often implies a rosy and positive image of the past that people long for.[3] In other words, nostalgia is often understood as a longing for a perfect and timeless past when things were unspoiled. The nostalgia for the socialist past, however, is not so much about longing for a perfect past. It is commonly acknowledged among my Bulgarian interlocutors that life under socialism was never perfect. However, people still evaluate some parts of the past positively in comparison to the present because the past is perceived as "better" (more tolerable) than the present. Creed (2010) makes an astute observation regarding the nature of socialist nostalgia in Bulgaria: the neoliberal discourses in Bulgaria have been too ludicrous that ordinary Bulgarians' nostalgic expressions should be viewed more as a critique of the present than a desire to return to the socialist past. Furthermore, he argues that it was telling that the term "socialist nostalgia" became more popularly circulated after Bulgaria entered the EU and there was no fear of turning back to socialism (see also Ganev 2013). This further confirms that the nostalgic accounts by some Bulgarians should be considered as a critique of the present.

Among the things Bulgarians listed as more positive during socialism was affordable access to basic necessities and the notion that those basics were not "garbage" (*bokluk*). Repeatedly, my Bulgarian interlocuters pointed out how consumption is actually not less grievous now, even though the lines are gone and there are seemingly more items and choices in the markets. These comparisons only highlighted the social values they deemed important and confirmed how these values are expressed and constructed as civic ideals to strive for. For my Bulgarian interlocutors across different age cohorts, the present denies them of many needs that were regarded as central for an existential normality they enjoyed (despite the flaws of the system) during the socialist era. This sense of existential normality—namely, the feeling of living a meaningful and dignified life—continues to be important to my interlocutors in Sofia. The sensory excitement they evoked when remembering shopping at CORECOM (see chapter 2) or lining up for various goods and housing, hoarding,[4] and utilizing social networks simultaneously stir up positive and negative aspects of the past. Given such a local understanding, it would be difficult to claim that Bulgarians' constant complaining in the present was simply because of their nostalgia for the socialist past. Rather, the present consumer discontent should be understood from the perspective of how civic ideals are constructed in the present. The fact that daily mundane consumption practices were always channeled through the state (allocation mode) or in relation to the state (black-market mode) was an important experience through which postsocialist citizens articulated their values and ideals.

Needs and Civic Ideals

Summer trips to the Black Sea were another practice commonly brought up as an example of a deprived need in the postsocialist era among my Bulgarian interlocutors. When my friends were starting to budget as summer approached to make sure that they could afford at least three or four days at the Black Sea, I was perplexed because I knew very well how economically constrained most of them were. I also could not help but feel that taking a summer vacation seemed rather like a luxury and for me would perhaps be a lower priority than saving money for other more needed things such as winter heating or buying clothes and shoes. In other words, I could not understand why seaside travel was regarded as a need for many Bulgarians. Whenever I expressed such opinions, my friends would always refer to the socialist period when "everybody" could and did go to the seaside, which was why they perceived it as an important need for their existential normality.[5] To be clear, there were still people during socialism who could not afford to go to the seaside during the summer, as my friend Maya explained to me. Her mother was a low-level factory worker, and her father was a machine technician. She said her parents could not afford to take the children to the seaside every summer, but she did admit that her family went several times during her childhood. During socialism, a lot of work organizations or associations (such as the unions of writers, water engineers, seamstresses, and so on) had their own vacation facilities at one of the many Black Sea resorts. This meant that the workplace guaranteed a generous, state-subsidized accommodation at the resort during the summer months for a nominal fee or sometimes no fee. If one happened to be better off or had good connections, one could pay more to rent a nicer place, such as a cottage on the waterfront. In any case, it was not hard for ordinary Bulgarians to afford a summer vacation at the seaside. Therefore, when my friends count "travel" as a need rather than a want, they are not merely referring to traveling abroad to Western Europe, for example. "That would be nice," as Yulia mentioned, "but I mean even traveling to the seaside for the summer, as was usually the case during socialism. I think it is really depressing to think that it is so hard nowadays to fulfill such needs because we simply cannot afford it. It used to be so basic and cheap—I mean, everybody could go to the seaside during the summer. Sofia was always empty during the summer."

This particular aspect of the socialist experience is selective in the memory of Bulgarians and gets reproduced in different age cohorts and becomes central to what they consider "normal," a significant reference point in constructing their civic ideals. In some cases, my older friends, whose children are now in their 20s and 30s, agreed with me that they wished that their children would instead save their money and use it for something more "needed," like a computer. In the summer of 2002, Mariella, a university assistant professor who supplemented her meager income with private tutoring to children of wealthy families, and her son Anton, who was a university student, got into a big fight because of summer vacation. Although Mariella could have given her son the money to go to the sea, she refused. She told him that she would pay for his education but not for his "playing." Her son fought back, arguing that it was not fair for her to deprive him of his needs and that she should know better because she knew what the summer vacation meant to Bulgarians. "What is wrong with being normal?" he asked me. In the end, Mariella did give him the money. She said that it was hard for her to convince her son that he had to work to pay for his "playing" expenses now that things had changed, especially because her son knew she could afford to pay for his summer trips to the seaside. When I retold this incident to Ina, another friend of ours, she laughed and said that while rationally she could understand Mariella's logic, she also thought that if it were her, she would have given the money to her son so that he would not be considered as "abnormal" among his friends. Again, seaside vacations during the summer were simply part of life in Bulgaria that offered a sense of existential normality. Not everybody was as lucky as Mariella's son to have a parent with means. Many Bulgarians I knew had to work to afford a seaside trip. It was particularly surprising when I understood that some of these friends who could not afford winter heating instead saved their money to go to the seaside in the summer. I must admit that during my fieldwork it was challenging for me to accept the local understanding of normality in this regard. Vacations, to me, always seemed a nice extra but never something essential or basic to count among my needs or to assure my existential normality. Yet these practices could also be understood as trying to live up to the civic ideals shaped by past experiences. This is another instance that illustrates how ideas such as needs and normality in the postsocialist period are anchored in social values shaped from the socialist experiences and not necessarily shaped by an imagined West or Western modernity. The civic ideals in postsocialist Bulgaria are manifested in these kinds of mundane consumption practices and demonstrate how citizen-consumers conceptualized their needs and prioritized their consumption practices accordingly.

These examples of heating, home ownership, and seaside vacationing show how thinking about the civic elements of everyday consumption under conditions of postsocialism and EU integration can illuminate new insights on consumption and its relation to the state. This approach goes beyond the common notion that situates consumption studies more exclusively within the realm of the market economy and rarely analyzes the state as a meaningful category in understanding consumption practices. Conversely, it also offers a comparative discussion of the anthropology of the state in which the state is represented primarily through bureaucratic encounters and political elections (Sharma and Gupta 2006; Herzfeld 1992, 2005b; Gupta 1995) or urban planning (Scott 1998) and systems of welfare (Caldwell 2012; Muehlebach 2014). The state, as I hope to have demonstrated thus far, is also intimately experienced and imagined through everyday consumption practices and is manifested as civic engagement and civic ideals. Moreover, following the discussion in the anthropology of the state (Sharma and Gupta 2006; Thelen, Vetters, and von Benda-Beckmann 2014), I consider both the state and consumption practices as culturally constituted and suggest that the EU, as a supranational entity and social context, is a particularly interesting arena that can offer insights into larger issues of the nature of the state within the transnational frame and under conditions of neoliberal globalization. The new postsocialist EU member states, such as Bulgaria, provide an interesting case because their consumers' relationship and expectations to the state was affected dramatically by the collapse of the state socialist system, yet such a relationship and expectation continued to inform their ideas on rights and responsibilities in the neoliberal milieu.

Scholars of postsocialism have questioned why civil society (as the counterbalance of the state) with a neoliberal agenda disappointed rather than enlightened people (Hann and Dunn 1996; Sampson 2002; Kideckel 2008) and diminished rather than encouraged civic engagement (Creed 2011). One way to think about this question is that civil society was often understood through the presence and practices of NGOs (through projects) rather than other alternatives (Caldwell 2012), which posed challenges for ordinary citizens to see the relevance in their daily lives that revolved about balancing access and choice. Another way to think about this question is to frame consumption practices as expressions of civic engagement, both in terms of voicing consumers' fears and frustrations and also articulating their shared future visions as members of their societies. Daily anxieties and fears can be turned into dreams or fantasies of a new capitalist future in the space of consumption. Advocating for rights (entitlement) is central in the political participation in a civil society. Yet notions of rights and debates on how one expresses such rights have created tension among different social actors who view concepts like rights differently in postsocialist Bulgaria. Bulgarian consumers described in this chapter show how they enacted their own visions of rights, thereby producing a space of civic engagement through consumption.

Notes

1. During the socialist era of the 1970s and 1980s, 1,500 leva was considered a large amount but "savable" considering daily expenses. Monthly salaries of various professions were as follows: average workers were paid 300–350 leva for what was called "first category labor," mine engineers were paid 750 leva (highest payment in the worker's category), teachers were paid 220 leva, full professors were paid 400 leva (assistant professors, 260 leva), and doctors were paid 250–300 leva. Someone working for the state's foreign trade enterprise or as editor-in-chief of a major publishing house (an ideological arm of the socialist state) received 800 leva, which was regarded as "an extremely high salary." To put wages into context, household bills such as electricity and central heating were about 15–20 leva each, one loaf of bread cost 30 stotinki, and a container of yogurt was 23 stotinki. In the 1980s, meat cost 4 leva per kilogram and was considered "expensive" especially compared to potatoes and tomatoes, which cost 15 stotinki and 30 stotinki, respectively, for example. A small studio apartment (locally called *garsoniera*) cost about 9,000 leva during the 1980s. Medicine and education were, of course, free of charge. Many Sofians remembered these figures, which is indicative of

how consumption was a form of civic engagement rather than merely a matter of individual choice.

2. This practice was called *pripisvane na apartment* (designation of apartment).

3. See, for instance, "structural nostalgia" (Herzfeld 1987, 2005a) and "imperial nostalgia" (Rosaldo 1989).

4. For vivid ethnographic details, see, for example, Ries 1995, Berdahl 1999, Humphrey 2002, Jung 2007, Caldwell 2009b, Keller 2004, and Shevchenko 2010.

5. See also Kristen Ghodsee's (2005) ethnography on the transformation of tourism in Bulgaria based on the experiences of female workers in the tourist industry at the Black Sea.

5

CONSUMER POLITICS AFTER STATE SOCIALISM

The New Phase of Consumer Politics in Post-Accession Bulgaria

Bulgarian consumers' frustrations about recent social changes can be understood as both a defense against further disappointment and as civic engagement through the space of everyday consumption practices. While the path to EU accession was often viewed with skepticism by many Bulgarians in its promise that EU membership would restore for them a sense of a normal (dignified) life, it nevertheless was perceived as the only realistic alternative for their country in the aftermath of state socialism. Despite the continuous caution expressed by my Bulgarian interlocutors not to be too hopeful for an anxiety-free future in post-accession Bulgaria, when the country finally joined the EU in January 2007, I noticed a sense of positive excitement during my visit that spring. Even my entry point to Bulgaria, the Sofia International Airport, boasted a brand-new structural presence with the new building's exterior and interior symbolically manifesting its changed political status. At least formally, Bulgaria had completed the transitional phase. Although EU membership was granted under stricter conditions for Bulgaria and Romania than for other postsocialist states that had joined the EU in 2004, Bulgarians put aside their ambivalence for a moment and took comfort in the fact that they were finally in. As a member state of the EU, their vote in the EU Council counted just as much as the vote of Germany or France, as Alex, a Bulgarian colleague and entrepreneur who worked part-time for BNCA, smilingly put it. Moreover, the appointment of then EU minister Meglena Kuneva, a Bulgarian, as the EU commissioner for consumer protection let my (usually) skeptical Bulgarian friends express some sort of national pride. As my friend Yana joked, winking humorously, "Romania took the 'multilingualism' commissioner position and Bulgaria got the 'consumer protection' one—guess what this means?" It seemed that Bulgarians understood that consumer protection was not an issue that was taken lightly in the EU, and they expressed some expectations regarding the improvement of consumer problems in their country.

Interestingly, Kuneva's position as the commissioner in charge of EU-wide consumer affairs posed an ironic situation for strengthening Bulgaria's consumer movement and the status of its consumer NGOs. On the one hand, Bulgarian consumers' general attitude toward consumer activism as well as toward EU consumer policies seemed more receptive than pre-accession, and the motivations and activities of consumer NGOs became less suspect. Consumer activists had started to gain more positive public attention from this momentum—reflected in their more frequent and regular appearances on national TV shows and radio programs. The visitors count at BNCA's website and its message boards set up for those seeking information, for example, also showed a growing interest in the consumer organization's work. On the other hand, having an EU-level consumer expert (namely, Kuneva) left Bulgarian consumers, activists, and bureaucrats (specializing in Bulgarian consumer affairs) with an even stronger sense of ambivalence and helplessness. Their expectations for Kuneva to address the plight of many former socialist citizens regarding access and choice was not fulfilled. By the time she stepped down from the position at the end of her term in 2010, her contributions to advancing the consumer sector in Bulgaria turned out to be minimal according to my interlocutors (both consumers and consumer experts).

This situation raised other questions regarding consumer politics after state socialism: What is the relationship between NGOs, the state, and the EU in the consumer sector, and what ought it to be according to consumers and consumer experts (activists and bureaucrats)? These questions are important in considering how postsocialist citizen-consumers reenvision the nature and role of the state that is central to everyday experiences of consumption in the postsocialist era.

I sensed a bit of commotion in the usually calm BNCA office when I visited in November 2008. Bogomil Nikolov was talking to three other staff members in the office and, judging from his tone and gestures, seemed upset. Kuneva had given an interview with the Bulgarian press the previous day during which she commented that while Bulgaria had made some progress in consumer protection, further improvement and development of consumer organizations were necessary. She had determined that there were no well-functioning consumer organizations in Bulgaria. To BNCA, this was not only inaccurate but also deeply demoralizing. It was a huge blow to these consumer activists, who had endured many difficult moments just to keep their work going without much support from either the public (consumers) or the state. Bogomil and his colleagues could have given up earlier in the year and closed the office when their financial situation was so bad that they had to rely on Bogomil's personal loans just to pay the rent. They persevered and eventually managed to secure some funding through various EU-sponsored projects. A symbolic gesture of validation from the EU commissioner of consumer protection would have meant a lot for the consumer organizations in finding their own meaningful position (categorization) vis-à-vis the consumers, as well as vis-à-vis the state, given the legacy of state socialism.

It was no secret among the consumer experts that BNCA people were the ones who "saved the face" of Kuneva whenever consumer representatives from different EU member states convened in Brussels for various presentations and conferences. In fact, in the consumer affairs circles in Brussels, BNCA staff members had gained a good reputation and were regularly invited to participate. (Since joining the EU, they traveled to Brussels and/or other European cities on a monthly basis.) They had a good command of English, gave interesting and professional PowerPoint presentations, and were good discussants. As Alex pointed out, it was BNCA who showed that Bulgarian consumer organizations not only existed and functioned but were also ahead of other consumer organizations from the EU's new Eastern European member-states in terms of their engagement with contemporary consumer advocacy work. After all, BNCA had managed to publish ten issues a year of the specialized consumer magazine *Potrebitel* since January 2007 (figure 5.1). The other new postsocialist member-states did not have such specialized magazines for consumer rights and protection, or if they did, they were in the form of newsletters consisting mostly of anecdotal stories or announcements. In comparison, *Potrebitel* was a substantive magazine that presented expert information about consumer problems with colorful graphics and aesthetics that made the magazine readable.

Modeled after the American magazine *Consumer Reports* and the German *Test*, the most prominent features of *Potrebitel* were the independently and professionally done comparative product testing results, encompassing

5.1 *Potrebitel* (2009, vol. 6) magazine cover
Bulgaria's consumer magazine is published by BNCA, the most active consumer organization in Bulgaria. *Reproduced with permission of Bogomil Nikolov.*

both global brand-name products (such as computers, cell phones, electronics, and cars) available in the Bulgarian market as well as domestic products such as Bulgarian food items and other commodities. With support from different EU grants, BNCA was able to become a paying member of International Consumer Research and Testing (ICRT, based in the United Kingdom), an international consortium of independent consumer organizations carrying out joint research and product testing.[1] This membership granted BNCA access to product testing results commissioned by the consortium and allowed it to publish those results in its own consumer magazine. For domestic product testing, BNCA used independent research labs affiliated with the Bulgarian Academy of Sciences (*Bulgarska akademiya na naukite* [BAN]). *Potrebitel* also contained sophisticated articles on pertinent and timely consumer issues in Bulgaria ranging from fraudulent (*mente*) organic food products to the GMO controversy, from cell phones to banking problems, and so on.

Bogomil once showed me the newsletter of BNCA's Czech colleagues, which was about twelve pages long and printed on low-quality paper that looked faded even though it was published earlier that year in 2008. He put it next to BNCA's consumer magazine, which was colorful, technologically advanced in terms of its design, and forty pages full of independent consumer information with the latest international product testing results. *Potrebitel* was priced at about 3 leva (a little less than US$2 then), which was similar to other specialized magazines and belonged to the median price point in the newspaper kiosks around Sofia. Earlier, before he heard the news about Kuneva's media interview, Bogomil had proudly told me that Kuneva's office was very approving of BNCA and presented its publications to consumer representatives from other EU member states as examples of fine consumer advocacy work.

The staff at BNCA therefore found it even more puzzling that Kuneva, by suggesting that consumer organizations in Bulgaria still had a long way to go, gave such a negative assessment of BNCA during a media interview when on other occasions she would project a different opinion on the consumer organization's work. They pointed out that her comments were simply untrue and demoralizing. They felt as if they had to go back to square one to convince Bulgarian consumers that their work was not corrupt and was useful for Bulgarian consumers and that there had actually been much progress in Bulgaria's consumer sector. It was interesting to me that Kuneva's comments in a press conference would be thought to have such direct effects on the evolving Bulgarian consumer movement and consumer organizations. This ethnographic moment revealed again the symbolic importance that the EU-level authority represented at the local level. In the perceived absence of an accountable state that could not live up to the consumers' expectation to help balance access and choice, the sense of helplessness among Bulgarian consumers, NGO activists, and state officials remained—that is, consumer problems under the present neoliberal regime could not be solely solved by the state, yet consumers still expected the state to do something. The presence of the supranational entity of the EU offered consumer activists new means to articulate and circulate consumers' interests, ideologies, and practices of daily consumption. One of these new means was the consumer organization's transnational network including the EU and its political position within this network, which in turn provided the symbolic capital of the organization vis-à-vis skeptical consumers. The making of a consumer protection regime in postsocialist Bulgaria, therefore, entailed a dialectical process in which consumers continually reshaped their perception of their nation-state as well as the supranational statelike entity of the EU. As Aradhana Sharma and Akhil Gupta (2006: 11) argue, even the states that appeared structurally similar could be very different from each other when it came to the meanings people attached to their states. Both the heating incident (see chapter 4) and BNCA's disappointment in Kuneva's negative assessment of its efforts suggested that for the majority of postsocialist consumers the "state" as the ultimate source for accountability was not always anchored at the level of nation-state. Such perceptions and representations of the state affected the way consumer regimes were being made and understood in the EU and influenced how citizen-consumers imagined the different regimes of power.

Challenges of Disseminating Independent Consumer Information

Despite numerous challenges, BNCA persisted with its mission to develop a viable consumer sector in postsocialist Bulgaria. According to the global regime of consumer rights, consumers have three basic rights: the right to be informed, the right to be protected, and the right to participate in decision making (Garon and Machlachlan 2006: 8). BNCA worked toward disseminating independent consumer information that it saw as the primary means for consumers to be protected. In the first phase of the organization's development (1999–2006), BNCA relied on press conferences and interviews with journalists (in print and on radio and television) to disseminate relevant consumer information. During 2005–2006, BNCA started to publish a monthly newsletter (not yet the magazine) *Potrebitel*, which was distributed for free from their office. In 2007, the organization achieved one of its biggest goals by launching the full-fledged magazine *Potrebitel* with its primary focus on providing independent comparative product testing information. The newsletter version also contained some comparative product testing results, but the magazine's information was much more extensive with more goods and services reviewed. BNCA published ten issues per year, and each magazine featured extensive independent testing results for at least one product. BNCA had launched its website in 2003, but with the publication of the magazine four years later, the website became more robust and included the magazine's online content in addition to relevant consumer laws, information on state agencies, and links to relevant institutions in the EU and other international consumer organizations (e.g., CI and BEUC) to which BNCA belonged as a dues-paying member. It also started to use the website to recruit its own dues-paying members and made the magazine content available online for paid members. While *Potrebitel* continued to be sold in major newspaper kiosks across Sofia and in other provincial towns where BNCA had branch offices, sales were relatively weak. According to Alex, the magazine did not get widely distributed even though people who saw it agreed that it was full of practical information. Yet my Bulgarian interlocutors continued to complain that they could not trust anything that was out in the market and searched for independent and reliable information.

This incongruity, however, did not turn out to be as perplexing as I initially thought. In the past decade or so, online forums such as BG-Mamma (www.bg-mamma.com) and SETCOM (www.setcombg.com) have become popular among Bulgarian consumers who share peer reviews of consumer products and services.[2] In 2013, my friend Genka, a freelance writer and mother of a teenager, mentioned that she frequently referred to BG-Mamma for consumer information and felt that it was trustworthy, beneficial, and efficient. In a way, these kinds of online forums were seen as grassroot communities with more efficacy than consumer organizations in terms of reliable consumer information. Yet, not everyone was able to participate in these online forums—one needed access to the internet and some degree of technological literacy. And while the information sharing was considered a positive aspect, Genka also admitted that if there was a problem with the product or service, these online forums could not really resolve it; the consumer still had to resort to a state institution or the producers themselves.

Potrebitel (renamed *Aktivni Potrebiteli* in 2010) was published for seven years, but sales continued to be weak and as the publication appeared to be unsustainable it was discontinued at the end of 2014. In 2015, Bogomil told me with a deep sigh how his organization tried but ultimately had to give in to the idea that Bulgarian consumers were not ready to pay for reliable and independent consumer information. He thought that if consumers saw the quality of information they might change their minds, and such information would help address consumers' grievances. The discontinuation of the magazine was a defeat for Bogomil (which he described as a mistake) because it was a project in which he had invested much both professionally and personally.[3] This experience echoed the comment that Ivan Bakalov, the founder of *Mente i Originali* (see chapter 1) made to me earlier in 2009 that he did not think Bulgarians would ever pay for consumer information because they feel entitled to access such information for free. Bogomil thought perhaps his consumer magazine was a bit ahead of its time. We had a chance to talk about the magazine again in the summer of 2016, when he also reminded me of a focus group interview we had witnessed together in 2009 (see chapter 1). He noted how the participants in that focus group had mentioned that they would rather donate money to the consumer organization than become dues-paying members. "Perhaps I should have paid more attention to those sentiments then and changed the financing approach. In hindsight, a 'donation-model' might have saved my magazine project," he told me. For now, BNCA continues to disseminate consumer information through a new online-only platform called *Buletin Aktivni Potrebiteli*, which includes three (compared to ten when he published the magazine) independent product testing results per year (the most his organization can afford with the current budget). The information in this *buletin* is available for free to the public, and people can access it through the website or receive it by email.

NGO-State Relations

In 2010, BNCA had another turning point: it changed its name to Bulgarian National Association Active Consumers (BNAAC), using the short form Active Consumers (*Aktivni Potrebiteli*) as its public name (figure 5.2).[4] It had reached a point in the organization's development when it felt that it

5.2 *Aktivni Potrebiteli* (2011, vol. 3) magazine cover
BNCA and *Potrebitel* underwent rebranding in 2010. Still a quality magazine, *Aktivni Potrebiteli* continued to specialize in independent comparative product testing and was modeled after similar consumer magazines such as *Consumer Reports* (US), *Which?* (UK), and *Test* (Germany). *Reproduced with permission of Bogomil Nikolov.*

needed a change with its public image especially to boost magazine sales and engage with consumers. BNCA applied for funding from the EU that would allow it to have an active campaign promoting the magazine and its organization and to rebrand itself. It thought "Bulgarian National Association of Consumers" sounded "old-fashioned" and, from a public relations standpoint, "terrible," as Bogomil described it to me in 2012. BNAC received the funding, given its productive track record of the past ten years initiating and successfully implementing EU projects and partnering with other consumer organizations across Europe. Its reputation within the consumer affairs circle in Brussels was also reassuring to the funders. Bogomil thought the group had two options in moving its advocacy work to the next level: one was what he called "the state factor," meaning the state had to help consumer organizations more actively in order to improve consumers' general ambivalence and skepticism vis-à-vis NGOs and cultivate trust from consumers. The other was the common EU narrative based on the neoliberal agenda—namely, Bulgarian consumers had to come to terms with the idea that it was worth paying for membership (which included a magazine subscription and free consultation) in the consumer organization to access objective independent consumer information that would help consumers protect themselves.

Bogomil reminded me of the case with ECC Bulgaria, which was established right after Bulgaria joined the EU. Technically an NGO sponsored through the EU-wide ECC Network with EU funds, ECC's mission was to help EU consumers when shopping and traveling within the EU. When Bogomil heard about this center in 2006, prior to accession, he actively sought to manage the Bulgarian office through BNCA. He knew that many EU members let the consumer organizations manage the ECC in their countries, considering it a natural fit since consumer consultation was one of the main activities of consumer NGOs anyway. Bogomil's bid was unsuccessful, however, because of the politics with the bureaucrats in the state institutions for consumer affairs. He was disappointed: "You know the state and us [BNCA], we are legally connected—we are not in a conflicting relationship. But those people [at the state], at least some of them, often consider us as their competition. It is nonsense, but that is the fact." Hosting this EU-sponsored center would have meant that BNCA could really capitalize on the symbolic status of the EU as a statelike entity, which would place the consumer organization in a less ambiguous category than NGO. It would also have meant that BNCA did not have to do numerous small grant projects just to maintain its advocacy work such as the publication of *Potrebitel*. In the end, ECC Bulgaria was managed by CTCP (*komisiyata*) thanks to the active support of the Ministry of Economy. In Bulgarians' categorizations, it made sense that the center was part of a state institution (the ECC was technically not a state institution although its association with the EU made it appear so in people's perception) and provided free information and consultation. Had BNCA been given this opportunity and provided the same service, it would have helped in reestablishing the consumer organization's relations vis-à-vis both the consumers and the state. For the former, this would have resulted in improving Bulgarian consumers' social trust of NGOs, and for the latter, it would have furthered the partnership with civil organizations by understanding their relations not as mutually exclusive, even though the dominant Western civil society discourse often depicted them in such terms (namely, civil society as the counterforce of the state and the market) (see, for example, Hann and Dunn 1996). In many European states, Bogomil pointed out, the consumer NGOs have actually always had a tight relationship with state institutions for consumer affairs—the states were not competing with the NGOs. This logic, however, did not apply in postsocialist Bulgaria.

Domesticating an EU Consumer Regime?

During my stay in Bulgaria in the fall of 2008, I received a PowerPoint presentation from Bogomil that he had prepared to deliver in Brussels the following week. Earlier, he had told me that he was invited to present about the achievements and challenges of the new member states regarding consumer advocacy work in front of a group of EU officials dealing with consumer policies. I opened the file unsure of what I would see. After the first couple of slides, I could not help smiling. I knew that Bogomil had perused my dissertation (from which this book was developed) with keen interest when I sent it to him. When I asked whether he liked my analysis, he nodded in affirmation but did not offer much substantive feedback on it. I felt a bit gratified as I went through his PowerPoint slides. It was clear that he appreciated my analysis regarding the challenges of consumer activism in Bulgaria. It appeared that my identification of the expected role of "the state" as a significant legacy of state socialism that affected consumer politics in the postsocialist era resonated with him. In the slides, he identified that the Bulgarians' perceptions of the state as the regulatory power and ultimate accountable subject were key challenges to advance consumer advocacy work in Bulgaria. He therefore concluded that the new member-states from the former socialist countries should think about addressing these particular ideas about the state for developing a stable consumer sector comparable to that in the Western member-states. In a way, he was suggesting a domesticated approach rather than merely following the model from the Western EU members, which put the questions about individual choice and responsibility as core principles of consumer politics in Europe.

I was eager to learn about the EU officials' responses to Bogomil's presentation when he returned from Brussels. He shrugged his shoulders and said that the audience found his presentation "very refreshing" and "interesting" and showed lots of sympathy. Ultimately, however, they had pointed out that they would not know how to translate this situation into a more adequate prescription for future development of the consumer sector in the enlarged EU. The difficulty of translating local problems (description) into viable solutions (prescription) has long been identified as one of the problems of development projects worldwide (see Ferguson 1990 and Escobar 1995, among others), and this was no exception. Bogomil looked a bit defeated. I asked his colleague Alex, who was listening to our conversation, what they would do next. Alex said that Brussels (i.e., the EU) could actually help the Bulgarian consumer movement if it could officially acknowledge this perceived difference of the role of the state in the new member-states, thereby helping to validate the work of the consumer NGOs under such circumstances. Such an EU-level "endorsement" through public forums (media interviews, conferences, etc.) would help change Bulgarians' perception of consumer organizations and their work. It would also help consumer organizations with their own relationship to the state, because under the EU's framework, consumer organizations should be working closely with state agencies and are entitled to receive state subsidies, albeit very nominal ones. Thus, rather than simply promoting "technical assistance" and "financial aid," which generally stipulated a one-way transfer of knowledge, Alex felt that a word from Brussels identifying the local specificities in relation to the respective historical and cultural legacies could help overcome the challenges facing consumer NGOs at the local level. Alex's comment resonated directly with the earlier disappointment to Kuneva's negative comments on Bulgarian consumer organizations and reconfirmed the symbolic importance that Bulgarian consumers and activists alike assign to the authority of the EU in the (perceived) absence of the postsocialist state that "cared."

Development studies scholar John Rapley (2007: 185) notes that "postdevelopment thought" was discussed in the mainstream with the fall of the Berlin Wall and the end of communism. These discourses on postdevelopment were triggered by criticism against the tautological argument of development (people seek development because it is desirable, and it is desirable because people seek it) as well as the increasingly neoliberal international development policies promulgated by international institutions such as the World Bank and International Monetary Fund (IMF) (Rapley 2007). Such an argument led to dismissal of the older development doctrine regarding the "one size fits all" model, which was long rejected as an inadequate way to tackle development problems. Despite this legacy in the development world, the postsocialist developments—especially in the context of EU integration—did not appear to have benefited from older development failures. Gerald Creed (2011) calls this failure of taking advantage of the familiar cultural resources that could have resonated more with local people "cultural dispossession." He has examined the seemingly archaic and esoteric Bulgarian mumming rituals (in which people wear costumes with menacing masks and loud bells and go around villages asking for food, drink, and money in exchange for invocations of luck [fertility, fortune, etc.]) popular in many Bulgarian villages called *kukeri* (or *survakari*), the practice of which survived state socialism although socialism actively promoted scientific modernization. Intrigued by how villagers who often struggled for basic necessities continued to invest resources for these rituals, he found that these practices could be seen as cultural resources that could have proven useful during the transition period. His insights offer a convincing critique as to why the neoliberal agenda of civil society produced more disappointment than enlightenment in the postsocialist era and speaks to similar sentiments that Bulgarian consumers and consumer experts persistently conveyed. I heard from my Bulgarian interlocutors that the plight of their country was that it always had to start anew, meaning that historically, Bulgaria always had to destroy what it had built rather than building upon the past. This kind of public discourse became most tangibly experienced when Bulgarians witnessed how socialist monuments, for example, were destroyed with explosives after the fall of the communist regime. At the same time, hegemonic power dynamics make it very challenging to take advantage of locally viable alternatives during intensive political and economic transformation, especially if they cannot translate those local resources effectively to counter the hegemonic global hierarchy of value (Herzfeld 2004). As Michael Herzfeld (2004: 209–210) argues, resisting hegemonic forces could only risk further marginalization because of the complex political economy attached to these global processes. In the Bulgarian consumer politics after state socialism, reenvisioning the nature and role of the state could have served as locally viable resources. Instead, because civil society in Bulgaria was seen as a democratic performance to civilize and establish governmentality of globally hegemonic powers and values (Creed 2011), civil society initiatives, including the development of a viable consumer sector in the context of postsocialism and EU integration, only reproduced earlier development failures. As an EU candidate country, Bulgaria was unable *not* to follow the EU model for a viable consumer sector. Bogomil and Alex thought the EU-level endorsement, especially since the EU commissioner in charge of consumer protection for the EU was a Bulgarian, could offer the tools for shifting the language of development to postdevelopment. Yet such validation did not occur, and Bulgarian consumer activists continued to search for ways to domesticate the EU's consumer regime.

Creed makes another important point that supports the arguments I make in this book: "Postsocialism is not just the situation of former socialist countries. It is the condition of the world in the aftermath of global Cold War that derogated socialism and laid the groundwork for cultural dispossessions" (2011: 7). Ultimately, development can be understood as a process of control (such as modernization projects). In the context of postsocialist development, the craving for the state is premised on a vision of the state that can ensure collective access and protect citizen-consumers from the abuses of the market so they are able to balance access and choice. Even in the neoliberal milieu, the dilemma over access and choice demands a different relationship between citizen-consumers, the state, and the market. Furthermore, how to put civil organizations such as consumer NGOs within this relationship was another important issue that was rarely debated. It was a given that the democratization process meant the development of a civil society that countered state power. In order to develop a civil society, as the dominant discourse before EU integration constantly reminded Bulgarians, there had to be NGOs. What the role of the NGOs within the relationships between citizen-consumers, the market, and the state ought to be, given the particular legacy of state socialism, was never questioned but merely assumed.

Why Consumer Politics Matter under Conditions of Postsocialism and Neoliberal Globalization

Hilton (2009) makes a convincing argument that defining consumer society based on choice is not only reifying it as a monolithic entity but also eclipsing the complex tension that different consumer movements underwent to shape them. According to his examination of consumer movements since World War II, consumer activists have undergone various phases of success and defeat and continue to struggle over dilemmas of balancing the demands of the poor and the affluent. The consumer politics in Bulgaria after state socialism certainly reflects this struggle but has been complicated by Bulgaria's inevitable path to EU integration. Consumer politics in the EU has revolved primarily around the language of choice as its dominant ideology since the 1990s. This had implications in how ideas on rights and responsibilities were articulated, contested, and debated, for and by consumers.

In this book, I discuss the perspectives of postsocialist citizen-consumers in facing the dilemmas of balancing access and choice in their everyday consumption practices. In the aftermath of state socialism, especially in their first decade of transition (and for Central and Eastern European countries during the years leading up to EU accession), many postsocialist countries were heavily led by a developmentalist logic that had been utilized in the developing countries in the Third World (Creed and Wedel 1997). From the perspectives of development aid experts, external circumstances in Bulgaria in the early 1990s appeared similar to those in Third World countries with large impoverished populations and clear development goals. Postsocialist Bulgarians were once again put in the familiar trope of having to work for the ideals of social progress only to realize that they had to debate the issue of access that they thought state socialism had achieved. In the market economy, they were now also offered the language and practices of individual choices in the free market supplied by abundant goods and services. Their rights as consumers with choices now entailed that they had to keep vigilant in informing themselves with credible consumer information. For some, having choices was a welcome change, but for others these were perceived as false choices because many ordinary consumers did not feel that they had much choice, since their daily consumption was about survival (access) and not pursuing a good life (choice as preference). Many consumers gradually found themselves comparing the postsocialist experiences to their socialist past, when they felt they had a relatively normal and anxiety-free life compared to the present. As consumer issues such as *mente*, affordable housing, seaside vacations, or *parno* repeatedly frustrated ordinary Bulgarians, they resorted to their past experience under socialism to make sense of the changes that made their life harder in the postsocialist setting. And this led to a common phenomenon in postsocialist Bulgaria that can best be explained as an enduring conundrum of distrust of the state (it is corrupt, it does not care about its citizens) on the one hand but also demanding accountability from the state on the other. This, I suggest, is a palpable tension of the politics of modern consumption that raises moral dilemmas over abundance and deprivation, especially as social stratification and inequality worsen under conditions of neoliberal globalization.

Postsocialist citizen-consumers felt that they faced the dilemma of having to solve both access and choice, but the EU rhetoric and practice of consumer movement offered no alternative to this dilemma. Many consumer problems were framed in terms of individual choice and responsibility and how independent consumer information was vital to fulfill rights as consumers. Collective actions were rarely suggested as a vision for a good life for everyone, and neither did they validate particular local circumstances in which the role of the state and state-citizen relations were conceptualized differently. The lack of collective actions, however, did not mean that consumers were disengaged. To them, everyday consumption practices were a form of civic engagement through which they cast their civic ideals and articulated visions for the future.

Consumer politics after socialism highlights a particularly acute problem in the contemporary world—namely, how to define and shape a vision for the future that can address both access for everyone and choice that guarantees even the less affluent are protected from the abuses of the capitalist market. Postsocialist citizen-consumers have firsthand experience in making the forceful claim that choice cannot be only an individual matter but also a matter of civic engagement. They require different relations between citizen-consumers, the state, the market, the NGOs, and the EU. This is why postsocialist Bulgarians see the role of the state as vital.

I have attempted to weave a story of postsocialist transformations using the lens of everyday consumption practices that involved consumer experiences both from the socialist era and transition period as well as the development of a consumer regime through consumer activism in the context of EU integration. In response to my initial questions raised in the beginning of this book—namely, questions regarding the nature and role of the state in modern consumption practices—I offer the following concluding thoughts.

As with any experience of social engineering projects, daily consumption practices under state socialism formed a peculiar relation to the state that dominated consumers' daily experiences. Because the socialist state's experiment can be understood as a shortcut to modernity, the mutually constituting experiences of socialism and postsocialism offer new insights into a seemingly homogenizing path to a consumer society under conditions of neoliberal globalization. Development in the enlarged Europe and within the context of an evolving consumer society entails one to acquire a European or global citizenship that allows both participation in global consumerism but also subjection to different forms of governance that often compel consumers like those in postsocialist Bulgaria to be complaisant rather than resistant or complicit. While the future of postsocialist societies will likely be just as diverse as their past experiences, I argue in this book that examining consumption as a site of civic engagement in which civic ideals are cast, as opposed to a site where identity and aspirations are expressed through individual agency, allows for new insights for understanding everyday consumption practices.

Postsocialist consumption practices are rich resources to understand the dynamics between the daily representation of the state, the market, and the EU, and how they affect citizen-consumers' ideas of rights and responsibilities. Furthermore, these ideas inform visions of social progress in the post–Cold War era. The socialist experiences remind us that the state is neither only a paternalistic entity that promised to take care of its citizens (hence its characterization of "weakened" in the aftermath of socialism) nor just a political structure against which people positioned themselves in mutually exclusive terms. Rather, the Bulgarian stories remind us that if we look through the lens of everyday consumption practices and how such experiences affected the formation of a consumer society, we learn that one's relationship to the state under conditions of neoliberal globalization is much more complex, inconsistent, and full of tensions. The experiences of postsocialist citizens with the paternalistic socialist state did not make the citizens infantile. Instead, the unfulfilled promises by the postsocialist state simultaneously generated not only a high level of skepticism and a constant anxiety about the future but also persistent demands for redress and accountability. While some of these circumstances resulted in increasingly autonomous consumption behaviors and attitudes, they did not make the state become invisible or insignificant in everyday consumption practices. When the postsocialist state failed to address the problems, consumers looked to a statelike entity such as the EU, even if it would not bring about concrete consequences. This was a way for casting their civic concerns and ideals. Rethinking the forms, relations, and histories of the analytical category of "state" itself in relation to consumption practices, therefore, provides new insights in understanding the continuing tensions between the neoliberal state, and the market, and civil society that govern our daily lives in the contemporary world.

So, what is the state that postsocialist citizen-consumers in Bulgaria imagine as they reenvision the nature and role of the state in post–Cold War Europe? Because of their complex experiences with the socialist state, Bulgarians expected the state to be a significant moral agent accountable for the plight of vulnerable consumers in the neoliberal milieu. Bulgarians want a state that can fulfill its obligations as an accountable object assuring and reinforcing social order and justice. This, perhaps, is not only Bulgarians' vision for the future. What is being demanded here is the realignment of the state, society (citizen-consumers), and the market that can ensure a better life for all.

Consumer politics after socialism suggests that the material abundance (but also growing inequality and poverty) the world has achieved in the past decades now must frame consumer issues not only around choice but around the balance of access and choice. In the case of postsocialist Bulgaria, citizen-consumers demanded actions by the state regarding how to make choices from the abundance of junk (the *mente* phenomenon) that flooded the market. This modern paradox of deprivation amid abundance is not only a problem of postsocialist societies but has implications for other contemporary societies in which consumers increasingly experience risks, vulnerabilities, and even market exclusion in the midst of seemingly abundant choices.

Notes

1. For a history of consumer product testing campaigns in the EU, especially in regard to EU enlargement, see European Commission 2009. Matthew Hilton (2009) provides an extensive overview of the history of comparative product testing within the larger context of consumer movements particularly in his chapter 1.

2. BG-Mamma started in the mid-2000s as an online forum to share parenting advice among mothers. Gradually, it grew into a comprehensive online forum where all kinds of topics including consumer issues were discussed and shared. In 2010, BNCA (under its new name, *Aktivni Potrebiteli* [Active Consumers]) partnered with BG-Mamma for anti-GMO protests and mobilized an unprecedented number of people for civic protest that lasted for over two months (see Jung 2014a). At the time, this was considered the largest protest since 1989/1990 when state socialism collapsed. SETCOM primarily offers reviews of small appliances, electronics, and cars, something equivalent to CNET in the United States. Whereas BG-Mamma is used by both males and females, SETCOM is frequented mostly by males.

3. This project with its independent product testing compelled him to get a doctorate in Economics with a specialization in Commodity Science in 2014. He took out personal loans to maintain the organization and publication of the magazine in 2009.

4. For consistency, I continue to refer to this organization as BNCA throughout.

EPILOGUE

"Enough Is Enough"— The Moral Commitment of the State

On June 16, 2013, I was on my way back to Sofia from a provincial town in northwestern Bulgaria. I was to return to the United States the following day. I received an urgent text message from Bogomil, my old friend and Bulgarian interlocutor for the past decade. The text message read: "Go to the Independence Square in front of the old communist party building. You will see something really interesting—there will be a big protest. Trust me and just go. And don't forget to take your camera with you." (Bogomil himself was traveling out of town.) I was intrigued. Bogomil's message contained a sense of excitement that I had not seen in him for several years as he was growing more and more disengaged from Bulgarian politics in general. A few hours later, as I was getting ready to leave my host family's apartment to visit some old friends, I was still undecided about whether I wanted to go to the seemingly big political event. I received another text message, this time from another old friend, Irena, who was away at her villa in the country: "Yusonka, you must witness this before you leave tomorrow. Go to the square in front of the old communist party building at 6:30 p.m.—there will be a big event." Needless to say, by the second message, my friends' urgings had finally compelled me to head out toward the square. To be honest, I went without expecting much because I was convinced by then that collective mobilization or large-scale civic protest was not likely in postsocialist Bulgaria. In my experience, Bulgarians did not believe in the possibility of grassroots-initiated changes after repeated disappointments and disillusion from the hopes of the early years of postsocialism. While my Bulgarian interlocutors were still engaged in discussing various aspects of politics, the discussions almost always ended with cynicism and political apathy. I did not think Bulgarians would actually go out to the streets again en masse with enthusiasm as they did in early 1990s right after the fall of the communist regime and in 1997 when hyperinflation was at its peak.[1]

E.1 Civic protest in Sofia, Bulgaria, June 16, 2013
Crowds protest the appointment of Delyan Peevski as head of the State Agency of National Security. This was the first day of a civic protest that eventually lasted for more than six months. Peevski's appointment was withdrawn as a result. *Photograph by author, 2013.*

I was completely dumbfounded as I approached the square where the protest was supposed to happen. Although it was not yet 6:30, hundreds of people—perhaps over a thousand—had already gathered and were chanting and taking pictures of each other (figure E.1). It appeared serious yet quite festive, too:[2] a number of citizens were blowing horns and whistles, waving Bulgarian flags, and chanting short slogans. I saw elderly couples dressed in their Sunday best who looked like pensioners, young professionals seemingly out with their dates, families with young children and strollers, and groups of families and friends noticeable in the way they addressed each other. I hung out for a while taking pictures and observing the participants and eventually left for my friends' house. After several hours of visiting with them, I took a cab back to my host family and instructed my cab driver to drive through the square area because I was curious to see what it looked like after the protest—I simply assumed that the protest was over. To my surprise, however, the cab driver gestured quite animatedly and raised his voice, saying that we had to drive around it because there were still hundreds of protestors out on the street. The family I was staying with happened to live by the main boulevard that led to the square about a couple of miles away. I could see the crowd from the apartment's balcony, and later that evening I could hear them from my bed. The crowd stayed out on the street (the boulevard was eventually closed to cars) until the wee hours of the night.

This massive public gathering turned out to be the first of over six months of civic protests participated in by tens of thousands of nonpartisan citizens. It was sparked by the appointment of a 33-year-old oligarch (and reportedly shady media mogul who controlled powerful media outlets), Delyan Peevski, to head the State Agency of National Security (*Darzhavna Agentsiya Natsionalna Sigurnost* [DANS]; the Bulgarian equivalent of the FBI in the United States). Earlier in the year in February, Bulgarian consumers had been angered by yet another sudden increase of their utility bills (primarily electricity but also heating [the focus of chapter 4] and water). Thousands of citizens had taken to the streets and protested in more than thirty cities against GERB (Citizens for European Development of Bulgaria), the ruling party. As a result, Prime Minister Boyko Borisov (GERB) resigned, and Bulgaria went through the electoral accountability process by holding an early election in 2013. It was considered the largest protest since 1990 and primarily mobilized lower-income people including the rural population who joined the protests in the cities (see also Ghodsee 2013; Stoilova 2013). While GERB still won the election, it won with such a small margin that it failed to form a government. A coalition of the Bulgarian Socialist Party (BSP), the center-right democratic Movement for Rights and Freedoms (DPS) party, and a populist and xenophobic nationalist party (ATAKA) was formed to constitute the government. Ultimately, the leader of the socialist party, Sergei Stanishev, nominated a close colleague, Plamen Oresharski, as prime minister, and he was the one who appointed the highly problematic Peevski to head the country's law enforcement agency.

Peevski's appointment brought Bulgarian citizens, primarily urban middle-class (and even wealthy) people, who had been cynical of and apathetic toward politics since the late 1990s, believing that politics was inherently corrupt, out to the streets. It mobilized a strong civic engagement that continued for over six months (the number of protests waned through the winter). As the prominent slogan of the June protest suggested, "Enough is enough" (*Taka poveche ne mozhe*), but what compelled these cynical postsocialist citizens to act this time on that prevailing sentiment?

Venelin Ganev has written an excellent account of the series of protests in 2013 and calls it the year of Bulgaria's "civic anger." His analysis is very relevant to the arguments that I make in this book as he relates the collective outburst of Bulgarian citizens to "non-electoral democratic accountability" (2014b: 34). According to Ganev, nonelectoral democratic accountability could be a way to hold political elites directly accountable in the democratic process that does not involve the usual form of vertical accountability of election through which citizens can remove leaders whom they do not like. Ganev suggests that civic protests can be triggered by either a case of bad governance (regardless of "democraticness") or "when 'democraticness' leads to civic mobilization provoked not by socioeconomic crises but rather by the damage that certain elite acts inflict on the quality of a country's democracy" (34). The latter case is what he calls nonelectoral democratic accountability. When someone like Peevski—who epitomized the so-called postsocialist political mafia with stereotypical gold chains, big SUVs, and an entourage of *mutri* (thugs, many of whom are former wrestlers and are described by Bulgarians as having thick necks around which they display gold chains) and folk singers—was about to gain formidable power that could allow him to ignore the rule of law, even the most cynical and politically disengaged citizens thought the ruling power had gone too far. Citizens felt that the elected politicians had now blatantly violated the last bit of moral tolerance of Bulgarian citizens, and this turned into a "civic anger" that Ganev refers to as a "scarce transformative political resource" (37–38). Peevski did not become the head of DANS, and eventually the civic protests faded out after more than six months of continuous mass engagement. The coalition government and Oresharski stepped down in July 2014, a year after the first anniversary of the protest. According to Ilia Iliev (2014), these civic protests did not achieve many concrete political changes despite the enthusiastic participation of the citizenry because the protesters "framed their protest as the ordinary people's fight against 'political mafia.'" In other words, the protests had much enthusiasm but not an ideology that could offer political alternatives to address the civic anger in productive ways. This kind of vagueness of political goal was in a sense deliberate because the protestors refused to be associated with any political parties or foreign-interest groups such as the Soros Foundation (Ganev 2014b; Gueorguieva 2015; Stoilova 2013).

Some of my old friends in Sofia whose stories were shared in this book were enthusiastic participants in the protests. During my visit in 2015, I asked them how they assessed the results of the civic protests of 2013. They were not completely happy with the outcome, but they thought the protests at least explicitly expressed the moral demand of the citizens—namely, an accountable state—and showed how even the most cynical and tolerant citizen could be mobilized if promises went unfulfilled. What they demanded was a state that was morally committed to its citizens. One way citizen-consumers could experience such a state was in the realm of their everyday consumption practices. Their demand was neither a return to a paternalistic state nor a neoliberal state, but a state that could balance the demands for access and choice for citizen-consumers. My Bulgarian interlocutors said their civic goal was rather modest: the moral commitment of the state, a state that can be held accountable, a state that showed it cared. This kind of state is the cultural ideal in the postsocialist era, and that is why the state becomes such a meaningful category despite repeated disappointments in various state practices in the past. If postsocialist reformers had paid more heed to addressing the significance of this cultural category of the state, Bulgarians' postsocialist experiences would have been less agonizing and more anxiety-free (*spokoino*).

Mundane sites of consumption animate debates about the state and allow citizen-consumers to experience the state in everyday encounters. In looking through the various grievances postsocialist Bulgarians expressed in the domain of everyday consumption, it is clear that their demand for an accountable state is essentially a request that the state fulfill its promises to its citizens. That is, the state that is being imagined here is one that can ensure basic rights to both access and choice. The state that Bulgarian citizen-consumers expect is one that is morally committed to offer a system that allows them to balance access and choice. The cultural logic here is that by doing so, ordinary people will be able to restore their civic confidence and social trust in the system, which would allow them to have the normal and less-anxious life that Bulgarians value so much.

In the spring of 2015, I shared some of my research on consumer culture in Bulgaria at a conference in Sofia organized by my Bulgarian colleague Evgenia Blagoeva-Krasteva. I presented a historical overview of the *mente* phenomenon and presented some of the ideas that I have explored in this book. The Bulgarian audience was receptive, and my presentation generated a lively discussion. One comment from Bulgarian colleagues particularly stuck with me: "Please also remember that there are different kinds of *mente*. You laid out the wide range of meanings well, from fake/fraudulent to garbage/quality stuff, but *mente* also refers to global brands that are different here even if they are not counterfeit." Several Bulgarian colleagues then started to list examples, one of which was laundry detergent. A global brand sold in Western Europe washed "better" than the same brand sold in Bulgaria, one colleague said. Another colleague concurred and said that her acquaintance who lived in Slovakia experienced the same thing and told her that some Slovaks would cross the border to Austria to buy the "real" stuff to avoid *mente*. When I asked whether it was simply a perception that the laundry detergent sold in Western Europe washed better than the one in Bulgaria, one colleague firmly insisted that there was actually an investigation and it turned out that the company used different "recipes" (the detergent formula) for different markets.³ The audience gave approving nods and knowing smiles to this last comment. Moreover, the colleague continued, the laundry detergent manufacturer used cheaper chemicals for the Bulgarian market and that was why the same brand sold in Bulgaria washed differently. This was, of course, not a new discourse. In the late 1990s and early 2000s, *Mente i Originali* had raised similar discussions regarding products such as Coca-Cola (see chapter 1). Aside from the authenticity debate, however, now in 2015 this comment had an oddly familiar resonance.

During my recent research on food politics in Detroit, Michigan (Jung and Newman 2014; Jung 2014b), I have heard similar questions from Detroiters regarding Whole Foods Market, an upscale grocery store. It was the first national chain grocery store to return to the city in almost a decade since the last regional supermarket chain closed all its stores in the city. In several community engagement meetings between Whole Foods and the residents, Detroiters asked whether Whole Foods was going to carry the same items in the Detroit store as in the suburban stores (or in other places nationwide). They insisted that whenever a national chain store came to the city, it carried different things for the Detroit market. These commentaries also brought back memories from my youth when South Korea was a developing nation. In the 1980s and 1990s, many South Koreans also thought some global commodities sold in Korean stores were different from those sold in their places of origin. In all these instances, citizen-consumers were expressing that having access to "lesser" things was beyond their control as individual consumers and related them to regimes of power (the state or local government that can influence corporate powers), which ideally should ensure fair access and choice for citizen-consumers. It would be too simplistic to assume that consumer problems and anxieties can be solved through increased purchasing power of individuals, reminiscent of an evolutionary development model. By voicing their grievances of mundane consumer matters such as *mente* and *parno*, citizen-consumers are also asking the state and other regimes of power to play their fair role. In the context of postsocialist Bulgaria, this is most explicitly expressed as demands for state practices that show a level of moral commitment to its citizens and that fulfill its part of the social contract.

The protests of 2013 did have a substantial civic outcome in terms of collectively expressing a shared vision regarding Bulgarians' expectation for an accountable state and good governance. It also connected the mundane grievances of everyday consumption (from *mente* to *parno*) to a more explicitly articulated demand to the ruling powers. Essentially, many Bulgarian citizen-consumers have been hoping for a state that can simply ensure a level of fairness and a degree of transparency that can make them feel more normal and less anxious (*spokoino*). That is what the state owes to its citizenry, especially in the aftermath of state socialism during which citizens thought of themselves as complaisant (unable *not* to follow) first to the vagaries of the authoritarian and paternalistic state and then to a corrupt neoliberal state. And this demand to ensure a level of fairness and a degree of transparency, perhaps, is not only the desire of postsocialist Bulgarians in a historical time in which the moral failures of politics and economy are questioned globally.

Notes

1. There had been intermittent street protests in the past decade, but those were not as massive and were relatively short lived.
2. In the early 1990s, I had witnessed political protests in South Korea during the tail end of the democratic movement. Compared to the Bulgarian crowd, Korean students and citizens looked a lot more militant wearing masks and headbands.
3. See also a recent report in the *Guardian* about this phenomenon (Boffey 2018).

APPENDIX

An East Asian Ethnographer in Eastern Europe: Notes on Fieldwork and Positionality

Doing Ethnography in Urban Bulgaria

Located in the Balkan peninsula, Bulgaria is a small country of less than eight million people. It borders Romania to the north along the Danube River, Greece to the southwest, Macedonia and the former Republic of Yugoslavia (Serbia) to the west, Turkey to the southeast, and the Black Sea to the east. Connecting the so-called East (the "Orient") and West (the "Occident"), Bulgaria features the mountain ranges from which the term "the Balkans" originates. Bulgarians often describe themselves as geopolitically unimportant, referring to their relative lack of heroic history compared to those of the neighboring Serbs, Greeks, and Turks (Ottomans). This self-representation always struck a chord with me as someone from South Korea, a small country between China and Japan. Growing up in Seoul, I, too, became familiar with this kind of modest self-representation.

I often heard Bulgarians lament that their country has usually been on the wrong side of history (see also Ghodsee 2015), hence its marginal status in the global hierarchy of geopolitical importance. Russia has had a particularly tight political relationship with Bulgaria in the modern period, liberating Bulgaria from the Ottoman Empire after the Russo-Turkish War in 1878. Bulgaria sided with the Germans during World War II as an ally of the Axis. The Soviet Army also helped push out the Nazis from Bulgaria in 1944 (Crampton 2007). During the Cold War, Bulgaria was considered the closest Soviet ally, earning its nicknames "the last (sixteenth) Soviet republic" or the "Soviet's younger brother." The legacy of historical ties with Russia/Soviet Union has had lasting political and cultural influences even after Bulgaria became a member of the EU in 2007 and continues to be evoked in mundane social commentaries among ordinary people.

While post–Cold War Bulgaria has attracted relatively little interest in anthropological scholarship compared to its Balkan neighbors (such as the former Yugoslavia or Romania), Bulgaria makes an interesting comparative case.[1] A relatively homogeneous nation with a comparatively small number of minorities (mostly Turks and Romas) who are considered (arguably) well-integrated,[2] Bulgaria has adapted fairly easily to surrounding political circumstances in the Balkans and Europe without political obstacles such as the ethnic conflict in Yugoslavia or a legacy of harsh dictatorship like its neighbor Romania—I refer, of course, to Nicolae Ceaușescu. During state socialism (1944–1989), it reproduced the closest Soviet system among the former communist Eastern European countries and was regarded as the most "obedient" satellite of the Soviet Union (Crampton 2007). While economically not as affluent as the GDR or Yugoslavia, my Bulgarian interlocutors considered their economic well-being often superior to that of the Soviet Union by comparing the lines for everyday purchases and accessibility of goods in the two countries. Some of my Bulgarian interlocutors who often traveled to the Soviet Union remembered that lines were longer there than in their home country and considered their lives to be better than those of citizens in the Soviet Union.

After the collapse of state socialism, Bulgaria adopted a series of reform policies modeled after the West including both the US and EU examples. These helped shape and implement Bulgaria's nascent democracy and transform the centrally planned economy into a market-oriented one. Bulgaria quickly set out on the path toward the EU by transforming itself into a potential member state (Bulgaria adopted thirty-one *acquis* chapters in 1995) and eventually toward inclusion in the global economy through the EU (see also Crampton 2007). In my eyes, as a highly interested foreigner, Bulgaria showed an incredible flexibility for political leaderships between the years leading to EU accession in 2007 and its aftermath. I witnessed these transitions between 1998 and 2016, first as a tourist and later as an ethnographer. To give an example, I learned that it did not matter to many Bulgarians whether the former monarch, Simeon Saxe-Coburg-Gotha, who became prime minister in 2001, was compatible with a socialist president in a parliamentary representative democratic republic. The former "tsar" was perceived as the only alternative who could facilitate Bulgaria's membership to the EU. In the parliamentary election on June 17, 2001, the former Bulgarian king Simeon II Sakskoburgotski (the Bulgarianized name for Saxony-Coburg-Gotha) led his newly created party, the National Movement for Simeon II (*Natsionalno dvizhenie za stabilnost i vazhod*, NDSV;

formed in April 2001), to victory and formed a coalition with the Turkish minority party of Bulgaria, the DSP, to become prime minister of the Republic of Bulgaria. "Tsar Simeon II," as Bulgarians refer to him, had become king of Bulgaria in 1943 when he was just six years old following the mysterious death of his father. He is a descendent of the Hungarian branch of the House of Saxony-Coburg-Gotha and is related to other European monarchies. At age 9, Simeon II was expelled from Bulgaria in 1946 with charges of the royal family's collaboration with the Nazis through a popular referendum that abolished the monarchy. He spent his exile primarily in Spain and returned to Bulgaria in 1996 after the collapse of the socialist regime. His political victory has been explained as a result of populist sentiments by Bulgarians who turned to the former monarch out of desperation. Although his political promises were not very different from those of the opposing parties, he convinced the Bulgarian public that he could improve their impoverished situation, thereby enabling Bulgaria to join the North Atlantic Treaty Organization (NATO) and the EU. The bids for NATO and the EU had actually been placed by the former government controlled by the Democratic Forces (*Sayuz na demokratichnite sili*, SDS) party. Bulgaria joined NATO in 2004, signed the EU accession treaty in 2005 (during the tenure of Simeon II as prime minister), and became a full member of the EU in January 2007.

Another seemingly incompatible political alliance was formed in 2006—an alliance of the party that supported a former monarch (NDSV), the successor party of the former communist party (BSP), and a moderate right-wing party of democratic forces (SDS). Although they looked like strange bedfellows to outsiders, Bulgarians often justified their acceptance of this coalition as a result of having no better alternative (hence, exhibiting a complaisant attitude). In 2009, a former firefighter and head of police and internal affairs, Boyko Borisov, took over the political leadership as prime minister and formed a coalition with both the far-right nationalist party and Turkish minority party and later with the socialist party. My Bulgarian interlocutors again embraced this seemingly awkward political alliance in hopes for a more prosperous future. In a way, Bulgaria's relatively stable democratic politics relinquished the economic aspect of social life as a prominent trouble zone.

My Bulgarian interlocutors in Sofia represented a cross-section of society, including journalists, economists working for state agencies, public relations experts, consumer experts, NGO employees and activists, lawyers, university professors, college students, cab drivers, current and retired school teachers, retired former actresses, a seamstress/designer, mid-level and low-level civil servants, a meteorologist, secretaries, an aspiring actor, employees of small companies, entrepreneurs, restaurateurs, a physical therapist and yoga instructor, engineers, a museum employee, Korean expatriates, and Chinese immigrants and businessmen. While some of them had college degrees, others had only high school diplomas including several journalists who entered college but did not finish due to economic reasons. They also represented a wide age range from people in their 70s who remembered the times before communism to younger informants who were in their 20s when I started fieldwork in 2001. The political allegiance of my interlocutors also ranged from avid supporters of the BSP (heir of the Bulgarian Communist Party) to enthusiastic and committed supporters of the Democratic Forces party and supporters of "Tsar Simeon's Party"; some had deep family ties to the partisans fighting against fascism, others suffered as descendants of fascists during the communist era.

Most of my interlocutors considered themselves as "Sofians" whose parents or grandparents migrated to Sofia after World War II. Some informants came to Sofia from provincial towns more recently either for work or for school. Most of them lived in the homes that they themselves or their families owned, which was quite typical. Even if they rented a place, their families who lived in the provincial towns were homeowners. It is worth noting that owning (as opposed to renting) a home in Bulgaria does not imply wealth. Rather, it should be considered a cultural phenomenon that puts much social value in home ownership (see chapter 4). Regardless of their employment status, however, most of them were cash poor and struggled to balance access and choice as consumers. Elderly pensioners often received help from their children and grandchildren to get by or relied on supplementary income by renting out rooms in their apartments if they could do so.

These interlocutors could be roughly grouped into three social networks around which my ethnographic research revolved. BNCA, the consumer rights advocacy organization where I volunteered, was founded in late 1998 and was registered as a not-for-profit NGO in early 1999. This organization particularly benefited from the timing because the Bulgarian Parliament passed the first consumer law in Bulgaria's history, the Law of Consumer Protection and Trade, on March 18, 1999. I started my preliminary fieldwork that summer and was fortunate to be able to follow the evolving consumer politics in postsocialist Bulgaria from its inception. Creating the consumer law was part of an effort to align Bulgaria's system with that of the EU under the objective of *Acquis Communautaire*. During the socialist period, consumer protection legislation was very limited and fell broadly under some sections of civil law referring to product guarantees, laws of standardization, civil contracts, and so forth. Thus, the creation of a separate consumer legislation to eventually protect consumers under the market economy system was an entirely new event for postsocialist Bulgaria.

My involvement with BNCA under such circumstances allowed me to better understand the social and cultural dynamics of postsocialist Bulgarian consumers. Since my fortuitous first encounter with a member of the board at a Chinese restaurant in Sofia, who subsequently introduced me to the executive director, Bogomil Nikolov, I participated in much of their activities between 2001 and 2002 (thirteen months); in 2007 (three weeks), 2008 (six months), and 2009 (two months); and I followed up with core members during short-term trips (two to three weeks) in 2012, 2013, 2015, and 2016. These activities included public seminars, workshops, conferences, press conferences, training sessions in Greece for their staff and Bulgarian journalists supported by EU accession funds, a series of organizational meetings with a German partner organization that took place in Sofia over several months and was supported by the German government, and participation in a seminar with Turkish consumer activists visiting the Bulgarian consumer NGOs and bureaucrats after EU accession in 2007, this time supported by the EU funds they won through EU project competitions. I also observed the internal politics among the different consumer organizations in Bulgaria by participating in their domestic workshops and conferences. I helped the BNCA staff apply for project funding from Western donors (primarily related to programs sponsored by the EU), observed consultation sessions for consumers, and followed the development of BNCA's consumer magazine *Potrebitel* as well as its website postings since its launch in 2007. Except for a small government subsidy, the funding for BNCA projects implemented during my stay came primarily from EU-sponsored programs such as Phare ACCESS and Leonardo da Vinci. After the accession, BNCA has been maintained with grants through EU structural funds for the consumer sector and has won funding for projects by partnering with other junior members of the EU (i.e., mostly former Eastern European countries that became new members) as well as EU candidate countries. Before the accession, BNCA was also funded by other EU member states as part of their programs promoting civil societies in Eastern Europe, as was the case with the German partner organization Verbraucherzentrale Bundesverband (Jung 2010).

I socialized with staff members (consumer experts) outside of the organization as well. I was often invited to their homes for a glass of *rakiya*, beer, or wine, and to birthday parties and name days celebrated either at home or in restaurants and bars; I accompanied them on shopping trips, to their (summer) villas in the suburbs of Sofia; and to their parents' homes in other cities. Moreover, my social capital (in the Bourdieuan sense) widened as I was introduced to their respective social networks as well. The relaxed setting over drinks and *meze* always offered an ideal environment for meaningful discussions.

The consumer experts that formed my first group of interlocutors mostly described themselves as professionals with college degrees. Some were third-generation Sofians (i.e., their grandparents migrated from villages or other towns to Sofia after World War II) and others came to Sofia from provincial towns for a university education. Most of them belonged to an age cohort in their late 20s, 30s, and early 40s in 2001.[3] Among the experts who were BNCA board members, some of my interlocutors were in their mid-40s and mid-50s. Most of these people were former state employees who had lost their jobs after the democratic changes in 1989, and they provided links to the government structures as well as to social networks. They represented the organization along with the younger professionals in official events such as consumer conferences and seminars as well as press conferences. It almost seemed like a division of labor: the older cohort took care of the domestic networking and publicity aspects while the younger cohort was in charge of international networking and reputation, which basically meant securing funding for the organization by writing project proposals (usually in English) and attending international consumer conferences representing Bulgaria. Over the years, the older cohort gradually retired.

Except for the executive director and one supporting staff member (a secretary) who received a regular monthly salary from the organization, none of the experts involved in BNCA had a regular income from it. Rather, they were paid by honoraria or on a temporary payroll system that depended on the various project grants available at different times. While BNCA published *Aktivni Potrebiteli* between 2007 and 2014, the organization hired two to four part-time staff members who were in charge of writing for and editing the magazine. The organization did not collect membership fees until it launched the magazine's website and offered access to comparative product testing results as part of membership privileges. Thus, some experts had primary jobs and occasionally received secondary income in the form of monetary compensation from various projects: they wrote articles for the newsletter and magazine, which was funded by an EU harmonization program on youth consumer education, for instance. This structure was common in other consumer organizations in Bulgaria, although gradually more and more organizations seemed to exist only in name as EU funding opportunities decreased and Bulgarian consumers did not respond to consumer advocacy organizations through memberships.

I regularly engaged with the social networks of these consumer experts including their friends from high school, college, or hometown as well as colleagues working in other civil organizations such as NGOs for children or NGOs for organic farming with whom the experts at BNCA had conducted joint projects. They, too, became an integral part of my own social network.

Over the period of my visits to Bulgaria since 1999, I got to know twelve families very well. These families and their respective social networks formed another important group of interlocutors for my research in urban Sofia. Their ages ranged from 32 to 91 (as of 2015), and they considered themselves "normal" people belonging to the middle class although they did not articulate "class" to identify their social and cultural belongings. I was able to follow them consistently over the past decade. None of them were the so-called *nouveaux riches* although a few had friends in that category. They were also not members of the former ranked party elites (*politburo*), although one of my landladies had close ties to them. Their economic statuses were similar as they owned their residences but not always a car (and if they did own cars, they were used cars; none of the people I knew bought brand-new cars), and they relied on relatively modest incomes that had to be supplemented by irregular second jobs or assistance from children, parents, or relatives. I cooked and ate with these families; went shopping with them; accompanied them to hospitals and doctor visits; strolled with them in parks and neighborhoods; hung out with them in coffee shops, bars, and restaurants; and participated in their private events such as birthdays, name days, Easter, Christmas, New Year's Eve, weddings, and memorial services. This group of informants spans different age cohorts. When it came to getting around Sofia and Bulgaria, I joined them for trips to the mountains to hike and ski or on visits to folkloric village festivals as well as on summer seaside vacations. For traveling, I benefited significantly from people in my age cohort among my social networks. These friends were the ones who had the economic means to afford such trips. In present Bulgaria, young adults in their late 20s and 30s are believed to be the most active consumers with the largest amounts of disposable income.

Finally, the third group of people with whom I associated regularly consisted of my academic colleagues in Sofia who were mostly university professors, researchers, or students. They first offered technical and logistical support to my research but gradually also became interlocutors who would contest, offer alternative views, and reconfirm or challenge my findings from the first two groups of people. They were also instrumental in widening my network by introducing me to their respective social networks. As Bulgarians put it, Sofia, with its population of roughly one million, is not a big city compared to capital cities elsewhere.[4] My friends in Sofia joke, "Everybody knows everyone else in the city" or "We are all brothers and cousins in Bulgaria," especially if one relies on one's extensive social networks. From my own experience, this was true only to a certain degree. Some of my third circle of friends and one of my host families overlapped significantly, but rarely did any other groups that I socialized with overlap with each other directly. Rather, they came to know each other through me, and some from different social groups had become very good friends and had expanded their own social networks.

Regardless of their self-proclaimed middle-class status, based primarily on education and occupation, most of my interlocutors shared a similar economic background and identified themselves as "normal/ordinary" Sofians who struggled to make ends meet and often had to supplement with second or third incomes. They were affected by the country's precarious economic situation that did not guarantee financial security (especially for retired people). Thus, the ethnographic data obtained from these three groups of interlocutors offered valuable insights into postsocialist consumption practices, both positive and negative, but particularly from the grievances associated with everyday consumption. I could not overlook the frequent grumbling and complaining about daily consumption that at times appeared like a daily greeting for the people with whom I interacted in Sofia. Whether it was in the context of formal consumer complaints in either the state institution or NGOs or in the context of informal in-depth conversations among neighbors and friends, consumer grievances prevailed in the social life of Sofia's residents.

The landscape of Sofia, especially in the 2000s, was one with many contradictions, contrasts, and ironies—just like the history of Bulgaria itself, as my interlocutors repeatedly explained. They said that Bulgaria was an impoverished nation with a high unemployment rate, but it also had many cell phones when it was very costly for an average person to maintain one; moreover, in the city, the cafés, bars, and restaurants were always full of people. My friends in Sofia continued to list the contrasts: the country had beautiful European turn-of-the-century architecture next to bleak Stalinist concrete structures, and Mercedes-Benzes and Volkswagens drove side by side with Russian Ladas, Moskvitches, and East German buses and Hungarian trolleybuses. And as a friend Yana ironically put it in 2001, "Bulgaria is a Republic but with a former monarch as prime minister and a socialist president! Where in the world do you see this?"

One of my fieldwork routines was to walk down the Boulevard Vassil Levski toward *Popa* (a popular square where the monument of *Patriarh Eftimii* is located) from my home near Sofia University every day. I rented a room in an apartment owned by a retired former actress. This building was located immediately behind the grave of Alexander of Battenberg, the first prince of Bulgaria (who ruled from 1879 to 1886) after its liberation from the Ottoman Empire in 1878.[5] After going by the Iranian Embassy, I crossed the underground path of the Sport Palace (*Sportnata Palata*) and passed by a couple of *klek* shops (described in the book's introduction). The urban landscape of Sofia reflects many characteristics of a busy consumerist urban community with bursting commercial activities. At the same time, in relative terms, Sofia also appears as an impoverished place, especially in older neighborhoods where apartment blocks with peeling paint and fading colors still await a makeover. In 2001, the Bulgarian National Statistical Institute reported an average monthly income as 132 leva (about US$66) per person (National Statistical Institute [NSI] 2002). This income was barely above the poverty line considering the rising cost of living in the capital city. The official average monthly income in 2007, the year Bulgaria joined the EU, was 430 leva (about US$310) (NSI 2007), and had increased to 850 leva (about US$480) by 2015 (NSI 2015). Although one cannot simply rely on numerical data, which do not take unreported secondary income (such as my rent to my host families or private tutoring fees to my Bulgarian language teachers), into consideration, many of my Bulgarian interlocuters confirmed that even in Sofia (which is still much better off than the rest of the country), many people continue to try to "survive" on a meager income sometimes even lower than the official average income. For these people, saving was often not a relevant concern. While not all Sofians were poor, the rising inequality between those who managed to accumulate wealth quickly in the aftermath of state socialism and the rest added to a perceived sense of poverty resulting in constraints regarding consumer choices, thereby intensifying debates about consumption and state-citizen relations.

An *Asiatka* in Sofia

Whenever I introduce myself as an anthropologist working in Bulgaria and Eastern Europe, I am always asked why I (a native South Korean) chose Bulgaria as my field site and what it was like to conduct ethnographic research as an Asian in Eastern Europe. I share the following notes on my fieldwork experience in Bulgaria with the hope that they may be useful for discussions on ethnographic research in the globalized world and in thinking about issues of positionality of ethnographers vis-à-vis the research subjects under such context.

I have always been fascinated by the Cold War and its effects on everyday life, having lived in West Germany in the late 1970s and early 1980s and in South Korea until the late 1990s. While East and West Germany reunited after the collapse of state socialism in 1989, Korea remains a divided country with North Korea and South Korea under armistice for over sixty years. Given this personal background, it may have been a more natural choice for me to go back to the reunified Germany to study the social and cultural transformations after state socialism. As an aspiring anthropologist, however, I was drawn to the more exotic Balkans. Ever since I first set foot in Bulgaria in the late 1990s out of serendipity, I have had an exciting and memorable time learning about an unfamiliar country, its language, its people, and its culture.

Bulgaria in the 2000s was visibly poor, defeating most stereotypes I associated with Europe as a developed, tidy, and wealthy place. Having witnessed firsthand South Korea's intensive (and quite dramatic) economic and political development since the 1980s (the so-called economic miracle that led to hosting the Olympic Games in 1988, alongside political transitions from military dictatorship to democracy), a poor postsocialist Bulgaria instantly raised many questions about development (both economic and political) and modernization, social engineering projects, and sociocultural attitudes toward the future as well as people's relationships to the world. South Korea in the 1980s, especially until 1988 when it hosted the summer Olympic Games, was poor. In fact, when I first visited Bulgaria, I could not help but notice parallels to South Korea during the development period following the Korean War (1950–1953). For example, the ugly concrete apartment blocks in the urban areas—a visible product of modern development regimes—dusty roads, cloth from cheap-looking fabrics, and unclean (and unreliable) public bathrooms all seemed familiar. Yet there were clearly differences that captivated an ethnographer's eyes. Despite my experience growing up in a developing South Korea in the 1980s, I found the urban environment in Sofia in the 2000s (especially the first half of the decade) challenging in terms of basic living conditions: stray dogs seemed omnipresent and aggressive, posing dangers for pedestrians; streetlights did not always work, creating fear for walking back home late at night. Ordinary things like heating and taking showers became issues due to water pressure and unreliable water tanks. Socializing at people's homes, cafés, and restaurants sometimes felt difficult because I knew of the financial constraints of most Bulgarians I met. I was young, single, female, and an East Asian in the Balkans, and I was interacting with a diverse group of Bulgarians across age, gender, and class. Generally, people stared at me at first because I was so visibly foreign, even in the capital city, but once they started to talk with me, they generally warmed up and became curious about why I was in their country. It helped that I spoke Bulgarian quite fluently, albeit with many mistakes. This was often the icebreaker in conversations. I found most Bulgarians accessible and relatively easy to talk to. Once I started to acquire my social networks, doing ethnographic research in Sofia proved not too difficult, and I got used to being the visible foreigner in various social settings. I was almost always introduced and accepted as a graduate student from Korea who was attending school in the United States (and later as a professor teaching in America). Because many Bulgarian students studied abroad in similar status as mine, my social position easily resonated with my Bulgarian interlocutors.

In the Anglo-American anthropology tradition, it is still relatively uncommon to learn about issues of positionality of a non-Western ethnographer studying Western societies.[6] Although my Bulgarian friends and interlocutors would probably give a friendly grin at my depiction of Bulgarians as Westerners (they would barely agree, and correct me that they were the Balkan people [*balkantsi*] or Slavic people [*slaviyani*], which differed from Westerners), I was doing research in Europe, and from my positionality as a native South Korean, Bulgarians were Westerners. This positionality often afforded me opportunities to reflect on multiple power dynamics between the researcher and research subjects and my own subjectivity. During my fieldwork, there were particular moments when I felt that my Asian (and maybe female)[7] identity had several advantages. One was having access to Bulgarian civil servants and the other was having access to and interacting with other Asians such as Chinese restaurateurs and diplomats as well as Korean entrepreneurs and employees of Korean companies in Sofia. When I started visiting Bulgaria as a potential fieldwork site in 1999, many Bulgarian civil servants mistook me for a potential foreign investor/client rather than a postgraduate researcher. It was interesting to me that I was usually able to meet and conduct an interview with them after my Bulgarian colleagues had made a cold call on my behalf. I was much less successful when I did the cold call myself, but it almost always worked when the initial calls were made by my Bulgarian friends (although they had no connection to the civil servants). The Korean conglomerate Daewoo (which went bankrupt in 1999 following the Asian financial crisis in 1997; one of its companies, Daewoo Motors, was bought by General Motors) had a particularly active presence in Bulgaria in the late 1990s and early 2000s with their cars and consumer electronics, and I suspect Bulgarians associated me foremost with the Korean company, given the frequent association people made with Daewoo once they learned that I was Korean (and later in the 2010s, Samsung and LG were frequently brought up). Some Bulgarian interlocutors also remarked how they felt I was different and understood them better because I was not a Westerner and came from a small country like Bulgaria (South Korea's area is a little smaller than Bulgaria's, but South Korea has a population of 50 million compared to Bulgaria's 7.3 million). The commonality of being citizens of a small country among big powers (Korea: United States-Japan-China-Russia; Bulgaria: EU-Russia-Turkey) often generated a sort of instant bonding between my interlocutors and me.

During my first long-term fieldwork from 2001 to 2002 (thirteen months), I lived with two Bulgarian families. I believed that this immersion would help me become fluent in the Bulgarian language faster, and as a visible single Asian female, I felt safer in such an arrangement. After spending one summer prior to my long-term fieldwork by myself renting an apartment in Sofia with limited socialization, possible only through my language instructor, I was convinced of the advantages of living with a Bulgarian family. Although Sofia is by no means a dangerous place for foreigners, the visibility of my Asian-ness made me self-conscious when moving around the city and the country by myself. (Of course, I became less conscious of my Asian identity over the years in my return trips, but that could be a combination of my changes in age and social status as well as my own growing familiarity with Sofia and Bulgaria and not necessarily because Sofia became more cosmopolitan.) During my stay in Bulgaria, I was also always aware that Sofia was one of the few former socialist countries in which a North Korean embassy was still present. As a South Korean citizen studying at Harvard University, I could not fully ignore my own cultural biases and Cold War indoctrination from my South Korean education and upbringing. It was perhaps a very remote possibility, but I was conscious that my elite identity could be used politically by the still existing Cold War situation between the two Koreas. Growing up in West Germany and South Korea, I used to hear stories of North Korean kidnappings of South Korean students studying in Western Europe (especially West Germany) for political purposes. As a South Korean national, I was also subjected to the South Korean National Security Law, which required South Korean citizens to report to the authorities if they accidentally met and talked to North Koreans while traveling abroad. During my long-term stay in Sofia, I was particularly sensitive to possible accidental encounters with North Koreans. Living with Bulgarian families eased some of these anxieties.

Asians in Bulgaria are very visible even in Sofia, which is more cosmopolitan than any other place in Bulgaria. Currently, the majority of Asians there are Chinese and are mostly involved in restaurant businesses or trading in open-air markets.[8] During the socialist era, a considerable number of Vietnamese used to live in Sofia when Vietnam and Bulgaria had an official agreement to exchange students and workers. They returned to their country in the 1980s, however, when the agreement ended. Besides the Chinese, there are a number of other Asians, such as Koreans and Japanese, mostly connected to embassies, businesses, missionary work (i.e., Korean protestants trying to convert orthodox Bulgarians), and classical music students. Most of these people live in Sofia or in large urban areas.

I was often referred to as *Asiatka* (Asian woman) and sometimes *Koreika* (Korean woman) by acquaintances who wanted to be more specific in describing my identity. My name confused my Bulgarian interlocutors regarding my gender because both my first and last names ended with a consonant. According to Slavic naming practices, female first and last names in Bulgaria end with a vowel, often an "-a." To avoid confusion, some friends and colleagues started to call me "Yuson-ka" or with the diminutive ending "Yuson-che" to express endearment toward me.

My being an *Asiatka* from the United States did not pose many obstacles for doing research in Sofia. Rather, I would like to think that this identity served as cultural capital. In many first encounters, I was asked whether I was Chinese, like the majority of Asians in Sofia. After I told them I was Korean, however, they often responded that they thought so because of the way I dressed and behaved. As my Bulgarian friends joked, socialism taught them a great deal about paying attention to details. I was equally perceived as an Asian and as a doctoral student from the United States (although rarely as an American citizen), and these identities broadened my accessibility to the lives of my interlocutors in Sofia. They often likened me to their children, cousins, relatives, or neighbors who went abroad to study or work. My Bulgarian interlocuters asked me as much about Korea and the "Far East" as they asked me about the United States.

In my experience, many Bulgarians are very open and sociable people. Usually, it does not take long after the first encounter between strangers to switch from the polite "you" (*vie*) to the casual "you" (*ti*). At least that was the case in Sofia, and numerous small chats with cab drivers attest to my observation. Above all, my Bulgarian language ability sparked lots of unexpected and productive conversations. Many Bulgarians reacted with a pleasant look of surprise and sometimes with disbelief that I spoke such good Bulgarian. My Bulgarian was never perfect, but my long-term stay improved my accent, and I was frequently complimented that I did not have a typical foreigner's accent. My language ability also differentiated me from other Asians in the city, most of whom spoke very little or, according to my friends, very "broken" Bulgarian. First drawn by curiosity toward an "exotic" Asian, they soon discovered cultural commonalities and translated the initial exotic and distant image into familiar references. Many Bulgarians were sympathetic to the political situation of North and South Korea and to the similarities of the Koreans and Bulgarians as small nations among big powers, which was particularly helpful in understanding their subjectivities.

Living with Bulgarian Host Families

It was not easy to arrange for host families in Sofia, although one might think that the financial constraints of Bulgarians would make rent an attractive secondary income. The fact that my host families were all of middle-class backgrounds, in the sense that, though they were cash poor, they had an education (at least a high school diploma) and owned their residence, was not a coincidence. As my Bulgarian friends explained to me, Bulgarians were not familiar with sharing their living spaces. In other words, rarely do they rent out a room to strangers, let alone foreigners. There seemed to be a social stigma associated with renting out part of one's living space. Only for financial needs would one consider doing so. My Bulgarian friends told me that leasing a room because one desired company (besides additional income) was unheard of in Bulgaria. Another hindering factor for finding a host family was the spatial limitations of many apartments in Sofia. This rendered only certain families eligible for renting out a room: pensioners who lived by themselves (the case of my second host family) or families whose children did not live with the parents anymore because they had gone abroad or lived independently (the case of my first host family). My host families were arranged through my primary contacts in Sofia, who were mostly professors at the universities and could vouch for me.

No fieldwork is complete without intimate engagement with local people and their lives on a daily basis. I was fortunate to have met two warm host families during my first long-term stay who welcomed me into their lives and cared for an *Asiatka* who wanted to research them. Had I lived by myself, I would not have been aware of the heating problem during the winter months because people did not openly talk about it. I would not have known that so many ordinary people were forced to turn off their central heating during the winter because they simply could not afford to pay the heating costs. They employed a variety of tactics to secure alternative heating, which I discuss in chapter 4. I would not have paid too much attention to these various arrangements had I not experienced the heating problem firsthand. Before my first thirteen-month sojourn in Sofia, I had stayed in the capital only during the summer months and had no idea about such winter conditions and Bulgarians' common anguish with heating in the postsocialist era.

The first three months of my first long-term fieldwork were indeed a time of enduring culture shock and initiated me into the phatic communion (community formed by the use of common language) of Sofia life. Although I had been to Bulgaria several times doing preliminary research before I launched the main project, living in Sofia during the summer versus experiencing a bitter winter made a big difference. I started to grumble and complain like any other Sofian going through the winter. My friends started to tease me that I had become a real Bulgarian. The Stalinist blocks and even the beautiful part of downtown Sofia with its gorgeous turn-of-the-century architecture could not be more depressing during the winter months with snow that nobody cared to clean up.

In these first three months, I lived in a residential quarter called *Mladost 1* (literally, Youth 1). This neighborhood was created by Todor Zhivkov, the communist leader who ruled the country for thirty-five years (March 1954–November 1989, the longest serving communist leader in Eastern Europe), in response to the needs of young families in the growing urban population. It was a typical outcome of socialist urban planning. Hence, eligibility was initially given to young families who did not own an apartment in Sofia and could no longer live with their parents because of lack of space. The neighborhood quarter, created in the late 1970s, followed the typical Stalinist architectural style with blocks of concrete buildings. *Mladost 1* was conveniently located off the main boulevard *Tsarigradsko Shose* (road to the tsar's city, meaning Istanbul) that connected the center of Sofia with its southern residential quarters. It was a fifteen-minute ride by bus or trolleybus. The apartment of my first host family had three rooms as well as a kitchen, a toilet, and a bathroom. One of the rooms was the children's room, which I rented and which was the largest room in the apartment. The other was the "adult" room that seemed to have two functions: it was the parents' bedroom, but it could also double as a dining room. The adult room was furnished with a sofa bed, dining table, and a few bookshelves.

My landlady occupied the adult room. In her early 50s and a mother of two daughters, she was a historian working for the history museum. Her husband was an engineer but had lost his job immediately after the political changes and worked temporary jobs in the villages of another city where he originally came from. Their marital status was a bit ambiguous: officially they were still married, but they were separated according to my landlady and her daughter. He would, however, come home once in a while, and I had seen him only once during my stay there. One of their daughters studied abroad, and the other daughter lived with my landlady's parents in a neighborhood closer to downtown. They were pensioners and had an extra room for her (which used to be the room my landlady and her sister shared when they were children), and she came home occasionally to spend time with her mother. Since I was occupying her room, when she came home, she shared the sofa bed with her mother. Although they were considered a middle-class family and once active members of the communist party (my landlady's father was a member of the *aktivni boretsi*, a group of people who fought against the fascists), their economic status had become very low over the years after the changes in 1989, and their main income relied on the meager salary of my landlady supplemented by my rent. Her older daughter held temporary jobs, but her income was primarily for her own expenses and did not contribute to the household income. My landlady and her older daughter were very kind and helpful in making me feel at home. They introduced me to their social network, which consisted of friends in the neighborhood as well as colleagues and friends beyond the community. My landlady had lost her job right after the political changes, but she was rehired by her former employer after being unemployed for almost ten years. Her position at her old job with a very modest salary (about 180 leva when the officially recorded average income in Bulgaria was 400 leva),[9] however, was precarious. She could lose it at any time and indeed she lost it during my first long-term fieldwork.

After surviving a couple of months of a very bitter winter without central heating, I was ready to move to a more convenient location with central heating. It was not an easy decision for me, especially because I knew how much my landlady relied on my rent, but I wanted heating and to be closer to downtown where I could walk to most of my field sites and meetings. The experience in *Mladost 1* in the winter, however, turned out to be a very valuable and sentimental one because it let me understand the reality that most of the people in Sofia and Bulgaria faced on a daily basis. It was also a turning point that gained me a level of cultural intimacy (Herzfeld 1997, 2005a) and included me as one of the Bulgarians who concealed from strangers the embarrassment of not having basic needs (such as heating). As soon as my interlocuters understood that I had experienced the heating problem firsthand like many of them, they revealed more intimate details of their lives. It was amazing how my experiences with heating made instant differences during interviews and daily interactions with my research subjects. Many Bulgarians did not seem to be embarrassed to talk about their low incomes, but topics regarding heating were not openly discussed with strangers or even among friends. It was considered a private and sensitive topic because heating was one area where the stratification of the population was more visible because the prices had gone up so dramatically in the market economy.

Not having central heating was unpleasant and uncomfortable. Worse still was the fact that my landlady had requested the heating to be turned off for her apartment because she could not afford it. And once it was turned off in the fall, it was impossible to have it turned on again during the winter, an example that was explained to me in terms of a lingering socialist bureaucracy. My landlady was very sorry for this arrangement and offered me an East German electric heater that her daughters had used in the 1980s, while she herself made do with a very old Russian electronic heater that she turned on for only a few hours each day before she went to bed in order to keep the electricity bill down. I did not understand this situation when I moved into her apartment in September. I did not comprehend why she and her daughter were constantly excusing themselves with "we do not have *parno*—we have turned it off." It was culturally not translating to me. Nor did I understand why they made such a concerned face whenever they brought up the topic of heating. The winter of 2001–2002 was very bad in the Balkans. It snowed an incredible amount to the point that Greece and Turkey had snow emergencies (which they rarely have) and the apartment buildings made of concrete became ice-cold. Having a small electric heater helped, but the sound it made was so loud that I could not leave it on during the night. Besides, I was afraid that the motor might burn out when it got overheated. Thankfully, my landlady gave me a very thick traditional blanket called *yurgan* (a word supposedly of Turkish origin) filled with dense cotton balls. The *yurgan* was my lifesaver and another traditional cultural reference I only got to know because of this winter experience.

After surviving the brutal winter without central heating in my first living quarters in Sofia, I spent the remaining ten months of my first long-term fieldwork with a former actress in her late 70s (and I have continued to return to her in my subsequent visits). She lived right in the heart of downtown Sofia, near the grave of Alexander of Battenberg. It was an apartment in a *kooperatsiya* built in the 1950s primarily for artists.[10] The building was six stories high and had two apartments on each floor. Almost half of them had been turned into offices of various companies in the 1990s, and only five apartments were occupied by original owners or their children. My landlady had been married to a once-active communist member (*aktivni boretsi*) for almost sixty years. Her husband (an editor-in-chief of a literature publishing house) passed away two years prior to my arrival. Although she had a son who was divorced, she did not live with him. It was definitely one of the bigger apartments in Sofia (about 120 sq m, compared to my first host family's *Mladost* apartment, which was about 90 sq m).[11] The apartment had three spacious bedrooms and was thus recognized as "bourgeois" by Sofians. My landlady rented out two rooms to supplement her state pension. She had been renting out rooms since the political changes in 1989 even when her husband was still alive. Although both of them had relatively good pensions (especially her husband), it was still not enough to maintain their apartment and the villa that they also owned. Given the usual Sofians' reluctance in sharing their living quarters with strangers, she and her husband were considered very modern in this regard, according to my landlady and my other Bulgarian friends who agreed with my landlady's explanation. Her apartment was decorated very nicely with what Sofians would describe as "old money" (*burzhoazni*). Expensive paintings by famous Bulgarian artists shined against the dilapidated but elegant wallpapers.[12] Her furniture was old but did not look like what I had seen at my first host family's apartment, which had been furnished in the 1980s. I understood that the furniture was gradually acquired from the late 1950s to the 1970s and that her most recent purchase was the washing machine acquired after the democratic changes. The old sofa in her living room was decorated with small cushions, the fabric of which my landlady had bought in Western Europe back in the 1970s and had sewn herself. Through her little balcony in the kitchen, I could appreciate an old enclosed European back courtyard inhabited by many feral cats. I could also see the golden dome of the Russian church (albeit from afar) and the huge dome of the Alexander Nevski Cathedral, one of the city's most emblematic architectural symbols.

My favorite view, however, was from my room's window. Through the tall trees, I saw the mausoleum of Bulgaria's first king in front of me and to my far left the statue of the Soviet Red Army (the Liberation Army) that was located in the park across the street and to my far right a big commercial sign for Valentine Scotch whiskey hanging by the stadium located across the park. This scenery aptly reflected the Bulgarian transition working its way up to join the EU: it was a situation in which a former monarch ruled as a prime minister with a socialist president who represented the nation in a new capitalist republic. In an interesting way, my two host families in Bulgaria reflected common realities of ordinary urbanites in the postsocialist era. They both owned an apartment but suffered hardships from living on low incomes (their pensions) and constantly encountered economic difficulties in their daily consumption practices. Living with these families provided me with intimate insights of the lives of Sofians in the new millennium.

In my subsequent visits, which included short-term visits during the springs or summers (2007–2016) as well as another long-term visit (six months) in 2008, I had different living arrangements: when I brought along my family, I rented an apartment, but when I was by myself, I rented a room usually with my second landlady or stayed with friends as their guests. When I rented an apartment, I did not have much social interaction with neighbors—in fact, I rarely encountered any neighbors, perhaps because my stay was not very long. The apartments I rented were all located in downtown Sofia and were all renovated with modern bathrooms and kitchens. Compared to my living spaces in the homes of my first two host families, the apartments I rented in the late 2000s were significantly better in terms of basic living conditions, and I never had issues with showers or heating. Many of my friends' apartments seemed to have also undergone a series of renovation projects over the years (mostly in bathrooms and kitchens), and when I visited my old landlady's apartment in 2013, hers was one of the few that was not able to have any modern updates. Overall, Sofia's urban landscape has significantly improved over the past decade with better public infrastructure such as better roads, new benches in the parks, better public transportation (including a subway), residential buildings with fresh paint, and cleaner public restrooms. While my Sofia friends hesitated to admit it, I saw gradual improvement in the urban landscape and citizens' living conditions.

Notes

1. A number of ethnographic monographs provide great insights into contemporary Bulgaria (Buchanan 2006; Cellarius 2004; Creed 1998, 2011; Ghodsee 2005, 2009; Kaneff 2004; Taylor 2006; cf. Sanders 1949 for an ethnography on presocialist Bulgaria). Most of them are based on extensive fieldwork in rural Bulgaria or provincial towns, whereas my research was primarily conducted in Sofia, the capital city of Bulgaria.

2. See Neuburger 2004, 2012 and Ghodsee 2009 for a more nuanced and complex account of minority relations in modern Bulgaria.

3. In light of the tumultuous changes in modern Bulgarian history, I define a group of people who were born in similar sociopolitical surroundings as an age cohort. For instance, those who were born in the 1950s and grew up in the so-called heyday of socialism comprises one age cohort. Similarly, those who were born in the mid-1970s and graduated high school after the collapse of socialism are categorized into another cohort. In terms of memories and practices of consumption, each age cohort represented a patterned narrative regarding their experiences such as in their renderings about the most meaningful purchases in their life.

4. Population of Sofia: 1876 (15,000), 1944 (300,000), 1989 (1.1 million), 2015 (1.2 million).

5. For more details of Bulgaria's modern history after its liberation from the Ottoman Empire, see Crampton 2007.

6. See the works of Sylvia Yanagisako (2002), an Asian American who conducted fieldwork in Italy, and Winnie Lem (1999), an Asian Canadian who conducted fieldwork in France.

7. A Korean male colleague who conducted ethnographic fieldwork in Poland in the late 2000s told me that he experienced strong racism against himself.

8. The Chinese population has been decreasing since Bulgaria became an EU member state and more Chinese started to move further West (see Jung 2012 for more details).

9. The currency rate of lev to US dollar was two to one at the time.

10. In the beginning of socialism, it was more common to own this type of apartment (see chapter 4).

11. It took about ten big steps to reach the family room from the entrance and another ten steps or so to the wall of the room at the other end of the apartment. From the balcony of the apartment to the bathroom that was situated at its opposite end, it was another twenty-five steps or so.

12. I was also struck by how my landlady managed to keep these artworks despite her destitute circumstances. She used to tell me that some of them are sought-after pieces and that some Bulgarians had visited her place and wanted to buy them. She refused and said, "Let my grandchildren have them. They may end up selling them, but to me, it is important that I leave these paintings and apartment for them." Wanting to leave something for one's offspring is considered a common cultural attitude in Bulgaria.

REFERENCES

Angelov, Stefan, ed. 1980. *Sotsialisticheskiyat Nachin na Zhivot* [Socialist way of life]. Izsledvaniya. Sofia: Izdatelstvo na Bulgarskata Akademia na Naukite.

Appadurai, Arjun. 1986a. "Introduction: Commodities and the Politics of Value." In *The Social Life of Things: Commodities in Cultural Perspective*, edited by Arjun Appadurai, 3–63. Cambridge: Cambridge University Press.

Associated Press. 2016. "Federal Emergency Is Declared in Flint over Contaminated Water." *New York Times*, January 16. https://www.nytimes.com/2016/01/17/us/federal-emergency-is-declared-in-flint-over-contaminated-water.html.

Avieli, Nir. 2014. "Vegetarian Ethics and Politics in Late-Socialist Vietnam." In *Ethical Eating in the Postsocialist and Socialist World*, edited by Yuson Jung, Jakob Klein, and Melissa L. Caldwell, 144–166. Berkeley: University of California Press.

Bach, Jonathan. 2002. "'The Taste Remains': Consumption, (N)ostalgia, and the Production of East Germany." *Public Culture* 14 (3): 545–556.

Bakalov, Ivan. 1998. "Editorial Note." *Mente i Originali*, no. 3, p. 5.

Belasco, Warren, and Roger Horowitz, eds. 2009. *Food Chains: From Farmyard to Shopping Cart*. Philadelphia: University of Pennsylvania Press.

Belk, Russell W. 1997. "Third World Consumer Culture." In *The Consumer Society*, edited by Neva R. Goodwin, Frank Ackerman, and David Kiron, 311–314. Washington, DC: Island Press.

Berdahl, Daphne. 1999. *Where the World Ended: Re-Unification and Identity in the German Borderland*. Berkeley: University of California Press.

Berdahl, Daphne, Matti Bunzl, and Martha Lampland, eds. 2000. *Altering States: Ethnographies of Transition in Eastern Europe and the Former Soviet Union*. Ann Arbor: University of Michigan Press.

Boffey, Daniel. 2018. "EU Moves to Ban Sale of Lower-Quality Branded Food in Eastern Europe." *The Guardian*, April 11. https://www.theguardian.com/inequality/2018/apr/11/eu-moves-ban-sale-lower-quality-branded-food-eastern-europe?CMP=share_btn_link.

Borelli, Caterina, and Fabio Mattioli. 2013. "The Social Lives of Postsocialism." *Laboratorium* 5 (1): 4–13.

Bourdieu, Pierre. 1977. *Outline of a Theory of Practice*. Cambridge: Cambridge University Press.

———. 1984. *Distinction: A Social Critique of the Judgement of Taste*. Cambridge, MA: Harvard University Press.

Bren, Paulina, and Mary Neuburger, eds. 2012. *Communism Unwrapped: Consumption in Cold War Eastern Europe*. Oxford: Oxford University Press.

Buchanan, Donna. 2006. *Performing Democracy: Bulgarian Music and Musicians in Transition*. Chicago, IL: University of Chicago Press.

Buchli, Victor. 2000. *An Archaeology of Socialism*. Oxford, UK: Berg.

Buchowski, Michał. 1996. "The Shifting Meanings of Civil and Civic Society in Poland." In *Civil Society: Challenging Western Models*, edited by Chris Hann and Elizabeth Dunn, 79–98. New York: Routledge.

Burawoy, Michael, and Katherine Verdery, eds. 1999. *Uncertain Transition: Ethnographies of Change in the Postsocialist World*. Lanham, MD: Rowman and Littlefield.

Buyandelger, Manduhai. 2008. "Post-Post-Transition Theories: Walking on Multiple Paths." *Annual Review of Anthropology* 37:235–250.

Caldwell, Melissa L. 2002. "The Taste of Nationalism: Food Politics in Postsocialist Moscow." *Ethnos* 67 (3): 295–319.

———. 2004. *Not By Bread Alone: Social Support in the New Russia*. Berkeley: University of California Press.

———, ed. 2009a. *Food and Everyday Life in the Postsocialist World*. Bloomington: Indiana University Press.

———. 2009b. "Tempest in a Coffee Pot: Brewing Incivility in Russia's Public Sphere." In *Food and Everyday Life in the Postsocialist World*, edited by Melissa Caldwell, 101–129. Bloomington: Indiana University Press.

———. 2011. *Dacha Idylls: Living Organically in Russia's Countryside*. Berkeley: University of California Press.

———. 2012. "Placing Faith in Development: How Russia's Religious Communities Contribute to a More Civil Society." *Slavic Review* 71 (2): 261–287.

Caldwell, Melissa L., and Jennifer Patico. 2002. "Consumers Exiting Socialism: Ethnographic Perspectives on Daily Life in Post-Communist Europe." *Ethnos* 67 (3): 285–294.

Canclini, Néstor García. 2001. *Consumers and Citizens: Globalization and Multicultural Conflicts*. Translated and with introduction by George Yúdice. Minneapolis: University of Minnesota Press.

Campbell, Colin. 1998. "Consumption and the Rhetorics of Need and Want." *Journal of Design History* 11 (3): 235–246.

Carrier, James, and Josiah McC. Heyman. 1997. "Consumption and Political Economy." *Journal of the Royal Anthropological Institute* 3 (2): 355–373.

Cellarius, Barbara. 2004. *In the Land of Orpheus: Rural Livelihoods and Nature Conservation in Postsocialist Bulgaria*. Madison: University of Wisconsin Press.

Cellarius, Barbara, and Caedmon Staddon. 1999. "Environmental Nongovernmental Organizations, Civil Society, and Democratization in Bulgaria." *East European Politics and Societies* 16 (1): 182–222.

Chelcea, Liviu. 2002. "The Culture of Shortage During State-Socialism: Consumption Practices in a Romanian Village in the 1980s." *Cultural Studies* 16 (1): 16–43.

Cohen, Lizabeth. 2003. *A Consumers' Republic: The Politics of Mass Consumption in Postwar America*. New York: Vintage.

———. 2006. "The Consumer's Republic: An American Model for the World?" In *The Ambivalent Consumer: Questioning Consumption in East Asia and the West*, edited by Sheldon Garon and Patricia Maclachlan, 45–62. Ithaca, NY: Cornell University Press.

Colloredo-Mansfeld, Rudi. 2013. "Consumption: From Cultural Theory to the Ethnography of Capitalism." In *The Handbook of Sociocultural Anthropology*, edited by James Carrier and Deborah Gewertz, 317–336. London: Bloomsbury.

Commission of the European Communities. 2004. *2004 Regular Report on Bulgaria's Progress towards Accession*. Brussels: Commission of the European Communities. https://ec.europa.eu/neighbourhood-enlargement/sites/near/files/archives/pdf/key_documents/2004/rr_bg_2004_en.pdf

Counihan, Carole, and Valeria Siniscalchi, eds. 2014. *Food Activism: Agency, Democracy, and Economy*. London: Bloomsbury.

Cowan, Jane K., Marie-Benedicte Dembour, and Richard A. Wilson, eds. 2001. *Culture and Rights: Anthropological Perspectives*. Cambridge: Cambridge University Press.
Crăciun, Magdalena. 2014. *Material Culture and Authenticity: Fake Branded Fashion in Europe*. London: Bloomsbury.
Crampton, R. J. 2007. *Bulgaria*. Oxford: Oxford University Press.
Creed, Gerald. 1998. *Domesticating Revolution: From Socialist Reform to Ambivalent Transition in a Bulgarian Village*. University Park: Pennsylvania State University Press.
———. 1999. "Deconstructing Socialism in Bulgaria." In *Uncertain Transition: Ethnographies of Change in the Postsocialist World*, edited by Michael Burawoy and Katherine Verdery. 223–244. Lanham, MD: Rowman and Littlefield.
———. 2002. "(Consumer) Paradise Lost: Capitalist Disenchantment in Rural Bulgaria." *Anthropology of East Europe Review* 20 (2): 119–126.
———. 2010. "Strange Bedfellows: Socialist Nostalgia and Neoliberalism in Bulgaria." In *Post-Communist Nostalgia*, edited by Maria Todorova and Zsuzsa Gille, 29–45. New York: Berghahn.
———. 2011. *Masquerade and Postsocialism: Ritual and Cultural Dispossession in Bulgaria*. Bloomington: Indiana University Press.
Creed, Gerald, and Janine R. Wedel. 1997. "Second Thoughts from the Second World: Interpreting Aid in Post-Communist Eastern Europe." *Human Organization* 56 (3): 253–264.
de Certeau, Michel. 1984. *The Practice of Everyday Life*. Berkeley: University of California Press.
Ditchev, Ivaylo. 2004. "The Forge of Consumers: An Essay on Communist Desire." Unpublished manuscript. Department of History and Theory of Culture, Sofia University "St. Kliment Ohridski," Bulgaria.
Douglas, Mary, and Baron Isherwood. 1979. *The World of Goods: Towards an Anthropology of Consumption*. New York: Routledge.
Dunn, Elizabeth C. 2004. *Privatizing Poland: Baby Food, Big Business, and the Remaking of Labor*. Ithaca, NY: Cornell University Press.
———. 2008. "Postsocialist Pores: Disease, Bodies, and the State in the Republic of Georgia." *American Ethnologist* 35 (2): 243–258.
Endres, Kirsten. 2007. "Spirited Modernities: Medium and Ritual Performativity in Late Socialist Vietnam." In *Modernity and Re-enchantment: Religion in Post-Revolutionary Vietnam*, edited by Philip Taylor, 194–220. Singapore: ISEAS Press.
Escobar, Arturo. 1995. *Encountering Development: The Making and Unmaking of the Third World*. Princeton, NJ: Princeton University Press.
European Commission. 2009. "Questions and Answers on the Promotion of Independent Consumer Product Testing." Memo 09-371, September 3. http://europa.eu/rapid/press-release_MEMO-09-371_en.htm?locale=en.
Featherstone, Mike. 1991. *Consumer Culture and Postmodernism*. London: Sage.
Feher, Ferenc, Agnes Heller, and Gyorgi Markus. 1983. *Dictatorship over Needs: An Analysis of Soviet Societies*. Oxford, UK: Basil Blackwell.
Fehérváry, Krisztina. 2002. "American Kitchens, Luxury Bathrooms, and the Search for a 'Normal' Life in Postsocialist Hungary." *Ethnos* 67 (3): 369–400.
———. 2013. *Politics in Color and Concrete: Social Materialities and the Middle Class in Hungary*. Bloomington: Indiana University Press.
Ferguson, James. 1990. *The Anti-Politics Machine: "Development," Depoliticization, and Bureaucratic Power in Lesotho*. Minneapolis: University of Minnesota Press.

Ferguson, James, and Akhil Gupta. 2002. "Spatializing States: Toward an Ethnography of Neoliberal Governmentality." *American Ethnologist* 29 (4): 981–1002.

Fine, Ben. 1995. "From Political Economy to Consumption." In *Acknowledging Consumption: A Review of New Studies*, edited by Daniel Miller. 127–163. London: Routledge.

Fitchen, Janet. 1988. "Hunger, Malnutrition, and Poverty in the Contemporary United States: Some Observations on Their Social and Cultural Context." *Food and Foodways* 2 (1): 309–333.

Fitzpatrick, Sheila. 1996. "Supplicants and Citizens: Public Letter-Writing in Soviet Russia in the 1930s." *Slavic Review* 55 (1): 78–105.

———. 1999. *Everyday Stalinism: Ordinary Life in Extraordinary Times, Soviet Russia in the 1930s*. New York: Oxford University Press.

Freeman, Carla. 2000. *High Tech and High Heels in the Global Economy*. Durham, NC: Duke University Press.

Gal, Susan, and Gail Kligman. 2000. *The Politics of Gender: After Socialism*. Princeton, NJ: Princeton University Press.

Ganev, Venelin. 2007. *Preying on the State: The Transformation of Bulgaria after 1989*. Ithaca, NY: Cornell University Press.

———. 2013. "Post-Accession Hooliganism: Democratic Governance in Bulgaria and Romania after 2007." *East European Politics and Societies* 27 (1): 26–44.

———. 2014a. "The Borsa: the Black Market for Rock Music in Late Socialist Bulgaria." *Slavic Review* 73 (3): 514–537.

———. 2014b. "Bulgaria's Year of Civic Anger." *Journal of Democracy* 25 (1): 33–45.

Garon, Sheldon, and Patricia L. Maclachlan. 2006. *The Ambivalent Consumer: Questioning Consumption in East Asia and the West*. Ithaca, NY: Cornell University Press.

Gilbert, Andrew. 2006. "The Past in Parenthesis: (Non)Post-Socialism in Post-War Bosnia-Herzgovina." *Anthropology Today* 22 (4): 14–18.

Gille, Zsuzsa. 2009. "The Tale of the Toxic Paprika: The Hungarian Taste of Euro-Globalization." In *Food and Everyday Life in the Post-Socialist World*, edited by Melissa L. Caldwell, 57–77. Bloomington: Indiana University Press.

Giordano, Christian, and Dobrinka Kostova. 2002. "The Social Production of Mistrust." In *Postsocialism: Ideals, Ideologies and Practices in Eurasia*, edited by C. M. Hann, 74–92. New York: Routledge.

Ghodsee, Kristen. 2005. *The Red Riviera: Gender, Tourism, and Postsocialism on the Black Sea*. Durham, NC: Duke University Press.

———. 2009. *Muslim Lives in Eastern Europe: Gender, Ethnicity, and the Transformation of Islam in Postsocialist Bulgaria*. Princeton, NJ: Princeton University Press.

———. 2013. "Bulgarians Take to the Street." *Anthropology News* 54 (2). https://anthrosource.onlinelibrary.wiley.com/doi/epdf/10.1111/j.1556-3502.2013.54204.x.

———. 2015. *The Left Side of History*. Durham, NC: Duke University Press.

Goodwin, Neva R., Frank Ackerman, and David Kiron, eds. 1997. *The Consumer Society*. Washington, DC: Island Press.

Graeber, David. 2011. "Consumption." *Current Anthropology* 52 (4): 489–511.

Grasseni, Cristina. 2013. *Beyond Alternative Food: Italy's Solidarity Purchase Groups*. London: Bloomsbury.

Gronow, Jukka. 2003. *Caviar with Champagne: Common Luxury and the Ideals of the Good Life in Stalin's Russia*. Oxford, UK: Berg.

Guentcheva, Rossitza. 2012. "Material Harmony: The Quest for Quality in Socialist Bulgaria, 1960s–1980s." In *Communism Unwrapped: Consumption in Cold War Eastern Europe*, edited by Paulina Bren and Mary Neuburger, 140–163. Oxford: Oxford University Press.

Gueorguieva, Valentina. 2015. "What Is the Lifespan of Reactive Mobilizations? From 'We Can't Take It Anymore!' to 'The Day after the Resignation.'" *Seminar_BG: Online Journal for Cultural Studies*. http://seminar-bg.eu/spisanie-seminar-bg/special-issue-3/item/450-what- is-the-lifespan-of-reactive-mobilizations.html.

Gupta, Akhil. 1995. "Blurred Boundaries: The Discourse of Corruption, the Culture of Politics, and the Imagined State." *American Ethnologist* 22 (2): 375–402.

Gupta, Akhil, and James Ferguson, eds. 1997. *Anthropological Locations: Boundaries and Grounds of a Field Science*. Berkeley: University of California Press.

Haney, Lynne. 1997. "'But We Are Still Mothers': Gender, the State, and the Construction of Need in Postsocialist Hungary." In *Uncertain Transition: Ethnographies of Change in the Postsocialist World*, edited by Michael Burawoy and Katherine Verdery, 151–188. Lanham, MD: Rowman and Littlefield.

Hann, Chris, ed. 2002. *Postsocialism: Ideals, Ideologies and Practices in Eurasia*. New York: Routledge.

Hann, Chris, and Elizabeth Dunn, eds. 1996. *Civil Society: Challenging Western Models*. New York: Routledge.

Hann, Chris, and Keith Hart. 2011. *Economic Anthropology: History, Ethnography, Critique*. Cambridge, UK: Polity Press.

Hann, Chris, Caroline Humphrey, and Katherine Verdery. 2002. "Introduction: Postsocialism as a Topic of Anthropological Investigation." In *Postsocialism: Ideals, Ideologies and Practices in Eurasia*, edited by C. M. Hann, 1–28. New York: Routledge.

Hansen, Karen T. 2000. *Salaula: The World of Secondhand Clothing and Zambia*. Chicago, IL: University of Chicago Press.

Harms, Eric. 2011. *Saigon's Edge: On the Margins of Ho Chi Minh's City*. Minneapolis: University of Minnesota Press.

Hemment, Julie. 2007. *Empowering Women in Russia: Activism, Aid, and NGOs*. Bloomington: Indiana University Press.

Herzfeld, Michael. 1987. *Anthropology through the Looking-Glass: Critical Ethnography in the Margins of Europe*. Cambridge: Cambridge University Press.

———. 1992. *The Production of Indifference: Exploring the Symbolic Roots of Western Bureaucracy*. Chicago, IL: University of Chicago Press.

———. 1997. *Cultural Intimacy: Social Poetics in the Nation-State*. New York: Routledge.

———. 2004. *The Body Impolitic: Artisans and Artifice in the Global Hierarchy of Value*. Chicago, IL: University of Chicago Press.

———. 2005a. *Cultural Intimacy: Social Poetics in the Nation-State*. 2nd ed. New York: Routledge.

———. 2005b. "Political Optics and the Occlusion of Intimate Knowledge." *American Anthropologist* 107 (3): 369–376.

———. 2009. *Evicted from Eternity: The Restructuring of Modern Rome*. Chicago, IL: University of Chicago Press.

Hilton, Matthew. 2009. *Prosperity for All: Consumer Activism in an Era of Globalization*. Ithaca, NY: Cornell University Press.

Holt, Douglas B. 2005. "An Interview with Juliet Schor." *Journal of Consumer Culture* 5 (1): 5–22.
Hsu, Carolyn L. 2005. "Capitalism without Contracts versus Capitalists without Capitalism: Comparing the Influence of Chinese *Guanxi* and Russian *Blat* on Marketization." *Communist and Post-Communist Studies* 38:309–327.
Humphrey, Caroline. 1995. "Creating a Culture of Disillusionment: Consumption in Moscow, a Chronicle of Changing Times." In *Worlds Apart: Modernity through the Prism of the Local*, edited by Daniel Miller, 43–68. London: Routledge.
———. 2002. *The Unmaking of Soviet Life: Everyday Economics after Socialism*. Ithaca, NY: Cornell University Press.
Humphrey, Caroline, and Ruth Mandel. 2002. "The Market in Everyday Life: Ethnographies of Postsocialism." In *Markets and Moralities: Ethnographies of Postsocialism*, edited by Caroline Humphrey and Ruth Mandel, 1–18. Oxford, UK: Berg.
Iliev, Ilia. 2014. "Bulgaria's Search for Political Alternatives in the Midst of Europe's Crisis." *Anthropology News* 55 (7). https://anthrosource.onlinelibrary.wiley.com/doi/pdf/10.1111/j.1556-3502.2014.55704.x.
Jung, Yuson. 2007. "Consumer Lament: An Ethnographic Study on Consumption, Needs, and Everyday Complaints in Postsocialist Bulgaria." Ph.D. diss., Harvard University, Boston, Massachusetts.
———. 2009. "From Canned Food to Canny Consumers: Cultural Competence in the Age of Mechanical Production." In *Food and Everyday Life in the Postsocialist World*, edited by Melissa Caldwell, 29–56. Bloomington: Indiana University Press.
———. 2010. "The Inability Not to Follow: Western Hegemonies and the Notion of Complaisance in the Enlarged Europe." *Anthropological Quarterly* 83 (2): 317–354.
———. 2012. "Experiencing the 'West' through the 'East' in the Margins of Europe: Chinese Food Consumption Practices in Postsocialist Bulgaria." *Food, Culture, and Society* 15 (4): 579–598.
———. 2014a. "Ambivalent Consumers and the Limits of Certification: Organic Foods in Postsocialist Bulgaria." In *Ethical Eating in the Postsocialist and Socialist World*, edited by Yuson Jung, Jakob A. Klein, and Melissa L. Caldwell, 93–115. Berkeley: University of California Press.
———. 2014b. "(Re)-establishing the Normal: Insights from Postsocialist Bulgaria and Postindustrial Detroit." *Gastronomica: Journal of Critical Food Studies* 14 (4): 52–59.
———. 2016. "Food Provisioning and Foodways in Postsocialist Societies: Global Belonging and Social Trust." In *The Handbook in Food and Anthropology*, edited by James L. Watson and Jakob A. Klein, 476–501. London: Bloomsbury.
Jung, Yuson, Jakob Klein, and Melissa L. Caldwell, eds. 2014. *Ethical Eating in the Postsocialist and Socialist World*. Berkeley: University of California Press.
Jung, Yuson, and Andrew Newman. 2014. "An Edible Moral Economy in the Motor City: Food Politics and Urban Governance in Detroit." *Gastronomica: Journal of Critical Food Studies* 14 (1): 22–31.
Kaneff, Deema. 2002. "Why People Don't Die 'Naturally' Anymore: Changing Relations between 'the Individual' and 'the State' in Postsocialist Bulgaria." *Journal of Royal Anthropological Institute* 8:89–105.
———. 2004. *Who Owns the Past? The Politics of Time in a "Model" Bulgarian Village*. New York: Berghahn.

Keller, Margit. 2004. "Needs, Desires and the Experience of Scarcity: Representations of Recreational Shopping in Post-Soviet Estonia." *Journal of Consumer Culture* 5:65–85.
Keyzerov, Nikolay M. 1979. *Patalogiya na potrebitelstvoto: kritika na burzhoazniya nachin na zhivot* [Pathology of consumerism: Criticism of the bourgeois way of life]. Sofia: Izdatelstvo nauka i izkustvo.
Kideckel, David A. 2008. *Getting By in Postsocialist Romania: Labor, the Body, and Working-Class Culture*. Bloomington: Indiana University Press.
———. 2009. "Citizenship Discourse, Globalization, and Protest: A Postsocialist-Postcolonial Comparison." *Anthropology of East Europe Review* 27 (2): 117–133.
Klein, Jakob A. 2013. "Everyday Approaches to Food Safety in Kunming." *China Quarterly* 213:376–393.
———. 2014. "Connecting with the Countryside? 'Alternative' Food Movements with Chinese Characteristics." In *Ethical Eating in the Postsocialist and Socialist World*, edited by Yuson Jung, Jakob A. Klein, and Melissa L. Caldwell, 116–144. Berkeley: University of California Press.
Klein, Jakob A., Yuson Jung, and Melissa L. Caldwell. 2014. "Introduction: Ethical Eating and (Post)socialist Alternatives." In *Ethical Eating in the Postsocialist and Socialist World*, 1–24. Berkeley: University of California Press.
Konstantinov, Yulian. 1996. "Patterns of Reinterpretation: Trader-Tourism in the Balkans (Bulgaria) as a Picaresque Metaphorical Enactment of Post-Totalitarianism." *American Ethnologist* 23 (4): 762–782.
Konstantinov, Yulian, Gideon M. Kressel, and Trond Thuen. 1998. "Outclassed by Former Outcasts: Petty Trading in Varna." *American Ethnologist* 25 (4): 729–745.
LaFraniere, Sharon. 2009. "2 Executed in China for Selling Tainted Milk." *New York Times*, November 24. https://www.nytimes.com/2009/11/25/world/asia/25china.html.
Lammer, Christopher. 2017. "Reworking State Boundaries through Care: 'Peasant Friends,' 'Greedy Entrepreneurs' and 'Corrupt Officials' in an 'Alternative' Food Network in China. *Vienna Working Papers in Ethnography* 5:1–30.
Lampland, Martha. 1995. *The Object of Labor: Commodification in Socialist Hungary*. Chicago, IL: University of Chicago Press.
Latham, Kevin. 2002. "Rethinking Chinese Consumption: Social Palliatives and the Rhetorics of Transition in Postsocialist China." In *Postsocialism: Ideals, Ideologies and Practices in Eurasia*, edited by C. M. Hann, 217–237.New York: Routledge.
Ledeneva, Alena V. 2003. "Informal Practices in Changing Societies: Comparing Chinese *Guanxi* and Russian *Blat*." Economics Working Paper 45. London: Centre for the Study of Economic and Social Change in Europe.
———. 2009. "From Russia with 'Blat': Can Informal Networks Help Modernize Russia?" *Social Research* 76 (1): 257–288.
Lem, Winnie. 1999. *Cultivating Dissent: Work, Identity, and Praxis in Rural Languedoc*. Albany: State University of New York Press.
Lemon, Alaina. 1998. "'Your Eyes Are Green Like Dollars': Counterfeit Cash, National Substance, and Currency Apartheid in 1990s Russia." *Cultural Anthropology* 13 (1): 22–55.
Liechty, Mark. 2002. *Suitably Modern: Making Middle-Class Culture in a New Consumer Society*. Princeton, NJ: Princeton University Press.
Lin, Yi-Chieh Jessica. 2011. *Fake Stuff: China and the Rise of Counterfeit Goods*. New York: Routledge.

Mazurek, Malgorzata, and Matthew Hilton. 2007. "Consumerism, Solidarity, and Communism: Consumer Protection and the Consumer Movement in Poland." *Journal of Contemporary History* 42 (2): 315–343.
Mazzarella, William. 2003. *Shoveling Smoke: Advertising and Globalization in Contemporary India*. Durham, NC: Duke University Press.
Merkel, Ina. 1998. "Consumer Culture in the GDR, or How the Struggle for Antimodernity Was Lost on the Battleground of Consumer Culture." In *Getting and Spending: European and American Consumer Societies in the Twentieth Century*, edited by Susan Strasser, Charles McGovern, and Matthias Judt, 281–300. Cambridge: Cambridge University Press.
———. 1999. "Working People and Consumption under Really-Existing Socialism: Perspectives from the German Democratic Republic." *International Labor and Working-Class History* 55:92–111.
———. 2005. "From Stigma to Cult: Changing Meanings in East German Consumer Culture." In *The Making of the Consumer: Knowledge, Power, and Identity in the Modern World*, edited by Frank Trentmann, 249–270. Oxford, UK: Berg.
Mihaylov, Nikolay. 1984. *Sotsializmat i Razumnite Potrebnosti na Lichnostta*.[Socialism and reasonable needs of people] Sofia: Partizdat.
Miller, Daniel. 1987. *Material Culture and Mass Consumption*. Oxford, UK: Blackwell.
———, ed. 1995a. *Acknowledging Consumption: A Review of New Studies*. London: Routledge.
———. 1995b. "Consumption and Commodities." *Annual Review in Anthropology* 24:141–61.
———. 1995c. "Consumption as the Vanguard of History: A Polemic by Way of an Introduction." In *Acknowledging Consumption: A Review of New Studies*, edited by Daniel Miller, 1–52. London: Routledge.
———. 1995d. "Introduction: Anthropology, Modernity and Consumption." In *Worlds Apart: Modernity through the Prism of the Local*, edited by Daniel Miller, 1–22. London: Routledge.
———. 1997. *Capitalism: An Ethnographic Approach*. Oxford, UK: Berg.
———. 2010. *Stuff*. Cambridge, UK: Polity Press.
———. 2012. *Consumption and Its Consequences*. Cambridge, UK: Polity Press.
Mincyte, Diana. 2009. "Self-Made Women: Informal Dairy Markets in Europeanizing Lithuania." In *Food and Everyday Life in the Postsocialist World*, edited by Melissa Caldwell, 78–100. Bloomington: Indiana University Press.
———. 2014. "Homogenizing Europe: Raw Milk, Risk Politics, and Moral Economies in Europeanizing Lithuania." In *Ethical Eating in the Postsocialist and Socialist World*, edited by Yuson Jung, Jakob A. Klein, and Melissa L. Caldwell, 25–43. Berkeley: University of California Press.
"Ministry Council Report no. 131." 1974. *Darzhaven Vestnik* (State Gazette), December 20. Republic of Bulgaria.
"Ministry Council Report no. 136." 1964. *Darzhaven Vestnik* (State Gazette), April 18. Republic of Bulgaria.
Mitchell, Timothy. 1999. "Society, Economy, and the State Effect." In *State/Culture: State-Formation after the Cultural Turn*, edited by George Steinmetz, 76–97. Ithaca, NY: Cornell University Press.
Muehlebach, Andrea. 2014. *The Moral Neoliberal: Welfare and Citizenship in Italy*. Chicago, IL: University of Chicago Press.
Nakassis, Constantine. 2012. "Counterfeiting What? Aesthetics of Brandedness and Brand in Tamil Nadu, India." *Anthropological Quarterly* 85 (3): 701–722.

National Statistical Institute (Bulgaria) (NSI). 2002. *Statisticheski Spravochnik* [Statistical reference book]. Sofia: Bulgaria.
———. 2007. *Statisticheski Spravochnik* [Statistical reference book]. Sofia: Bulgaria.
———. 2015. *Statisticheski Spravochnik* [Statistical reference book]. Sofia: Bulgaria.
Neuburger, Mary. 2004. *The Orient Within: Muslim Minorities and the Negotiation of Nationhood in Modern Bulgaria*. Ithaca, NY: Cornell University Press.
———. 2012. *The Balkan Smoke: Tobacco and the Making of Modern Bulgaria*. Ithaca, NY: Cornell University Press.
Newell, Sasha. 2013. "Brands as Masks: Public Secrecy and the Counterfeit in Côte d'Ivoire." *Journal of the Royal Anthropological Institute* 19:138–154.
Patico, Jennifer. 2002. "Chocolate and Cognac: Gifts and the Recognition of Social Worlds in Post-Soviet Russia." *Ethnos* 67 (3): 345–368.
———. 2005. "To Be Happy in a Mercedes: Tropes of Value and Ambivalent Visions of Marketization." *American Ethnologist* 32 (3): 479–496.
———. 2008. *Consumption and Social Change in a Post-Soviet Middle Class*. Washington, DC: Woodrow Wilson Press.
Patterson, Patrick H. 2009. "Making Markets Marxist? The East European Grocery Store from Rationing to Rationality to Rationalization." In *Food Chains: From Farmyard to Shopping Cart*, edited by Warren Belasco and Roger Horowitz, 196–216. Philadelphia: University of Pennsylvania Press.
Phillips, Sarah. 2008. *Women's Social Activism in the New Ukraine: Development and the Politics of Differentiation*. Bloomington: Indiana University Press.
Pritchard, J-P., ed. 1994. *Consumer Protection in Bulgaria*. Consumer Institutions and Consumer Policy Programme (CICPP). European Commission.
Rapley, John. 2007. *Understanding Development: Theory and Practice in the Third World*. Boulder, CO: Lynne Rienner.
Rausing, Sigrid. 2002. "Re-constructing the 'Normal': Identity and the Consumption of Western Goods in Estonia." In *Markets and Moralities: Ethnographies of Postsocialism*, edited by Caroline Humphrey and Ruth Mandel, 127–142. Oxford, UK: Berg.
Reeves, Madeleine, Johan Rasanayagan, and Judith Beyer, eds. 2014. *Ethnographies of the State in Central Asia: Performing Politics*. Bloomington: Indiana University Press.
Reid, Susan E., and David Crowley, eds. 2000. *Style and Socialism: Modernity and Material Culture in Post-War Eastern Europe*. Oxford, UK: Berg.
Ries, Nancy. 1997. *Russian Talk: Culture and Conversation during Perestroika*. Ithaca, NY: Cornell University Press.
———. 2009. "Potato Ontology: Surviving Postsocialism in Russia." *Cultural Anthropology* 24 (2): 181–212.
Rogers, Douglas. 2010. "Postsocialisms Unbound: Connections, Critiques, Comparisons." *Slavic Review* 69 (1): 1–15.
Rogers, Douglas, and Katherine Verdery. 2013. "Postsocialist Societies: Eastern Europe and the Former Soviet Union." In *The Handbook of Sociocultural Anthropology*, edited by James Carrier and Deborah Gewertz, 439–456. London: Bloomsbury.
Rosaldo, Renato. 1989. *Culture and Truth: The Remaking of Social Analysis*. Boston: Beacon Press.
Sampson, Steven. 2002. "Weak States, Uncivil Societies and Thousands of NGOs: Benevolent Colonialism in the Balkans." In *The Balkans in Focus: Cultural Boundaries in Europe*, edited by Sanimir Resic and Barbara Törnquist-Plewa, 27–44. Lund, Sweden: Nordic Academic Press.

Sanders, Irwin T. 1949. *Balkan Village*. Lexington: University of Kentucky Press.
Scott, James C. 1998. *Seeing Like a State: How Certain Schemes to Improve the Human Condition Have Failed*. New Haven, CT: Yale University Press.
Sharma, Aradhana, and Akhil Gupta. 2006. *The Anthropology of the State: A Reader*. Malden, MA: Blackwell.
Shevchenko, Olga. 2002. "'In Case of Fire Emergency': Consumption, Security and the Meaning of Durables in a Transforming Society." *Journal of Consumer Culture* 2 (2): 147–170.
———. 2010. *Crisis and the Everyday in Postsocialist Moscow*. Bloomington: Indiana University Press.
Skultans, Vieda. 2001. "Arguing with the KGB Archives: Archival and Narrative Memory in Post-Soviet Latvia." *Ethnos* 66 (3): 320–343.
Smith, Jenny. 2009. "Empire of Ice Cream: How Life Becomes Sweeter in the Postwar Soviet Union." In *Food Chains: From Farmyard to Shopping Cart*, edited by Warren Belasco and Roger Horowitz, 142–157. Philadelphia: University of Pennsylvania Press.
Smollett, Eleanor. 1993. "America the Beautiful: Made in Bulgaria." *Anthropology Today* 9 (2): 9–13.
Snavely, Keith, and Uday Desai. 1994. "The Emergence and Development of Nonprofit Organizations in Bulgaria." Working Paper Series. Washington, DC: Aspen Institute.
Steiner, Andre. 1998. "Dissolution of the 'Dictatorship over Needs'? Consumer Behavior and Economic Reform in East Germany in the 1960s." In *Getting and Spending: European and American Consumer Societies in the Twentieth Century*, edited by Susan Strasser, Charles McGovern, and Matthias Judt, 167–186. Cambridge: Cambridge University Press.
Stoilova, Maria. 2013. "Bulgaria's Summer of Dissent Extends into the Fall." *Anthropology News* 54 (11). https://anthrosource.onlinelibrary.wiley.com/doi/pdf/10.1111/j.1556-3502.2013.541104.x.
Sunshine. 1999. Directed by István Szabó. Toronto, Canada: Alliance Atlantis.
Taylor, Erin. 2006. *Let's Twist Again: Youth and Leisure in Socialist Bulgaria*. Berlin: LIT Verlag.
Thelen, Tatjana, Larissa Vetters, and Keebet von Benda-Beckmann. 2014. "Introduction to Stategraphy: Toward a Relational Anthropology of the State." *Social Analysis* 58 (3): 1–19.
Thomas, Kedron. 2009. "Structural Adjustment, Spatial Imaginaries, and 'Piracy' in Guatemala's Apparel Industry." *Anthropology of Work Review* 30 (1): 1–10.
Todorova, Maria, and Gille, Zsuzsa, eds. 2010. *Post-Communist Nostalgia*. New York: Berghahn.
Tracy, Megan. 2010. "The Mutability of Melamine: A Transductive Account of a Scandal." *Anthropology Today* 26 (6): 4–8.
———. 2013. "Pasteurizing China's Grasslands and Sealing in *Terroir*." *American Anthropologist* 115 (3): 437–451.
Trentmann, Frank, ed. 2006. *The Making of the Consumer: Knowledge, Power, and Identity in the Modern World*. Oxford, UK: Berg.
———. 2007. "Citizenship and Consumption." *Journal of Consumer Culture* 7 (2): 147–158.
Trouillot, Michel-Rolph. 2001. "The Anthropology of the State in the Age of Globalization: Close Encounters of the Deceptive Kind." *Current Anthropology* 42 (1): 125–138.
Vann, Elizabeth. 2006. "The Limits of Authenticity in Vietnamese Consumer Markets." *American Anthropologist* 108 (2): 286–296.

Vedwan, Neeraj. 2007. "Pesticides in Coca-Cola and Pepsi: Consumerism, Brand Image, and Public Interest in a Globalizing India." *Cultural Anthropology* 22 (4): 659–684.
Velinova, Iskra. 2004. "Za Potrebnostite, Potreblenieto i Konsumatsiata pri Sotsializma" [About needs, consumption and consumerism during socialism]. *Antropologichni izsledvaniya* 5. Sofia: Nov Bulgarski Universitet, Department "Antropologiya"
Verdery, Katherine. 1996. *What Was Socialism and What Comes Next?* Princeton, NJ: Princeton University Press.
———. 2002. "Whither Postsocialism?" In *Postsocialism: Ideals, Ideologies and Practices in Eurasia*, edited by C. M. Hann, 15–28. New York: Routledge.
———. 2003. *The Vanishing Hectare: Property and Value in Postsocialist Transylvania*. Ithaca, NY: Cornell University Press.
Verdery, Katherine, and Caroline Humphrey. 2004. *Property in Question: Value Transformation in the Global Economy*. Oxford, UK: Berg.
Warde, Alan. 2015. "The Sociology of Consumption and Its Recent Development." *Annual Review of Sociology* 41:117–134.
Watson, James L. 2006. "McDonald's in Hong Kong: Consumerism, Dietary Change, and the Rise of a Children's Culture." In *Golden Arches East: McDonald's in East Asia*, edited by James L. Watson, 77–109. Stanford, CA: Stanford University Press.
Wedel, Janine R. 1995. *Collision and Collusion: The Strange Case of Western Aid to Eastern Europe*. New York: Palgrave.
Wilk, Richard. 1995. "Learning to Be Local in Belize: Global Systems of Common Difference." In *Worlds Apart: Modernity through the Prism of the Local*, edited by Daniel Miller, 110–133. London: Routledge.
———. 2001. "Consuming Morality." *Journal of Consumer Culture* 1 (2): 269–284.
Wilson, Marisa. 2013. *Everyday Moral Economies: Food, Politics, and Scale in Cuba*. Oxford: Wiley Blackwell.
———. 2014. "Agroecology and the Cuban Nation." In *Ethical Eating in the Postsocialist and Socialist World*, edited by Yuson Jung, Jakob Klein, and Melissa Caldwell, 167–187. Berkeley: University of California Press.
Wolfe, Thomas C. 2002. "Cultures and Communities in the Anthropology of Eastern Europe and the Former Soviet Union." *Annual Review in Anthropology* 29:195–216.
World Bank. 2016. "GDP per Capita (Current US$), 2015." World Bank National Accounts Data and OECD National Accounts Data Files. Accessed April 9. https://data.worldbank.org/indicator/NY.GDP.PCAP.CD?end=2015&start=1960.
Yan, Yunxiang. 2012. "Food Safety and Social Risk in Contemporary China." *Journal of Asian Studies* 71 (3): 705–729.
Yanagisako, Sylvia. 2002. *Producing Culture and Capital: Family Firms in Italy*. Princeton, NJ: Princeton University Press.
Yotova, Maria. 2014. "Reflecting Authenticity: 'Grandmother's Yogurt' between Bulgaria and Japan." In *Food between the Country and the City*, edited by Nuno Domingos, José Manuel Sobral, and Harry G. West, 175–190. London: Bloomsbury.
Yurchak, Alexei. 2006. *Everything Was Forever, Until It Was No More: The Last Soviet Generation*. Princeton, NJ: Princeton University Press.
Zatlin, Jonathan. 2007. *The Currency of Socialism: Money and Political Culture in East Germany*. Cambridge: Cambridge University Press.

INDEX

abandonment, 10, 19–20
"access and choice," 5, 15, 47, 59
accountability, 21, 36–39, 75–76, 147–148; nonelectoral democratic, 153
Acquis Communautaire, 18, 83, 86, 89, 94, 161
age-cohort, 20, 24n10, 29, 177n3
Aktivni Potrebiteli, 138–139
anxiety-free, 10, 16–17, 22, 39, 82, 85, 98, 154
apartment and mortgage, 121–123, 129n1

Beriozka, 28n3
BNCA (Bulgarian National Consumer Association), 37–39, 84, 96, 160–162
"book for complaints," 64, 79n22, 98–99
Buchowski, Michal, 12
Bulet, 48

Canclini, Nestor, 4
China, 8, 79n19; Chinese, 169–170, 177n8
citizen-consumers, 4
citizenship, 4, 43. *See also* consumption and citizenship
civic engagement, 11–15, 119–120, 128–129; ideals, 126–128; protest, 149n2, 151–153; society, 12
civil society, 12, 14, 129
Cohen, Lizabeth, 1
"common luxury," 78n7
comparative testing, 37, 148n1
complaisance, 87, 106n5; complaisant attitude, 88, 156
"connections," 78n5, 121
consumer, 54–55, 79n14; activism, 83; activists, 57, 74 (*see also* consumer: experts); advocacy, 32; anxiety, 2, 19, 22; complaints, 43, 64, 75, 79n22, 98, 102–105; culture, 92–93; experts, 107n8, 162 (*see also* consumer: activists); fraud, 15; grievance, 11, 23, 29, 44, 71; law, 19, 88–89; magazine, 13, 37–38, 138; movements, 8, 11, 55, 145; NGOs, 13, 42–43, 89–95; organizations, 31–32, 37–38, 77, 90, 95, 99 (*see also* consumer: NGOs); politics, 2–3, 131–132, 145–146, 148; policies, 18, 30; protection, 34, 55, 75, 88, 94; rights, 63–66, 69–75, 96–99; safety, 7; sovereignty, 6, 29–30
consumerism, 5, 21, 48, 54–55; ethical, 55; global, 14
consumption and citizenship, 4; and poverty, 20–21; socialist, 5, 17, 51–53, 78n11; studies, 3–4, 24n3, 79n11
CORECOM, 24n4, 46–53, 78n1, 78n4, 78n10
counterfeit, 1, 15, 31. *See also* knock-off
Craciun, Magdalena, 16, 24n9
Creed, Gerald, 124–125, 143–144
Cuba, 8

deficit economy, 78n2
Ditchev, Ivaylo, 51, 78n10

EU (European Union), 21, 30, 65, 83–85; Accession, 158; Integration, 86–88, 90

fake, 1, 15–16, 24n9, 35, 154. *See also mente*
Fehervary, Krisztina, 58, 80n24
food safety, 8

Ganev, Venelin, 24n11, 42, 153
Ghodsee, Kristen, 130n5
globalization, 4, 9, 17, 145
global hierarchy of value, 144
Grasseni, Christina, 13
grievance, 10–11, 24n8, 43. *See also* consumer: grievance

Herzfeld, Michael, 12, 144
Hilton, Matthew, 5, 55, 102, 148n1

Iliev, Ilia, 153
independent consumer information, 136–138
institutional hierarchy, 119
Intershop, 78n3

191

Japan, 8

Kaneff, Deema, 24n11, 45n13
Kideckel, David, 43
Klein, Jakob, 8
knock-off, 15. *See also* counterfeit
Korea, 1, 9, 155, 156n2, 166–169
Kuneva, Meglena, 131–135

Law of Consumer Protection and Trade Rules, 83, 161
Law of Standardization, 81–83
Lin, Yi-Chieh Jessica, 15

mente, 1, 14–15, 24n1, 27, 44, 44n4, 96–98
Mente i Originali, 30–34, 39, 44n5
moral agent, 21, 154
moral commitment, 154

necessities, 29, 49, 79n16. *See also* needs
needs, 30, 46–50, 53, 79n16, 81, 92, 121–124, 126–128. *See also* necessities
normality, 82, 85, 92, 128
nostalgia, 125, 130n3

parno, 109–117, 174
paternalistic state, 19–20, 52

positionality, 24, 166–171
postdevelopment, 143
postsocialism, 20, 24n6, 145
Potrebitel, 38, 101, 133, 134, 137

quality, 15, 58, 66–67, 80n24, 80n26

role of state, 147–148

self-surveillance, 36, 92
shanzhai, 15
social distrust, 81, 84
social trust, 53, 76, 83, 141, 154
standards and control, 56–58, 65–66, 72–75, 81–83, 105
state-citizen relations, 6–10
stategraphy, 41

Thelen, Tatjana, 6, 44n12
Torgsin, 78n3
"transition," 65–66, 86

Velinova, Iskra, 54, 79n15

Warde, Alan, 19
Wilson, Marisa, 8

YUSON JUNG is Associate Professor of Anthropology at Wayne State University in Detroit, Michigan. She is editor (with Jakob Klein and Melissa Caldwell) of *Ethical Eating in the Postsocialist and Socialist World.*

Lightning Source UK Ltd.
Milton Keynes UK
UKHW020106030919
348881UK00019B/415/P